ON MY KNEES

MAINSTREAM SPORT

ON MY KNEES

THE LONG ROAD TO ENGLAND'S WORLD CUP GLORY — A HARRASSED HACK'S HOMAGE

STEPHEN JONES

MAINSTREAM
PUBLISHING
EDINBURGH AND LONDON

This edition, 2004

First published in Great Britain in 2004 by
MAINSTREAM PUBLISHING COMPANY (EDINBURGH) LTD
7 Albany Street
Edinburgh EH1 3UG

ISBN 1 84018 905 3

A catalogue record for this book is available from the British Library

Typeset in Galliard and Myriad

Printed and bound in Great Britain by
Cox & Wyman Ltd

ACKNOWLEDGEMENTS

I would like to thank my family and colleagues for all their support; also my Australian doctor, Alexander Hunyor, and my Australian nurses, Nick Cain and Barry Newcombe.

Also Bill Campbell, Ailsa Bathgate, Graeme Blaikie and everyone at Mainstream Publishing.

CONTENTS

'I distrust summaries, any kind of gliding through time, any too great a claim that one is in control of what one recounts; I think someone who claims to understand but is obviously calm, someone who claims to write with emotion recollected in tranquillity, is a fool and a liar. To understand is to tremble. To recollect is to re-enter and be riven . . . I admire the authority of being on one's knees in front of the event.'

Harold Brodkey, 'Manipulations'

'Steve. For Christ's sake, make sure we have your report right on the final whistle today. I've just spoken to the editor. He says if the first edition's not away on time, we're both f*****g sacked!'

Alex Butler, Sports Editor, *Sunday Times*

PART 1

Panic! – England Threaten the World

1. CAPTAIN CALMAC

July 2002 – Camusdarach Beach, Road to the Isles

On flat calm days, the Sound of Sleat shimmers like something molten, protected by its giant windbreaks offshore – the Small Islands of the Inner Hebrides, Rum, Canna, Eigg and Muck. In the wee small hours, from up on the hills outside Mallaig, the end of the road to the Western Isles, sleepless because of the draw of the majestic natural glory outside (or simply on your way for a piss), you can watch the firefly lights of the small trawlers bobbing on the Sound's vast expanse.

Down the coast are the sweeping white sands of Camusdarach Beach, setting for the wonderful *Local Hero*, the location as Burt Lancaster's chopper swept in and where Fulton Mackay's character had his beach shack. There is no village above the beach as there was in the film, because the village scene and the famous red phone box were filmed in another location and the beach is too far south to have the aurora borealis erupting overhead. But the film took the fullest advantage of the wondrous, mystical natural glories of the west of Scotland and the Western Isles.

And on Camusdarach, in the summer of 2002, I sketched out a change of life. I was in a privileged position, since few others reaching the sharpest end of their 40s can simply opt out and away. But I had reached that sharp end, was to be 50 in November 2003, had worked in the same job for 20 years when peers seemed to think that you have to move every two, given it what I considered a relentless, draining best, been away on tours for 20 consecutive English springs to hack it along, never taken a Saturday off outside a small summer window, fretted endlessly about it, panicked over its deadlines, let it rule too much of my life.

Probably, I had always remembered my father's words the day I started a holiday job in the lintel factory where he worked as wages clerk. 'Son. Always look busy. If there's nothing else to do, pick up a brush and start sweeping up.'

I'd swept up reports on rugby matches for two decades. If I was ever to make the break, it was now. There, on Camusdarach, in the lee of a vast rock over which the breezes from the Sound of Sleat whispered, and as I sketched a pressure-free future with an egg sandwich and a can of Scrumpy Jack, I decided to sell up in the soft south; I decided to become a CalMac captain.

Caledonian MacBrayne are the life force of the Western Isles. The company's fleet of black-hulled ships and boats – red funnels aloft – have been chugging and bashing among the myriad islands for generations, smelling of oil and tar and sick. CalMac recently introduced 'dinner cruises' where you can eat and drink as the scenery slips by. Nah! The concept seemed incongruous. CalMac boats are lifeblood, not tourist traps.

They bring sustenance and essentials. They shape and rule life – I recall taking the MV *Hebridean Isles* out of Oban to Colonsay on a winter Sunday some years ago, on a night so calm and clear that the wake stretched out ghost-white and unblemished for miles and the stars took up more space in the heavens than the black sky behind them. As Colonsay rose on the darkening horizon, it was merely a vast, featureless black shape.

As the ship slowed to dock, lights twinkled on, the jetty became alive with wharf workers, a small refreshment kiosk opened and a few hands prepared to unload the stores and greet the tourists, while vans arrived to carry essentials into the hinterland. The owner of the only hotel – who also turned out to be the chief fire officer, the secretary of the golf club and the special constable – fussed about. The boat unloaded, drew its ropes, reversed and set course for some other island. Colonsay, touched by its visitation of the outside world, returned to darkness. Only the CalMac boat had made it come alight.

And I decided that I wanted to sail them – maybe the MV *Loch Bhrusda* from Barra to Eriskay, or MV *Lord of the Isles* from Mallaig across the Sound, to Skye; or the bigger boats to the outer Hebrides, even the tiny tender from Sconser to Raasay, a distance for which Tiger could keep the woods in his bag. Some days I would mix with tourists with calm authority and on others, holding on grimly as stormy winds drew high Atlantic swells, smiling as only a sea dog can at the alarm of the landlubber passengers, I'd be reassurance in person.

Then on days off, I imagined hiking to the very top of the Cuillins, from there looking down on the whole wonderful panoply of the Hebrides, as far out as Uist and Lewis; in the evening, with all the ropes tied, I would golf at Traigh, every hole of its nine a new surprise; drink Red Cuillin Beer in local pubs, wearing ludicrous dazzling Batik pullovers; dine in fish restaurants of which only we locals knew; tend to the wishes of girls in every port; or given the tiring nature of such toil – CalMac services 20 ports – maybe just a girl in every other port.

Even my new home was all set. There's a giant traditional Scottish log cabin on the outskirts of Mallaig at the top of a steep hill, with glorious views. I'd take breakfast and dinner outside on the milder days, spreading out the *West Highland Free Press* and marvelling that the tiny paper had found the budget to enlist my favourite sportswriters, now including glorious essays by the superb Norman Mair and savage assaults by the ferocious Michael Henderson; I'd read books on Scotland and on life by John Prebble, the scholarly, acidic dramatic historian. And I would marvel that, as a gesture to his long-serving fans in the area, Bruce Springsteen forsook his arena tours and played open-air at Loch Morar. For a short season of a week, only.

There, after literally days of research in my shed, I would discover, and perfect, an antidote to the Lord God's one blight on the Scottish west: the midges, the unseen dive-bombers that ruin warm evenings, providing midge 'n' chips, insinuating themselves into the skin between your toes and behind your ears and up your nose. My potion, sprayed from a light aircraft, would rid the country around of midges; I would appear in the colour supplements and *Hello!* ('former London-based sportswriter rids Scotland of the midge menace').

And then I would become even more famous and even more adored. The lack of midges would bring thousands upon thousands of extra visitors, upsetting the frail eco-balance, tourism quotas and economic structure of the region. So I would destroy the formula for all time, returning the balance and the midges. On Camusdarach, looking across to the small islands, the Sleat still shimmered on the vision of a new life.

2. FISHING FOR GEMS

August 2002 – South Beach, Tenby

The old life, maddeningly, kept sticking its big nose in. I decided to abandon the bit about the girls in ports since it was unlikely that my wife would have enthusiastically embraced the concept. But I still stuck rigidly to ambitions of a career on the high seas – until a few weeks later when the family and friends went on a two-hour mackerel fishing trip round the bay in dear old Tenby in west Wales, on another calm day when the waves hardly lapped. I came over queasy walking up the gangplank, turned and walked back to the beach.

'Dad, Dad, it's OK, there's a radio on the boat,' said the kids, to reassure me just in case the (unforecast) tempest struck. Even though you could have almost walked back to the jetty from where the boat stopped to fish, I spent the hours on the shoreline, tossing flat pebbles, humiliated, till they all came back with wire looped through the mouths of their catches.

There was that, and the fact that covering rugby union for the *Sunday Times*, even in my 20th year of it, was the only thing I knew much about; that I was probably compelled to keep going not only because it had left me life savings of precisely nothing but also because, for good or ill, it was far too much a part of me to consider giving up. Too much of my social life was wrapped in it, too many of the people I most admired as characters or blood brothers were involved in it too, as colleagues or in various walks of rugby life.

Above all, way above the rugby, I adored newspapers, had always wanted to work for one and was never in the slightest bit tempted when people asked me to switch to the battery-driven media. I was doubtful that I had mastered the art of them or grown sanguine about their modern-day vicissitudes. Anyway, what really worried me was the onset of the feeling of relaxation if rugby and newspaper life was taken away.

The summer of 2002 marked the start of an 18-month rugby season, which would culminate in the Rugby World Cup, to be played in Australia in October and November 2003. England, not so much a bridesmaid at most World Cups as a reserve usher redirected to the wrong church, were favoured, at this early stage, to make a strong showing – though they had been favoured before, and the gloating, two-fingered hegemony of the southern hemisphere rugby teams had crushed them.

Yet even then, contemplating in a Tenby deckchair, there were a few signs. Not, yet, signs that England's campaign was to burgeon into a crusade of genuine, thrilling hope, which would absolutely horrify those in other countries where the prospect of an English sporting triumph is anathema – I was to come across several million of them. But those logo-covered jerseys on which the odd splash of white showed through seemed to contain something hard and shiny. English steel.

In charge of the would-be crusade was Clive Woodward, a head coach known in his early days as 'Mr Flaky', but who had begun to produce results, begun to knock off the southern hemisphere giants – and who had certainly developed a conviction amongst his charges that was on the verge of becoming un-English in its expectation of victory and refusal to look for excuses in the event that victory did not arrive.

In charge on the field would be Martin Johnson, formerly a clerk with the Midland Bank but now, probably, the greatest forward who had played the game and a relentless, glowering leader who dominated the opposition in the mental battle as well as anywhere else. Notably on the 1997 Lions tour of South Africa, he clearly intimidated opponents.

There seemed to be a hard core of grizzled experience represented by Neil Back, the relentless flanker; and also real footballing sizzle represented by Jason Robinson, a convert from rugby league who had adapted well to the more difficult code. In a sense, Woodward had rewritten the history of England as a staid and forward-based rugby species by setting his players free to attack.

Naturally, there was so much that could go wrong. 'We all know that England peak between World Cups, not during them,' said Andrew Mehrtens, the All Black fly-half. Eighteen months out, New Zealand were the bookies' favourites, with Australia, the home team after all, in second place. Third, heading a small pack including France and South Africa, were good old England.

Finally, amongst England's strengths was a player who scored many of their points, made many of their harder tackles and was so ferociously dedicated that he almost made the rest of an England squad welded to the work ethic look like a bunch of shirkers. He was a fresh-faced, unassuming lad that Rob Andrew and Steve Bates of the Newcastle Falcons had found in Frimley, Surrey.

I was going to see every game England played, God willing. Yes, I know few would not have swapped with me as I stuck pins and coloured dots on a double-year planner. 'Have a great holiday,' said Debbie, my friend, when I eventually set off for the World Cup. She was being serious.

Well, I had a free ticket for every match, could even meet and interview the players – provided I went through the RFC's media-relations department or a series of agents, and provided I could glean enough to produce a fascinating written portrait of the player and the man, illuminating all his greatness and influences and insecurities and vivid anecdotes, and all the tittle-tattle, all within an interview time-span of ten minutes. And after interviewing them once, I could then nod to them across crowded airports as if I was their old mucker. Providing they liked what I'd written.

And yet, to be fair, this ten minutes of their precious time, after which I was going to probably laud them for the four million or so readers of the *Sunday Times* – an advertisement you could not have bought for £250,000 – was always fixed as a one-to-one, outside the main press conference, just the two of us, apart from the times when it became the one-to-one hundred, with questions drowned out by bursts of light machine-gun fire as the snappers' shutters clicked and hordes of hacks gatecrashed the interview, including the charlatan from the new website on the block who was going to splash any pithy quotes he heard at my interview on to the web three days before my *Sunday Times* article appeared.

And then, just as my subject was about to say something of mild interest, he would be dragged away by the collar by the press officer to the next insightful one-to-er-one interview. Then, when I got back to the office after padding it all out, the sports editor would say: 'Didn't say much, did he?!' Or, if the player had come up with just a few industrial gems, given you just a few small pegs to hang something on, he would say: 'That thing's been spiked, the editor wants a piece on Jonny.'

'We did Jonny last week.'

'Well, do you think there's a new angle?'

The hurt could only be assuaged when I gathered with the other rugby writers at the end of the media (avoidance) session. 'What did he say, then?' I would ask, referring to the interview my colleague had just conducted with Hilly or Backy or Loll or Vicks or Jase or Woody or Robbo or Johnno or Daws.

'Fuck all.'

One day, *The Sun* had the brilliant idea of interviewing the team chef. Most of the squad had been flogged to death in the media, but here was a fresh slant. No one knew much about him. Perhaps there would be some insight into the team's favourite foods and foibles. Perhaps he'd be a breath of fresh air. Frankly, quite a few of us were a little anxious as Tony Roche, the *Sun*'s rugby correspondent, set off for the interview. No one likes being scooped.

'What was the interview like, Rochey?' we asked when our man returned.

'About as useful as an empty rifle at Rorke's Drift.'

'Well, what did he say?'

'Fuck all.'

It wasn't their fault, the poor old players, that the era of the lengthy and erudite media interview had almost passed. If you set every media outlet loose willy-nilly on the England team in this day and age they'd be on the phone longer than on the training field. Sometimes, of course, when the squad were not in camp, you'd manage to drag someone away from the hothouse, manage to spend some time with them, and they'd be as interesting as the old players you used to interview over seven bottles of wine. I interviewed Stuart Barnes once at the height of his playing career. When I played the tape back, most of it consisted of one or the other of us ordering another bottle. By 2003, media mixed zones and media-speak was to be the order of the year.

So was sheer, white-faced exhaustion. Panic. Black moods. Bystanders, even players, would see you marching off to a big match, or to a plane seat bound for adventure, see you downing a convivial drink late on at night. They never saw the faces drain near deadline, the pressure exerted by the ferocious competition between newspapers, the nonsensical hours imposed by the industry's continual slashing of costs (one of these days they are going to ask us to take cameras along to take the picture too), the seven-day operations favoured by some newspaper chains which would leave the poor hacks without a single day off, the industry's driven professionalism and the attendant fretting over every last comma and the agony if an error appeared in print.

And at Big Game time, the need to retain some kind of freshness while filing up to 12,000 words for one weekend's paper. The *Sunday Times*, which produces separate editions for Ireland, Scotland, Wales and England every week, was to send six reporters to the World Cup. 'But you only work one day a week,' people said. 'Why do you need six?' Frankly, ten would have found a full week's work.

And they never grasped that conviviality late on was all that stood between you and mental disturbance, even forms of insanity; all that stood between you and loneliness and the feeling that only you were going through it.

Anyway, you'd still swap with me. You could have finished a match report of 1,200 words, transmitted it on a hissing phone line to a slow copytaker who was obviously a deaf pensioner wearing boxing gloves, who couldn't spell Robinson, let alone Dallaglio or Harinordoquy, to the background noise of 70,000 roaring Frenchmen, and have it on the screens of the sub-editors back at the office in Wapping, plus 25 words each on every one of the 30 players in the match plus replacements plus a mark out of 10, before the match had actually ended, couldn't you? And still tell yourself, masochistically, that you loved to death being in the newspaper game.

'Course you could.

Yet the most terrifying prospect was not of the non-interviews, or the endless build-up, or the sheer hard yakka involved in covering the England bid for the World Cup itself (with only rare relief in following someone else's fortunes, as English newspapers have become increasingly Anglo-centric). Most of it still felt, overwhelmingly, like a privilege, which I took for granted not for one second.

It was one game that caused me a deep anxiety. It lurked in the far distance. It was a domestic affair, not even involving much work, lying in wait on 29 November 2003. It was the first Saturday after the World Cup final ended. There was a kind of void on my planner after the World Cup, bearing no pins. There it lurked.

Call me a pessimist; accuse me of not living for the moment. But I knew that a few days before that first game back on the domestic beat, the great adventure in Australia would have ended, the sense of let-down would be profound, and we would be suddenly pitched, jet-lagged, into a dark British winter with short days, after the brightness of the summer of the Big Island Down Under.

And I knew also that I would return an exhausted 50-something. How would it all feel? Would I find that the newspaper spark and the sporting spark had gone; after 20 years, that I didn't need the stress and deadlines and all the unseen vicissitudes any more; that I'd been to Welford Road and Kingsholm and Kingston Park too often to be bothered to go there again because it all bored me? Or, worst of all, that I had to be bothered because there was nothing else to switch to.

The 18-month colossus of a season, the World Cup monster, and then the dreaded 29 November. I was grimly fascinated to wonder what the dawn of that distant day would bring.

Indeed, even by the autumn of 2002, before the big final push ever started, it was already time for change. Martin, my chiropractor, had fiddled round for weeks with a painful area in my back. He'd clicked and wrenched, but it would not settle. The area was associated, so he said, with the adrenal gland. 'It's your lifestyle,' he said. We spoke about what passed for one.

Apart from work-related socialising and hanging out with my local friends – and a raging affair with music, which I listened to on the way to work – I had not a single hobby or diversion or a way to relax. I did coach my son's team at Maidenhead Rugby Club, which by season 2002–03 had reached the Under-15 group and was highly successful. I loved the lads, their banter, their guts in adversity, the times they produced something word-perfect that we'd done in training.

But, as a result of the insight gained from being around Woodward and scores of other coaches (poor Phil Larder, Andy Robinson and Brian Ashton, the national academy manager, were all pressed for hints and advice, and, staggeringly, not once did they ever demur), and the tiny bits that had rubbed off after studying rugby for ever, the sense of satisfaction I gained from their success was often swamped by the knowledge of how much more we could be doing with the boys. The odd prattish parent (and the real prats rarely realised it) I could take, but what I disliked was the sense of under-achieving. That was, well, stressful.

'You're bound up with your work and you are too tense,' Martin said. 'You have to find a diversion. You have to relax. There's no point in you coming here all the time till you make changes.'

That Sunday evening, mindful that I had to find a distraction, I went to the pub quiz in The Pickwick Arms in Eton Wick. Tim, the *Independent on Sunday*'s golf writer – a man of such famous dryness of wit that dust has been known to congeal on his lips – and myself formed a team. The quiz was in three sections and you were supposed to pass your paper to another team after each section. We knew no one else, so marked our own.

After the first section, we were pitifully far behind, way out of contention. The whole pub jeered when we called out our interim score. We struggled through the second section. As they began to call out the answers to the second section, I had had enough. 'For goodness sake,' I said, 'fill in a few blanks and mark them correct.' At the end of the second section, having past-posted and filled in several answers, and altered others so they were correct, we were still way adrift.

In the final segment, we filled in every answer we didn't know, scored a last-leg maximum and, even though we finished last, at least were in touch with the field. They were just about to hand over the money to the winning team when a regular walked behind us and looked over our shoulders at our answer sheet. 'Lads,' he said, 'don't you know it's two points for a correct answer? You've only given yourself one.'

We muttered that we'd settle for it this time. But he took the paper away and a recount was done; despite our teeth-clenched protestations, our score was doubled, and, by the expedient of filling in the answers when they were called out, found that we had romped home. There was a tannoy announcement. There was a respectful ripple of applause. 'Fucking ringers,' someone called out from a corner.

'We've got to say something,' I said.

'Stuff it,' said Tim. 'Keep quiet.'

We did. We won £11.

3. ETERNAL PALACE OF SWEAT

11 August 2002 – Pennyhill Park, Bagshot

It was time to prepare for the autumn international series, and Woodward's men gathered at what was to be their base for the whole, interminable experience. In Bagshot, the leaves were beginning to tumble, to be raked away by the gardeners of stockbrokers and drug dealers. England's bill for preparations was not beginning to tumble. By a conservative estimate, to bring their side to what they hoped was a perfectly honed peak for the World Cup would cost £20 million.

There was one thing I never understood about the era when hordes of true-blue officials would uphold the sacred concept of amateurism in rugby, saying that rugby was nothing without it (and wouldn't you know, hardly any of them resigned when the game went pro; they liked the limelight, international tickets and claret). But if they didn't want to pay the players then why did they not at least mollify them by giving them the very best of everything?

I once went to interview Jonathan Davies on a Wales tour of New Zealand. I was to see him at the team hotel. To get to it, I had to drive through an industrial estate and bump across a disused railway line, eventually finding the building skulking amongst some scruffy factories and sheds. It was one of the memorable Kiwi motels in which your door opens directly onto a concrete outside corridor. Jonathan had his tracksuit on over his pyjamas.

'Bloody cold last night,' he said.

These days, it is a five-star existence. England have dispensed with the notion that players can get too pampered, can find resolution softening in elegant spas and rooms with a view and room service and giant divans and flunkies bowing and scraping. England's headquarters, indeed their home from home for the two years prior to the World Cup, was

Pennyhill Park, west of the M3 in Bagshot. As Jason Leonard said: 'Everything is laid on, everything is beautifully organised, down to the last detail. But what that creates is a no-excuses environment. Before in England teams, people might say that the beds were uncomfortable or the food didn't agree with them or that their back was playing up. All that has gone. The back-up and the coaching and the medical assessments and treatment are spot on. The perks are nice, but if you don't perform, you are out.'

You enter the hotel's long drive, with a golf course to the right, and, eventually, come upon an illuminated sign that welcomes you to the hotel and posts your car registration number. It's hard to say how you feel about this: is it a snazzy way to welcome you to the hotel, to add a human touch? Or is it to let you now that, literally and figuratively, they've got your number, squire?

And did that secretive bugger, Woodward, put them up to it? Much more likely, given Woodward's mania for secrecy and his insistence that people were spying on him; it would be something for him to keep harping on about till the World Cup was over. ('Look at him over there. That's not a real lawnmower, you know.')

On the left of the long drive you could just crane up and see the tops of some rugby posts. The hotel had specially installed a pitch for the squad. As preparations wore on, a gym was installed in a giant marquee near the field so that the players could put in their heavy work before breakfast number one. (In their daily feeding cycle, set down by their nutritionist, there were two breakfasts. Number two came after the heavy stuff.)

The hotel entrance was to be found across a courtyard, to the left of which was the new spa centre. There were large function rooms for media conferences, of which there were around 150 in the year leading to the World Cup, not including unofficial briefings. The players had a large room each, while Woodward, his chief lieutenants and his captain had palatial suites. If soft living makes you a soft team, then England would enter the World Cup a bunch of soppy retriever puppies.

It was in this ivy-clad pile that the team sweated and fretted, and that, in team rooms full of whiteboards and video screens, the strengths, weaknesses and predilections of opposition teams were pored over, where everyone and his wife had his say, where treatment was administered by the doctor and physios, where the throws coach helped the lineout, the front-five coach powered the scrum, the kicking coach put the boot in, where rough edges were planed smooth. And from where, on home match days,

England filed on to a coach, en route to take part in that 80 minutes for which, it must have seemed sometimes, they had been preparing for 80 years.

How much memory did the human on-board computer actually hold? Most probably, the players had to delete some important old stuff just to find room for the latest input, fad, brilliant idea or golden nugget that one of Woodward's staff had come up with. Wonder their heads didn't explode.

England's players were to spend more than 80 nights at Pennyhill Park before they left for the World Cup. No doubt it was luxurious, in its ivy-clad graciousness. No doubt the staff were good, no doubt the players were often stupefyingly bored. Many of them were intelligent, a few read widely, a few simply could not summon the energy after sessions to do anything bar sleep.

And, no doubt, a few subsided into that worrying torpor of professional rugby, lying around in tracksuits frying their brains on computer games. I once asked George Smith, the Wallaby flanker, if he had any distractions to freshen his mind when he was not training. 'Yeah, mate,' he said. 'I'm on my PlayStation most of the time.'

Loneliness, most probably, was never a problem. Clive Woodward's team at the start of the autumn series of 2002 had him at the head. Andy Robinson, the former Bath flanker, was the coach. He perpetually had a furious expression on his face. When you delved deeper, however, you found that, usually, under the furious expression, he was furious. Phil Larder, the defensive coach, lean as a whippet and one of those people with a worryingly deep tan way out of summer season, was outwardly more relaxed than Robinson. Inwardly, he fretted so much that when a try was scored through his beloved defence he looked ashen. Larder's career as a top rugby league coach was pretty well chewed up by the mid-1990s, as he had gone to the top with Great Britain and ended unsuccessful and frustrated. Woodward drafted him; he served a hard apprenticeship with Leicester and then England. By the early years of the new millennium, his reputation as a defensive coach was such that people playing against his teams often fell over anyway, without needing to be tackled.

As the Long Season went on, the on-site back-up team grew like Topsy. At its height, 3,000 men and women were slaving in the back room. Or so it seemed. 'What the hell does she do?' someone asked as a youngish women walked by in an England tracksuit.

'She's Woody's gofer.'

'Ah. Now I see. And her?'

'She's the visual awareness coach.'

'What's that?'

'She makes you aware, visually.'

And local delights in Bagshot? Who knows? No one ever went out to find any.

4. GARDEN OF RECOVERY

10 October 2002 – Cookham, Berkshire

The World Cup was to begin exactly a year today. I wanted to gauge whether excitement was growing in Clive Woodward, and whether he had aimed his dreams a year ahead. 'The answer's no. I can't. I'm sorry if it knackers the line in your story, Jonesy, but I have to be focused on what's next. Tell me another way to say that I want to take one game at a time, and I will say it. But I have learned that the World Cup will take care of itself.'

It was already two years since he had lost to a southern hemisphere team. The European Grand Slam had remained elusive, because in every year of his reign, the oppressed had found a champion to knock England over – in sequence, Wales, Scotland and Ireland. But he was on his way.

In his playing days, Woodward was known as a dreamer, a superb footballing talent who could lose concentration. He lost matches through it, unforgivably drifting offside right at the end of a Wales–England match at Cardiff – when it was obvious to the world and his wife that Wales would try to draw any Englishman offside – and conceding the losing penalty.

It is remarkable, but true, that he was by no means first choice when he was appointed as England coach in 1997, and in 1999, after England had been rudely ejected in the World Cup quarter-finals, he kept his job, at least in part, because there was no one else of any real stature who was available. Dick Best, who was sounded out, contented himself by drawling: 'I'd rather stick needles in my eyes than work for that lot.'

Sitting on a warm autumn morning, in a secluded corner of Royal Berkshire with Mrs Jayne Woodward talking us through the plants in their magnificent garden, being briefed on the latest achievements of the Clan Woodward, it was possible to believe that Clive had not changed and was still too nice to be the man who could drag England to the very top of world rugby. I like him, and always have. He can be just a little scatty: in his early years in the job he'd make a round declaration one day and the opposite of it the next. But he is never, in my experience, pompous; he is honest, courageous and loyal (provided the loyalty is reciprocated).

But by 2002, you'd only have doubted his mettle if you'd missed the flash of the steel in all his activities. Woodward, preparing for the autumn Test match against New Zealand, had already revolutionised the whole operation of the squad. He had abandoned the notion, rampant in international rugby before he started, that you always pick your teams with an eye on the future. He realised that every match had to be treated as a mighty one-off. That was the staple of his success.

He was already engaged in putting together an expensive and high-octane back-room staff; the philosophy behind it would be repeated in most international rugby camps and throughout sport. He had, with the aid of a crucial core of experienced players with relentless self-belief, such as Johnson, Dallaglio and Back, replaced the mush of England's inner man with an expectation of victory against any opposition. He had, with a little judicious seeding of the media, ended a stand-off between Team England and Premier Rugby. Woodward, as we spoke, had just landed an agreement in which the professional clubs gave him their international players for an incredible 80 days in a calendar year.

He had already withdrawn his men behind closed doors, jealously guarding the inner secrets behind a battery of media officers and the principle of super-secret training sessions. That process continued, so much so that it was possible to tour with England for a fortnight and never see some of the players, except at matches. I have not watched England train for two years. If I had tried to attend a session, an assortment of leather-jacketed goons with earpieces would have seen me off.

Clearly, Woodward had already, as we spoke, created a hothouse atmosphere in which honesty was prized; dissent – up to a point – tolerated only if it stayed internal. 'We do listen to what the players have to say,' he told me. Do they then act on it? 'Sometimes.'

Clearly, he kept a distance, the distance of command. 'I've been reading some of the players' columns,' he said. 'Very interesting. They are all saying how much they are looking forward to the World Cup next year. I'm dying for next week when we meet for the New Zealand game. I want to remind them they might be a little presumptuous.'

In the year, England were scheduled to play a whopping 13 matches. If they somehow managed to battle through to the World Cup final, then they would be playing 20 times in just over a calendar year. No sermons here, for now, about over-playing and cheapening of international rugby's currency. But I can still see the indignation on the face and the spittle on the lips of a member of the Irish Rugby Union when he was told, less than ten years ago, that his national team would be playing a full six matches in the season ahead. Six! 'It smacks of professionalism,' he said. Rubbish, of course. It smacked of exhaustion.

Many of the planned England matches were in bona-fide events. Others were cash cows fulfilling the dreaded reciprocal agreements between unions, which festoon the whole rugby year with Test matches. Paraphrased only slightly, these reciprocal agreements state solemnly that all major national teams promise to play all the others, every month. Into infinity.

Of the 20 games England hoped to play in their bid for ultimate glory, the first three would come in the 2002 autumn series against, in sequence, New Zealand, Australia and South Africa. Three reverberating collisions, although how sad it is that these days we have moonlight flits in and out of Heathrow instead of proper and much-loved tours.

Of even greater significance would be the five matches in the New Year, comprising England's programme in the 2003 RBS Six Nations. Woodward was preparing for his sixth attempt on a Grand Slam, after five straight, agonising failures and the famous succession of last-ditch defeats against Wales, Scotland, Ireland and then France. Woodward made no bones about it. As ever, he shut off his own escape route. He could easily have claimed beforehand that to lose a Slam again would not be the end of the world. But that would have been a lie: 'The Grand Slam is an essential goal. We want to go to the World Cup as champions of Europe.' An essential goal, and slippery as a greased eel that had been taking evening classes in extra elusiveness.

With the domestic grail hopefully in the bank, the next two matches would both be in the southern hemisphere in June 2003 – New Zealand lurked again with a match arranged for Wellington and then, a week later, the world champions themselves were to be met in Melbourne. Even at eight months' distance, this Down Under trip looked fraught with peril, with every possibility of some kind of wounding and shaming defeat as a tired England side saw their confidence blown away.

After that, the contractual-obligation games. August and September would see World Cup warm-up matches – one against Wales in Cardiff, one against France at the notoriously riotous stadium in Marseilles, and then, what amounted to the departure match, a return against France at Twickenham. At least this pre-tournament occasion had a ring of authenticity about it. In 1999, England ponced about playing matches against something called the Premiership All Stars, events that did their cause no good whatsoever.

Those who had decided not to take one match at a time may even have looked a year hence, briefly pondered England's four Pool matches at the distant World Cup, and even dared to dream of them reaching the knockout stages. But all that was so far in the distance – still to come were months of rugby grind and millions of column inches.

I asked Woodward how many players he could pen in to his starting team. He reckoned about half, say seven. This is not for a moment to say that he was sanguine about all their chances of still being alive, let alone in form, after the brutal programme of build-up and playing which was ahead of them. But in a world of rampaging uncertainties there were a few names you could write on the team sheet, if not in pen, then at least with a sharp pencil.

He refused to name them, so I had a crack. Jonny Wilkinson, barring an accident, which would have amounted to a national catastrophe, was going to be England's fly-half. Will Greenwood, uncertainties of his early career behind him, was almost certain to find a place in the centre, and Ben Cohen, the giant and yet sizzling wing, was an easy front-runner too.

In the forward positions, Steve Thompson, hardly known in the world game at large at the start of 2002, had come thundering through the ranks in England and was already threatening to rampage through the World Cup as the finest hooker England had ever fielded and the finest hooker of his era in the sport. Alongside him, Gloucester's Phil Vickery, still a young man by the standards of grizzled front-rowers, had cemented himself into the tight-head position, while the great Martin Johnson, England's captain, was obviously going to lead his men into battle in Australia. In the back row Richard Hill, regarded as one of the greatest match-players of the era, would fill one of the flank positions.

Half a team, a year before the World Cup. Not the worst situation to be in. You'd like a few bankers but you'd also like some areas into which players could grow, especially if they were players who had so far avoided the baleful glare of video analysts of the other major teams. Fred Trueman used to mock slow bowlers with a loop in their delivery. He said that he could be in form when the ball was bowled and out of form by the time it landed. So, certainly, England's top players could lose form in a year and play like drains when the time came.

Furthermore, as well as the seven, it was obvious that Jason Robinson, who had made such a wonderful – if lonely – transition from rugby league, was almost certain to make the team in some position, especially if he managed to take his game onwards after the video analysts managed to slow his initial electric performances.

Yet there were problem areas. There was something missing in the back three of wings and full-back; there was no one who was both brilliant and consistent to play at outside-centre, where Woodward was hoping and praying for a real dazzler to come through to cut people up out wide.

Furthermore, at scrum-half, the perennial battle between Matt Dawson and Kyran Bracken, both with their champions like medieval jousting knights, was, as ever, in some kind of deadlock. Both players were finding injuries easy to come by. The further dilemma was provided by the revival in the career of the engaging Andy Gomarsall, the Gloucester scrum-half.

In the forwards, and bearing in mind that even the steadiest Eddies would not win a World Cup, there were vacancies at loose-prop, lock and in the back row. Graham Rowntree is one of the sport's most fantastic warriors on the loose-head but England probably needed someone with an extra edge in the loose and an extra megaton of power.

But perhaps the wicked conundrum for Woodward lay in sport's endless debate about age, and, frankly, the endless attempts of rugby's media to retire backs when they reach the age of 29 and to retire forwards when they reach the age of 32. The truth was that when Woodward, figuratively speaking, nosed around Somerset House for birth certificates, he found that even the indestructible Johnson would be 33 by the time of the tournament; that the hitherto unstoppable Neil Back would reach a codger-like 35 shortly after the tournament ended; that Dorian West, his reserve hooker, would end the tournament old enough to be Jonny's father.

Lawrence Dallaglio, the number 8, was a relative stripling at 31, but he was still fighting the after-effects of a serious knee reconstruction, which had cost him nearly a year of rugby. Would all the bones and ligaments and cartilages and other bits and pieces have the recovery rate and necessary elasticity and endurance to see Dallaglio anything like back to his best form? Jason Leonard, meanwhile, had long been a 30-something; some of us had even urged Woodward to jettison him after the 1999 World Cup.

Granted, Jason and the others were ploughing on quite magnificently. But where, oh where, did Woodward draw the line? He knew full well that the programme of endurance training and conditioning ahead of his veterans was enough to drive lesser men into early retirement. And he was brave enough not to admit it, but there is always the dreadful possibility if you back your older players to go the distance through a 20-match programme, that you find them suddenly waning on the eve of the big matches, and younger players you could have groomed through eight or nine Tests are callow with lack of experience.

'I don't even want to think about the World Cup until it actually happens,' he said. 'But I remember that when I played for England we had some great players but the organisation was a shambles. In the next year, I want to give these guys the very best chance to fulfil themselves.'

And what of the populous back room? 'In my estimation, the top four or five teams at the next World Cup will be of roughly the same ability, and will be coached roughly as well as each other. The key factor could be which team can find that extra edge somewhere. I am determined that we will leave no stone unturned.'

26 October 2002 – Stakis Hotel, Leicester

Woodward's dilemma about his older players was personified by Neil Back. I had doubted the tiny, rather foppish-haired pocket dynamo when I first saw him playing for England Under-21s, in furnace heat in a concrete jungle stadium in Bucharest in 1989. The main England game had been moved into the cooler evening; the younger hopefuls struggled on through the hottest part of the day. Neil Back was everywhere. But what relevance did he have for international rugby?

A little later, as he struggled to establish himself in the England side, always relentless and always declaiming that the number 7 jersey should be his, I doubted him again – this was an era when rugby could become kicking tennis, and in some games he simply craned his neck as the ball flew high, unable to bring the action to the closer quarters where he was brilliant.

It was now more than 13 years later, doubts long ago admitted and evaporated. Back had more than 50 caps, his hair was brutally cropped, his face was wreathed in stitches, or by the scars where they had once been inserted, with the little ridge they leave where they criss-cross. His relentless, pounding dedication had long been a byword; his steely, even stroppy driving of his own teammates at Leicester and England was already a legend.

So was his refusal to give credence to anyone's doubts, even those merely hinted at, even those he had anticipated you would bring up just to play devil's advocate. I asked him if he had learned from experience, so that his anticipation and rugby nous enabled him to run the shorter lines.

'What you're asking is whether I've lost speed,' he retorted. (I wasn't, actually.) 'My tests say that I'm quicker than ever, so there's no issue there.'

Yet I had brought along with me, in my head, his fixture list for the next year – a barrage of 13 internationals, 20 if he made the World Cup squad and if England reached the final; but alongside that barrage, a torrent – Leicester is not a club where you take a rest, but would he try some self-preservation?

'Johnno [Martin Johnson] and I love the game. We love getting out there and mixing it. We don't like sitting on the sidelines. We don't even like standing out of training sessions. That's from the heart.'

Fair enough, well spoken. But that gave him a Zurich Premiership campaign and a Heineken Cup three-peat attempt lying in wait, into the bargain. And had he found a way to live with himself if he did step back a little to preserve himself, an action which, considering all he had done for his club, every Tigers follower would find understandable? He thought for a bit. 'Well, not really. I still have a massive passion for it.' He had even instigated a new level of training – the pre-pre-season. 'After I'd been off a week at the end of last season, I started getting ready for a run. Ali [his wife] asked me what I was doing. She said I'd only had a week off. I really thought I'd had two.'

He was desperate to play in the World Cup. 'And I want to be the starting number 7. I don't want to be just in the squad.' But he was too bound up in the week-in, week-out thrash to get ahead of himself. He grasped the significance, the likely sense of achievement, if he could keep his form together. 'I don't have time to dream about the World Cup. I just know that it's out there somewhere.'

Who were his rivals? He had one in his own backyard, because the precocious Lewis Moody, a fellow Tiger, blond but bigger, was already well in the England frame and had been lauded by Clive Woodward. Richard Hill, for so long a partner in the celebrated Back–Dallaglio–Hill back row, was essentially a number 7 too. So even if Moody did not make a dazzling burst to reclaim the openside position, then a meteor at blindside could always see Hill move across. Was sizzling rugby on fast pitches at high temperatures any environment for a 34 year old, even the fittest, most artful and most focused 34 year old who ever played the game? It seemed not. And decisions could hardly be made on Back's own promise to stay the longest course. A man of such indomitable pride was never going to tap Clive Woodward on the shoulder and say: 'Sorry, Clive. Drop me. I'm shot.'

There were other problems. There was a new generation of

supercharged number 7s well established around the world, men of fantastic athleticism and pace – Oliver Magne for France, Joe van Niekerk of South Africa, Richie McCaw and Marty Holah for New Zealand, George Smith and Phil Waugh for Australia. Gleaming brightly, the lot of them. Surely, no one knew enough shortcuts to get there before that lot.

A week after we spoke, Woodward announced his team to play New Zealand. Woodward knew that to back his older generation was a risk that could backfire. He chose Moody to start, with Back on the bench. Was it the start of the Long Fade?

2 November 2002 – Grosvenor House, London W1

Meanwhile, in a land not far away, preparations for the World Cup were also progressing. It would be silly to say they were progressing in parallel, because England were building on a powerful platform and Wales were poking about in a pile of ashes, trying to relight something. Yet their relative fortunes would be compared throughout the next year or so. The teams, provided the draw worked out as it was meant, would meet in a quarter-final – a new twist in an old rivalry. If you could still call encounters between the teams a rivalry. More like a formality. Memories of the pre-formality days came flooding back on 2 November in Grosvenor House.

The dinner's had its day. I suppose the relics remain, club dinners with warm white wine in hot halls, the lads with top button undone, reeling about. I used to go to hundreds, would drive miles to be the guest speaker, always unpaid, always hated it. Frequently, there'd be a black-tie affair entitled, or it should have been, the 'No Apparent Reason Dinner', followed closely, as soon as you'd scraped the cold kidney off your lapel, by the 'Any Excuse Evening' (black-tie). 'Carriages at 2 a.m.' For years I'd stand on the pavement looking for a horse.

There was a nice warm feeling at the Gareth Edwards Tribute Dinner, a corporate shindig at Grosvenor House. Wales now had to come to England for its rugby thrills. This evening came from the Any Excuse genre, I suppose; but Gar himself was there, looking fit and happy and unassuming as ever. He didn't look much in need of a tribute, but lent his name to one anyway. Major companies supported it, and charitable donations were made to the Cardiff Institute for the Blind and Conservation Lower Zambezi. They could simply have cancelled the dinner, saved the cost of the food and room hire, added it to the sponsorship and sent all that to the charities, but let's not be too bleeding heart, there was a good night thrown in.

They were all there – Gareth, Barry, Merve the Swerve, JJ, Gerald, Pricey, Willie-John, recycling the same hoary anecdotes, saying nice things. I still can't believe that, because of my job, I talk to the people I once revered. I keep half-expecting Gerald Davies to tell me to buzz off and stop bothering him even though we've been friends and colleagues for years. Last year, I went into a bookshop in Tenby where Gareth was signing his latest work and was pathetically grateful, surprised and the hero of my (late 40s) mates and my sons, when his face lit up with recognition and he even remembered something I'd written.

The jokes flowed, the anecdotes, the memories. We were time travellers, back to an era when Max Boyce, Gren the cartoonist in the *South Wales Echo* and John the bloke up in Ponty who made the Grogg ceramics were the conscience of the nation. Me, Dad, the lads, the village, everyone, were united in glory and made patronising jokes about the English. On the night, Gareth told the one about Pricey, Gerald told the one about Merve; I was happily back in the north enclosure, swaying and fighting for a view of sporting glory.

Memories. Suddenly, as if a chill wind, even a shock wave, had passed through the Great Room, accompanying the beef Wellington, it was all suddenly exposed, at least in my own mind. Memories. I thought about the current Welsh team, the team we never dreamt could be so bad, the horrific administration, and the collapse of the great club rugby scene. The death of the dreams of glory on school playing fields. Memories. You see, they were all that we had left. And unless we found something, England would kill us.

PART 2

Hope – The Long Road to Heathrow

5. THE PRICKS OF ARROGANCE

9 November 2002 – England 31, New Zealand 28
(Twickenham)

Nation shall speak bile unto nation. It had been apparent to me for some time that some of the wholesomeness has disappeared from the arena of international rugby. It's something more than the mudslinging between coaches in the week prior to a big match – they cheat, we don't; they are boring, we are great to watch; they throw punches, we are choirboys; all that stuff. Read a New Zealand website post or listen to a New Zealand phone-in and you'll find something which, were it not dressed in rugby's regal robes of forgiveness, you might even call hatred – of England.

The emotion emerges as an accusation – that English rugby is arrogant. I have reported on England rugby players for more than 20 years, become as close to a few as it is ethically feasible for a reporter to be. I cannot remember one utterance that I would describe as going further than a hearty expression of self-belief, or what Barry John used to call the sporting arrogance needed by all great players.

Apparently, some New Zealanders have picked up things that I missed. Indeed, it seemed as 9 November 2003 approached that, as well as looking forward to a match, we were engaged in the play-off for the World Arrogance title. Andrew Mehrtens, the All Black fly-half, said: 'England are pricks to lose to.' Christian Cullen, the full-back, said: 'When they win, they make sure everyone knows about it as well.'

On this point, one would have thought that with a mass media of elephantine proportions following England's every move, Christian, people would have picked up the result without the England team exclusively revealing it, but wallow on, old chap. Taine Randell, New Zealand captain for Twickenham (latest in a line of poor Black leaders), felt that the dislike was widespread. 'It's not just the All Blacks who take that line on England,' he said.

There is one incident to which every Kiwi trying to make the case for arrogance always refers. A weak England team lost to New Zealand with a passably brave performance in 1997 in a one-off Test at Old Trafford, Manchester, and the England team walked around the ground waving to the spectators. This, every arrogance monitor from Mehrtens down tells us, is proof positive that rugby's master race even fancy themselves in defeat.

Pure poppycock, of course. People who may normally be football or rugby league followers in the great northern sporting heartland roaringly supported England in the Theatre of Dreams that day. The gesture was purely one of thanks, was well merited and well timed.

If England need an excuse (which they do not), here are two. First, the England media is so vast, the newspaper coverage of internationals so monumental, that defeated teams are apt to wake up in their hotel the next morning drowning in half a ton of reportage and celebration. Clive Woodward will be in every paper, apparently crowing like a strutting cock, yet all that will be appearing are slightly different versions of what is normally a single, often gracious, post-match chat. It is a matter of quantity, not tone.

Second, New Zealand has a problem with England. England is the mother country: too influential in too many fields, too much history and too much richness. They are just jealous, guys.

But there is more. The World Cup season was to prove, conclusively, for all time, that New Zealand are the breathtaking champions of arrogance and, by God, by the southern hemisphere spring of 2003, they were to pay dearly for it. If there was one reason I wanted England, or any northern hemisphere team, to win the World Cup it was to prick the bubble of pomposity and lack of self-analysis which combines to convince New Zealanders that they are great rugby players and guardians of the game by divine right, and necessarily better than their England counterparts.

I can still see the coldly smug face of Farah Palmer, captain of the New Zealand ladies team, at a women's World Cup press conference some years ago. Why did she think her team were favourites for the World Cup? 'Because we are All Blacks,' she said. No, young lady, you are favourites because you are, possibly, in this tournament, the best team. Just because you are All Blacks doesn't absolve you of the necessity to play better than the opposition on the day.

Let's be honest. New Zealand is a marvellous rugby nation. Most times, its top players are so focused, so driven, that their communal effort is always greater than the sum of their parts. They usually play with vast pride and simplicity. In the past, you might even say that if you took a New Zealand player with precisely the same physical attributes and technical ability as, say, an England player, then the New Zealand player would be better. No longer, but you get the point.

But what had arisen in the first years of the new millennium was that too many people involved in New Zealand rugby believed that all they had to do to win games was get out of bed. Perhaps Wayne Shelford is their champion, the man whose myopic devotion to the myth of New Zealand superiority not only rubbed everyone up the wrong way but also made him a very poor coach of Saracens in season 2002–03. The club decided to dispense with him after one dire season, much of which he seemed to spend ranting about how poor English rugby was and operating with all the deftness of a silver-fern sledgehammer.

'Your top 50 players in the country would be good for the Super 12, but they are scattered down amongst 12 clubs. There's a massive difference in skill between them and the players beneath . . . a big chunk of the players are a long way off Super 12 teams. Only nine players at Saracens are at a good level,' he once said. If he thought that, then maybe he would have been best going off to improve them rather than criticising them in public.

But that wasn't the point. It was to be proven in 2003, not to spoil the eventual outcome for my dear readers, that in terms of producing quality international class rugby players for New Zealand, the Super 12 was a load of old toss, a waste and a frippery. How many of dear old Buck's dear old Super 12 players could, instead of prancing about in mostly non-contact rugby for a mere 11 games per year, cope with the thunder of the Zurich Premiership season, with its 22-game slog? Certainly not the Kiwis he drafted during his Sarries time, who couldn't have set alight an Aussie forest in December.

Mark Evans, the Harlequins chief executive, had heard enough Buck bollocks to last a season. 'Nice bloke, but it's a load of rubbish. He's never coached a Super 12 side.' (A pointed reference to the fact that no Super 12 club ever got round to employing Shelford, even though he applied.) 'I could compile a list of players who were good in Super 12 and nothing special here,' Evans said.

New Zealand came to Twickenham with half a team. But they were, of course, All Blacks. John Mitchell, their coach, was realistic and gracious in public. Apart from him, you could scour press briefings, websites, New Zealand exile enclaves and you never found anyone who even considered the outside possibility that England might win. Josh Kronfeld, the great All

Black flanker who saw his career out in somewhat uninspiring fashion at Leicester, said of the English: 'I have never met a team, or a nation, or individuals, who talk themselves up so much.' I have, Josh. Kiwis.

It was to prove the richest autumn; rugby in warm colours. It began wonderfully, with a match which swept and surged, which expanded so that it hurtled up and down Twickenham's extremities, so that the touchlines hemmed it in, rather than providing distant boundaries for the action. It was a game between the two teams, which, according to the bookies, would contest the distant World Cup final, so it was a time to secure bragging rights. It was, also, apparently, a time for both coaches to assess players for the future.

Stuff that. These were concepts quickly, gloriously abandoned in favour of a pell-mell, short-term dash for one-off victory, and the future could go and hang itself. I loved it. Any international match in any sport that is played as a rehearsal for another does not deserve to take place. If your eyeballs are not popping, then keep your eyes shut. And the English won. Poor old Mehrtens.

First, the crowd found an antidote to the Haka. Opposing teams have tried ignoring it, jeering it, facing it down, winking at it and advancing on it in menacing fashion. Here, England followers tried to drown it. Carlos Spencer started strutting at the head of the team, but before he got the first 'Ka Mate' out, Twickenham countered with an uproarious 'Swing Low, Sweet Chariot'.

Harry Thacker Burleigh's old spiritual was to become rather familiar over the months to come. Aussies were, it turned out later, forced into counselling because they could not stop the bloody thing ringing in their ears. Poor chaps. I always hated the thing when our college team used to belt it out with appropriate lewd gestures. I never grew a taste for it. But as the season and the World Cup went on, there was a contextual magnificence about it that, thank God, submerged the mawkish banality.

Back to Twickenham. The twists were exquisite. New Zealand scored two early tries. Jonah Lomu scored after some hard New Zealand driving and then Doug Howlett, the other wing, scored after Matt Dawson had attempted an optimistic flip pass. Yet by the final quarter, England were front-running powerfully at 31–14.

Steve Thompson, surging in the loose, was at the heart of the action. New Zealand wanted to commit a couple to the tackle and subsequent ruck, keep everyone else in an orderly defensive line. Thompson kept barrelling into that line, drawing three or four. After one of his charges, brilliant play by Jonny Wilkinson and James Simpson-Daniel drew the remains of the defence, and Lewis Moody scored.

It was not the most comfortable try for a man desperate to establish himself (and who was to miss too much rugby with injury to make the complete case). Simpson-Daniel, as dangerous in one style as was Lomu in another, made space for Moody, but not quite enough. 'When I received the ball, I knew I was going to score but I also knew that I was going to be hurt because I was aware of two big guys coming at me. As I touched down, one landed on my shoulder and the other's knee punched into my kidney. It was a dream come true.' I think he meant the try, rather than the knee.

After half-time, Mike Tindall made his one surge, Simpson-Daniel shot away on an arc, and Wilkinson, head up and realising that the defence was flat, chipped and chased and scored. Ben Cohen then made a devastating finishing burst; it was 31–14, the young Kiwis, badly out-scrummaged, were shot. Carlos Spencer, chosen by John Mitchell to be his springboard, was jettisoned at half-time and Andrew Mehrtens came on to play against the pricks.

Yet the staggering Lomu reversed the momentum, almost single-handed, battering his way past three for a try, and another try by Danny Lee and some kicks made it 31–28. A hair-raising end game brought a tackle by Cohen on the flying Ben Blair that immediately became part of Twickenham folklore.

England held on, their sighs of relief causing a steady breeze. New Zealanders looked at the closeness of the scoreline and pointed to the fact that key players had been left at home, predicting revenge when the teams next met, Down Under in Wellington in June 2003; and then, surely, again towards the business end of the World Cup. England had won a battle; New Zealand clearly felt they were favourites to win the war.

Some of us did not agree. New Zealand's scrum was under pressure, and it struggled. They had forgotten how to scrummage because the Super 12 did not call for it. Furthermore, what were we to make of Carlos Spencer, installed by Mitchell as the team's rudder man? He had a few touches; he walked a bold walk. He had a repertoire of flicks and fancy tricks. Great. In the context of winning a tight and physical Test match, though, did King Carlos's talent really amount to anything?

That night, as they squeezed into their suits for the ridiculous, outdated ritual of a post-match dinner, at least two men were a little happier than most. Lomu had been decried in his own homeland, hounded by Mitchell for lack of fitness. The nephritic syndrome with which he had been diagnosed in 1994 was biting ever deeper, destroying his kidney. The condition was to worsen considerably. But here was Lomu playing in a country where he had always been revered, making mighty interventions. His legend lives on in Europe.

The other happy man was Trevor Woodman. The man with furry gerbils where other people have eyebrows had played a striking game. He was powerful in the loose, part of a palpably superior England scrummaging effort. He was playing in the loose-head position, where Woodward was by no means settled in his mind. No one at that stage was thinking 'World Cup', they were just celebrating a win. But with Woodward and Andy Robinson, as they both quietly admitted later, the performance of Woodman had registered.

Victory, after a memorable afternoon, went to the pricks. That evening, the final words sent through the ether to Wapping, we walked though a deserted Twickenham, through a clutter of discarded plastic beakers, on the way for a beer. Saturday evenings are hateful, hateful. The adrenalin and panic of the day may be over but the aftermath still boils. The car prevents you downing enough alcohol to calm down.

Over one beer, Nick Cain, my dear colleague, and I went through the number of times we had seen the All Blacks lose live. Halfway down the lone pint, we'd finished. Not many. So, momentous England.

On Sunday evening in The Pickwick Arms pub quiz, Eton Wick, one of the questions concerned drinks. It came at a critical stage because one of the strongest teams, Mean Machine, were only a point adrift of us.

Question: 'What are the component parts of a Black Velvet?'

There was a buzz of muttered but animated conversation. Unfortunately, the buzz was not loud enough to drown the urgent stage-whispered order at the bar from our teammate, Dave the policeman. At the precise moment when the conversation lulled, the whole pub heard him place his order, in a conspiratorial low rasp.

'Black Velvet, please,' he whispered, hoarsely.

6. THE CONTINUITY OF DEFEAT

16 November 2002 – England 32, Australia 31 (Twickenham)

Campbell's Coaches (well, the plural was wrong, there was only one) used to operate in our village. Campbell himself was a grim old stick. We used to call him 'Sourguts' as he drove us to Stow Hill baths once a week from school. He was keen on the idea of capital punishment, a sentence for which he would call in cases of murder, arson in Her Majesty's Dockyards and discarding an Opal Fruits wrapper in his bus.

Every Friday, he'd operate a mystery tour. Old couples used to turn up, as grim-faced as their driver; he'd grind it up through the gears as everyone wondered aloud as to which exotic destination they'd end up at this time. It was always, apparently, Penarth.

One day, someone altered the big black chalkboard outside his garage. 'Every Friday,' it said, 'Misery Tours.' I never went to Penarth on his bus, but I've been on a few misery tours since – only one, the Tour to Hell in 1998, was an abject affair off the field. It's silly to judge reporting trips purely on whether the team you follow lost. But I've had to laud moral victories and condemn wasted opportunities too many times.

The worst sporting misery came in 2001, when the British Lions toured Australia. It was a splendid trip, all in all. The British Lions played some excellent rugby, powered to a crushing victory over a mediocre Australian team in the First Test, crushed them again in the first half of the Second Test, and at half-time they really should have been out of sight, dropped over the horizon. Terry Smith, my friend in the Aussie media, leaned over: 'Jeez, the Lions are just too good, mate.'

In Shakespeare, you are not meant to attribute too much significance to relatively minor accidents. For example, although the discovery of Michael Cassio's (planted) handkerchief in Desdemona's boudoir is the vehicle by which Iago winds up Othello, it was actually the tragic forces at work (it was Othello's racism, so said our bearded prig of a left-wing

45

history lecturer – yes, you, Mr Paul O'Flynn) that brought about tragedy.

So following this through, the fact that a poor, speculative pass from someone called Jonny Wilkinson gave Australia a try early in the second half, utterly against the run of play, may just have been a small detail. Excuse me for thinking, now and then, that had the pass gone to a British or Irish hand then the Lions would have taken the series that day by a convincing margin.

By the time of the Third Test, a Lions team sent from Blighty and Sweet Erin, half-dead with exhaustion and carrying injury, was collapsing in a heap and way off the pace. They could and should have won that final match even tottering with exhaustion. Misery tour, all right. Graham Henry, the New Zealand-born coach, would not have been thrilled either. He did nine-tenths of a brilliant job, the bits he could control he did control. He was let down by miffed English on the field refusing to accept that they were not playing for England, and miffed Englishmen off the field who wanted to be known as Henry confidants but were not allowed to be.

All right, I was miffed too, because a Lions win would have proved my contention that the Australian team was fading, lacked the forwards to play real rugby and that Eddie Jones, the coach, even though he was genuinely unaware of it amongst his paeans of praise for his attractive side, was actually producing a team that was more straight-up, straight-line boring even than the paint-drying outfit produced by Rod Macqueen, Jones' predecessor, which had won the World Cup in 1999.

Jones, like Macqueen, still felt that it was wondrous entertainment if the ball was in play – being bashed up rugby-league style in a succession of semi-contested mini-rucks. I was miffed because I had a giant journalist cannonball with 'I told you so' chalked on it and at the end of the tour, I had to check it in, pay the excess baggage and drag it back to Heathrow.

But history also turned with that great Aussie escape. Graham Henry left Europe with reputation diminished when he was clearly an outstanding coach and student of the game. And Australia were smugly unaware of the fact that the game was changing, the rugby world was passing them by, forward play was back in vogue and, gradually, individual genius and attacking ideas were taking the place of the Aussie philosophy that if you keep the ball for long enough, one of the defenders will simply doze off.

I did suspect that Australia would not escape reality for long. That the day would shorten and darken. When they came to Twickenham for the second match in England's autumn almanac, they were roughly the same old Aussies – George Gregan and Toutai Kefu conspiring, George Smith off his feet in rucks but with the refs persuaded by Aussie propaganda that he was, in fact, floating like a human hovercraft in and out of post-tackle without putting his knees on the ground. Danny Herbert in the centre, depending on how you looked at it, was still either powering his way up the midfield or gumming up the works. Bill Young was still using any means he could think of, and the referee didn't grasp, in order not to have to scrummage legally. He was still doing it a year later in the World Cup.

England were not quite present and correct. Woodman, after making such an impression, was to miss several months with a neck injury he sustained against New Zealand. Ben Kay, not at his best for Leicester, had missed the New Zealand game but was back in for Danny Grewcock. Kay revealed that Grewcock had not only been the first to congratulate him, but as Grewcock had played against Australia extensively on the 2001 British Lions tour, he sat down with Kay and went through all the Australian lineout men. 'That's Danny,' Kay said.

And for this match, Woodward dropped Dallaglio, the first time that the great man had been left out of a game for which he was fit for seven years. 'Hopefully,' said Woodward, 'Lawrence will be a very angry young man. You have to be brutally honest with these players. No spitting of the dummy is expected from Lawrence.' Neil Back, thrown into the Angry Young(ish) Man category for the previous week, returned alongside Moody and Hill. It was a period when Woodward dropped icons like a drunken expert on the *Antiques Roadshow*. And our Clive got his wish. Lawrence was very angry indeed.

But the march of history, if it seemed it might work against Dallaglio, did not appear to affect the Australians too badly. There they were, the green and gold devils, leading at Twickenham by 31–19. England's dominance of the first half had yielded a clever try when the brilliance of Robinson and the sharpness of James Simpson-Daniel, growing into his Test jersey, made a try for the strapping giant of the flanks, Ben Cohen.

Jonny Wilkinson was kicking goals as Australia infringed but as another spectacular match unfolded, Australia began to break out, to run diagonals, forsaking their parallel lines. Against the run of play, Elton Flatley skipped through a large gap in a stretched England defence for a wonderful Aussie try and it was only 16–13 to England at half-time.

Yet England were not to know, as Andy Robinson railed at them in the dressing-room, that the Flatley try was only the first element in a scoring burst. Kefu performed a dazzling chip-and-chase and then sharp retention, and long passing put Wendell Sailor over in the corner. England tried to respond, coughed up the ball, and Flatley, feeling like a bit-part soap actor suddenly recruited by Hollywood, ran 80 metres with it to score. The kicks made it 31–16. Ah, well. They were reigning World Champs, after all.

However, England responded. There was something about their demeanour while Australia's lead was building that was striking. They seemed to be quiet, focused. Talking in small groups. They did not seem to be flapping. It was small gestures here and there, the lack of a slump in the body language. Maybe this team was indeed growing.

They attacked and attacked. Wilkinson kicked three goals. Then England, a team and a rugby nation deemed to be based on sweat and power, went for victory. Lewis Moody drove on Steve Larkham's restart kick after Wilkinson's second penalty, and in a move in which the nifty drayhorses, Phil Vickery and Jason Leonard, both handled, in which Robinson made more thrilling ground, the ball reached Simpson-Daniel, who had stepped in from his wing to midfield.

Cohen was outside Simpson-Daniel. Cohen wanted Simpson-Daniel to take the ball up under the noses of the Australian midfield defence and slip Cohen through the gap. But the crowd noise was too great. Both men looked, mouthed something, and when they could not make the communication connection, decided to hope for the best. Simpson-Daniel duly took the ball up, slipped Cohen through and Cohen unleashed a finishing burst of killing power and pace. He also brought off a spectacular swallow dive. Wilkinson kicked the goal, England held out. Two Southern scalps taken.

Amidst the acclaim for both teams for another epic, there was condemnation of Paul Honiss, one of the least popular southern hemisphere referees among European players, and, my God, there is stiff competition. Honiss watched and whistled as Australia infringed to kill the England flow. However, he appeared to have left his yellow cards at home in New Zealand. He did do the game one major service. Larkham, the greatest Aussie on God's earth (sportsman or not) or a frippery – depending on your point of view – has an unfortunate propensity for collapsing in a heap on the field whether tackled or not.

It is not that he is a diver of the Jurgen Klinsmann class, just that, shall we say, his efforts to stay on his feet after any kind of contact can be sporadic. He once bailed out Australia in a tough match against New Zealand Maori in Sydney. The Maori had scored while he sat on his backside and it could easily have been a match-turning try. But the touch judge brought the play back about half an hour and said that Larkham had been late tackled. The video, however, did not exactly provide him with grounds for a charge of assault and battery against the Maori.

On this occasion Larkham collapsed to the ground after an entirely fair English tackle. Over the referee communications system, we heard Honiss pipe up: 'Come on, guys, no Oscars today.' Good on Honiss. At least he got that right.

Individuals kept on waxing. The fresh-faced chap from Surrey scored six penalties and two conversions, tackled with a wincing brilliance and played regally. 'Jonny,' said Phil Larder, 'will be talked about in 100 years' time. A great player, a superstar.' Simpson-Daniel, too, was sharp. Could he yet become the carving outside-centre Woodward had always craved?

One Englishman left very little out on the field. He gave it all. Phil Vickery, the raging bull, gave a stunning performance. Tight-head props are still the foundation stones of any team, and Vickery, after some seasons when he kept coming up a degree short of world class, had, unquestionably, made it. And never mind the era, never mind how big scrummaging is allowed to be, if you have a cornerstone on your tight head, you are in business.

Our team in The Pickwick Arms pub quiz that night had a new recruit: Kate, the veteran barmaid, had a night off work and selected herself for the squad. In what film, ran the question, did one of the characters say: 'You're gonna need a bigger boat.' Easy. One of the characters in *Jaws*, when he realises how great the great white is.

There was a triumphant note in Kate's voice. 'I know this one,' she shouted. 'Fucking *Titanic*!'

7. REAL RUDI?

13 November 2002 – Royal Terrace, Edinburgh

South Africa has had some dreadful coaches. Carel du Plessis, who was around in 1997, never had the foggiest. He would have been out of his depth in your toddler's padding pool. Harry Viljoen, who came later, was, in many of his rugby theories, bonkers. 'Free thinking,' his more optimistic supporters said. Off his chump, in other words.

Of course, it is the most fiendish sporting post you will ever find. You have to bring together a rugby country still, to this day, fissured down racial lines, with Afrikaners, Europeans, blacks and coloureds often no more in harmony than they ever were. And down provincial lines. Even where there is harmony, there is always incoherence of selection and a stolid slowness in following rugby trends. But if you fail, they hate you. Carel and Harry failed massively.

Who would be next? Whoever he was, given the weighty list of responsibilities and the fact that England would face him in major matches that autumn and then, tumultuously, on 11 October 2003, he would instantly become one of the three most important people in world rugby.

Here he came now, ambling across the foyer of his team's genteel Edinburgh hotel, a foyer full of posh city residents having cake. His own media had already dubbed him 'The Lugubrious Moose' and from his demeanour, vocal delivery and appearance they had it on the button.

I was fascinated to talk to him. It was already long decreed that England and South Africa would play a seminal Pool game in the Rugby World Cup and therefore that each camp would strain for news from the other. But it was more than that rivalry – I have always been in awe of South Africa. It is a bewitching, dangerous, staggering, infuriating place. I have always felt humbled that rugby is big there and so it draws rugby hacks to cover it.

Rudi Straeuli extended a ham fist. He had the battered head, the lug ears, low vocal growl and mighty shoulder span of the old rugby warrior and an extract of Afrikaner farmer. Yet he toned down the hint of old vicissitudes with a chunky pullover, with a dry wit so understated that he would pause in conversation and make a throaty sound. Just as you were about to commiserate about his cold and call the night nurse, you realised it was his laugh at the joke you had missed before the pause.

But when he began to expand on his philosophies, I began to sense that this was no Carel P. or Harry V. He charmed me. He seemed to have a handle on the need to be multi-racial in head and team sheet. He said that problems and provincialism were declining. He had just lost to France in Marseilles and he was mad about it; any Springbok defeat brings a savaging back at home. But he was a few days away from reparation day, against the Scots at Murrayfield, where Springbok teams are forbidden by history to lose. He was to face England a week later.

You will find people in Britain who speak of Rudi Straeuli only in superlatives – the teammates he played with at lowly Penarth, for a start. Penarth had always been the whipping boys of Welsh rugby. They'd go seasons without winning. Straeuli went to Donkey Island, as it is called, to broaden himself, to escape the stultifying Afrikaner culture with apartheid still raging. 'We didn't vote for it and we were excluded from international rugby.' His power and pride helped Penarth to relative heights – they once hammered mighty Swansea and their South African scored two tries. 'I would have stayed, but was called up at home for military service.'

He came back at another horrendous time for another struggling club – as club rugby in England thrashed about at the start of the professional era, with new owners and new money (some of it well-earned and wielded by fine men; some of it dodgy and thrown in by shysters). In those heady and dangerous times, he came to coach Bedford, and with little budget or certainty, often with pay delayed, he forged a wonderful team spirit of which Bedford's diaspora, players like Andy Gomarsall, Junior Paramore, Jason Forster, Scott Murray and others, speak of with pride.

'We had a fantastic spirit in adversity. I never thought we were doing it to earn money. We were doing it so Bedford survived, so that the rich traditions laid down by people who had run it with passion and love would still continue.' He went further. 'Sometimes, I don't think the game was even meant to be professional. It's meant to have a camaraderie and an interaction.'

He warmed to the theme; I warmed to a man with rugby spirit coursing. It seemed. He spoke of the horrendous sterility of modern touring. He gestured out of the window where Auld Reekie glittered in late autumn sun. 'I don't know how many of my guys will even walk up to

Edinburgh Castle this week. When I played here, we went grouse shooting and salmon fishing. I met up with Doddie Weir the other day and we had a few whiskies.'

He clearly believed that lack of cultural exchange had just cost his team a Test match. 'Some of the guys had never been to France before. Suddenly, they're running out in Marseilles for a night Test. I like to get the feel of a place first, to understand the place, the people and their rugby.' I agreed utterly. France is profoundly different. French rugby is profoundly different. The Marseilles Experience (France have never lost there) is staggering. The young Boks were asked to absorb cavernous cultural shocks as well as the assault of the French team itself. Amazing they lost only by 30–10, really. Cultural exchange as a weapon for sporting betterment. Unbeatable. No thick farmer, this man. The man to revive the Boks, and to fill rugby's spirit to the brim of the glass.

Except two days later, his team lost, humiliatingly, to Scotland. And nine days later, his team collapsed in rank and file and spirit, conceding 50 points to England, trying to maim them and, it seemed, playing as if almost literally murderous.

Where did that leave Rudi and my warm first impressions of him?

23 November 2002 – England 53, South Africa 3 (Twickenham)

Jack Shoe, our violence spotter, was straight off the mark. Never before had he sprung into action before the anthems. 'Christ, did you see Labuschagne then?' he screamed, over the crowd noise from 75,000 as England took the field. We had. The South African team had lined up left of the halfway line, ready for the anthems, but as England ran on, Jannes Labuschagne left his team, raced menacingly across towards them, apparently shouting at them to make some kind of point to the England team, to show how fierce he was.

He and his pathetic gesture were pointedly ignored. Not one England player broke stride. But it did set the tone for an afternoon of Springbok thuggery on a gross scale. Jack Shoe called the shots throughout, claiming sightings on and off the ball until the end. Perhaps unbelievably, the naked eye suggested that Corne Krige, the captain, was usually involved.

By the end, Labuschagne was no longer among us. He was sent off by Paddy O'Brien, the New Zealand ref, for a crude late lunge on Jonny Wilkinson, so long after Wilkinson had kicked the ball that our eyes followed it into touch. Jack Shoe, primed never to miss a developing situation, saw everything. 'He's gotta go, he's gotta go.' He went. Well done, Jannes. You've just left your pals to play a man short for an hour. What a hard man.

England scored 50. As a response to thuggery it was perfect, studied, deadly. It was a marker big as a house for Destiny Day, ten months later, when the teams were to meet again in a World Cup Pool match. The team continued to build – Phil Vickery began to hit his straps, bosh-bosh-boshing through the phases, bull-necked and dominant. Ben Cohen played sensationally well, with a Herculean (or possibly Epicurean) appetite for the ball. Not so long ago, wings would gripe and groan because the ball never came their way. Cohen took the ball up the side of rucks and mauls, he stood way out on the opposite wing to chase kicks, and he took the ball as first receiver, changing his line as he approached the traffic so that the tacklers could not set themselves. He is big, he has gas and he can finish.

He scored the first try, slanting on the perfect angle alongside Phil Christophers after Matt Dawson and Lawrence Dallaglio bit off yards of territory. Will Greenwood scored twice, Neil Back, embedded in a maul and unseen, bawled the directions and scored under the writhing heap. O'Brien gave a penalty try as a nutcase-high tackle by Werner Greeff, the full-back, on Christophers, stopped him scoring a try. Greeff should have gone, too.

At the end, neutrals scented a chance for England to answer South Africa's insult to sport with England's 50th point. England put down a set scrum, and although South Africa loaded up with an extra back, they were brutally, yet deftly, shunted backwards, and the country where scrummaging is still a religion popped its collective bonce out of the scrum and found that Lawrence Dallaglio, disdainfully, had scored the pushover.

Afterwards, Clive Woodward was definitive. 'It was a brutal match. The England changing-room is like a field hospital. I commend Paddy O'Brien and I commend the England players for their discipline.'

Then, Rudi Straeuli rumbled into the room. The Lugubrious Moose. His demeanour was precisely that of a man who had brought the Boks abroad, played three Test matches and lost them all. He struck back when Woodward's attack was repeated. 'We have two players treated for concussion,' he growled. 'Do you think we gave ourselves concussion?' The answer to that question, as we were to discover in the days ahead, was surprising.

Meantime, England had thundered through their autumn and taken the three scalps. They had terrified their Southern detractors. They had added bits. The old year ended and they were waxing. The autumn series represented for me, at the time, the highest point England have ever reached throughout the years I had been watching them: from the time when I hated them, the squawking accents and silly brown trilbies, and to the end of 2002, when I admitted their excellence, dedication and wondrous spirit, and began to consider for the first time in four World Cups that, with the confluence of a few key factors, they really might become contenders.

Straeuli announced before the tour that his party in England would form the basis of the World Cup squad. When he eventually arrived in Australia, he was to have alongside him, of the 22 on duty at Twickenham 10 months before, a princely three players.

The week ended with South Africa angrily denying rough play.

10 December 2002 – *Rugby Club*, Sky Sports

You want to be a polemicist in the sporting media? You better be ready for ranting readers replying, for opprobrium on websites and in clubhouse bars. And you'd better be sure of your conviction. If you feel the need to apologise or change your slant, then how committed were you in the first place?

I like polemics. If you are making a powerful point or if you are angry about something in sport, why piss about, why present the alternative view, why wimp out by dragging in some contrary view? Get your own column, sonny. On the Thursday after the South African debacle, the finest journalistic item of the whole pre-World Cup period appeared on television.

Sky Sports' rugby coverage is so far ahead of that of the BBC and ITV through the era that it is embarrassing. I know that *Private Eye* have a column which monitors praise for Sky from employees of News International. Tough. Fuck off.

The Beeb have the history, but not the focus. They stick current players on the set who smarm and patronise and misfire their way through. ITV have not the focus, history or interest in the sport. Sky are superb, and of all the back-room people serving rugby out of sight of the rugby lover and viewer, it is entirely possible that Martin Turner, the station's senior rugby producer, is the most valuable. Turner is voluble. He is never a popular visitor to donkey sanctuaries due to an unerring ability to talk the hind legs off the incumbents. But he is sharp, clever and most of the initiatives of the recent past are his. You want to give an award for services to the game, you should give it to Turner. And tell him not to make a speech.

Four days after the Springbok assault and the Lugubrious Moose's denials, Turner and his square-eyed troops carefully and meticulously sifted the output of all 22 of their cameras, running all the angles. They compiled their dossier, they powdered up their experts – Stuart Barnes and Dewi Morris – ran the titles of *The Rugby Club*, the weekly magazine programme, and took aim. They struck relentlessly, with precision and with not a word from a Bok spokesman, nothing to dilute the purity of their message – that the Springboks had been an utter disgrace, as mad as hatters.

Morris, a former England scrum-half who used to get stroppy at media criticism then realised that viewers want opinions, not platitudes, was clearly, fiercely, on-message. 'Absolute thuggery,' he said.

They showed Straeuli posing what he thought as a rhetorical question: 'Do you think we gave ourselves concussion?' The artful Barnes cued in the evidence. Yes, Rudi old son, you sure did. Corne Krige was shown swinging a forearm wildly at Matt Dawson. Dawson ducked, and Krige struck Andre Pretorius on the head. Pretorius went off.

Krige played as if crazed. Immediately after he pole-axed his own man, he was seen kicking Phil Vickery and booting Lawrence Dallaglio. Later, he elbowed a prone Jason Robinson in the face; he threw two sneaky, low-level punches into the face of Jonny Wilkinson when Wilkinson was prone in a ruck. He took a huge swing at Dallaglio and just failed to connect. He delivered a flying head-butt into Matt Dawson. And that was just one man – there was psychotic mayhem from others too.

From England? Twenty-odd cameras and hours of poring found that Ben Kay had struck Bolla Conradie with a straight-arm tackle. Nothing else. And Barnes was able to consider the attitudes of the two captains. O'Brien called the captains together and warned them that the match was flaring up. Johnson turned back to his own men and bawled: 'Everybody! Nothing!' In his terse-speak: don't get involved. Krige merely went away and continued to play like a moron.

He was called to account afterwards. 'It was blown out of proportion,' he said. 'If you have twenty-two cameras around the stadium, you pick up far more incidents than you would with three or four.' Brilliant, Corne. So a vicious incident is not a vicious incident unless it is shown on television?

The two teams sat back for Christmas and aficionados of explosive sport looked forward to their return in Perth. Sky's chaps produced a withering gem of journalism. Right of reply? There's no answer to the evidence.

11 December 2002 – Stade Jean Bouin, Paris

Biltong, boerewors, brandy, kopstamp. You didn't need a degree in Afrikaans to make some sense of the aftermath of the thuggery, but it helped. So where was I with Rudi? Was he the urbane new influence to banish a grim past in South Africa? Or was he an unreconstructed Afrikaner who felt too much pressure? I was inclined to forgive him, as many of us assumed that Krige and senior players had lit the touch paper after Straeuli had left the changing-rooms before the match.

Nick Mallett, the former Springbok coach, disagreed strongly. Mallett, in exile coaching Stade Francais, based at the Jean Bouin Stadium in south-west Paris, had a fine coaching record in his term. Yet he fell between too many stools – he was of English descent so was caught without constituency between the Afrikaners and the non-whites. He was forced out of his position due to internal intrigue in the South African rugby football world and therefore this urbane, worldly, travelled, forceful man was lost at a time when he was most needed.

He attacked Straeuli. 'I have always thought that the way a team plays is a reflection of its coach. I have seen so many Afrikaner coaches resort to aggression and brutality to make up for their lack of technical skills.'

Mallett clearly had allies in the camp because he was well informed. 'After they lost to France, they were stunned. So the coach put them through a week of "kopstamp". It means head-banging and being beasted in training. Then, they played abjectly in Scotland. Where could he go then? He'd already worked them off their feet and verbally attacked them. He'd driven them into the ground. The only thing he could fall back on was to go down fighting.'

Mallett was savage on the state of South African rugby and the arrogance that expects world domination. 'The scene is unhealthy, intense and hugely unpleasant.' He called the rulers of rugby the 'biltong, boerewors and brandy set'.

Straeuli, in the genteel foyer, seemed the man of his legend; the man adored at Bedford; the new man for the Rainbow Nation needing new attitudes. Close up at Twickenham, close up under the cameras and in the words of a true man of the rugby world, he seemed shabby, one-dimensional, out of his depth, even prone to invoking violence on the field.

I suppose it showed that to purport to reveal all of a complex character after a one-hour interview is dangerous and pompous. We would know a year ahead which of the two extremes he really inhabited. Whether he was reconstructed and where on this earth he was coming from.

6 December 2002 – Endless match, Bromley RFC, Kent

On the day after the Twickenham debacle, Maidenhead Under-15s travelled to play Bromley, in Kent. We were denuded by injury, but played bravely. The match was set for the usual 30 minutes each way. The first half lasted only 28 minutes and we were decently ahead.

The second half was a tough affair. Towards the end, Bromley came back and trailed only by three points. They battered away. On my watch, the 30 minutes was up. Still, they battered. There had been very little injury time but the second half was still going strong – the 35-minute mark came and went; then 40 mins, then 45 minutes; 15 minutes of injury time on a 30-minute half.

The referee had to blow up in the end, with us still ahead. The match had started at 11 a.m., but it was now getting dark. The referee was Bromley's head coach. Unlike our pal Rudi, at least we know where he was coming from.

8. JASON'S HUNDRED

5 February 2003 – Stoop Memorial Ground

A certain immobility in the neck muscles was a hint that he had played a few international matches in the front row – 99, to be exact – and when we met, he was waiting to see if Clive Woodward would unleash him for the century and a wave to the pavilion, in the match against France ten days hence which would open the RBS Six Nations Championship as the next phase of the endless season.

If the crushing power of 12 years of scrummaging against some of rugby's beasts was not enough, he had once had a disc in his neck repaired by a surgeon taking bone from his pelvis and installing it in its new position through an incision in his throat. Tap Jason Leonard on the shoulder and you feel he would take around 20 minutes to turn round to see who it is.

Yet when he did turn round, the clue to the secret of his magnificent longevity was in his eyes. Bright and sharp as two new pins. Leonard's infectious enthusiasm for the game illuminated a deserted and rather dull bar area at the Stoop Memorial ground. Remarkably, his recall of events was splendid. I remember reminiscing with Jeremy Guscott about his own brilliant career and yet Guscott would hardly identify a single match from the amorphous lump of it. Leonard, who might have been forgiven for seeing it all as some kind of endless beavering scrum and ruck, was different. 'Name one of the games and there'll be something I can remember to trigger things off.'

These would normally be anecdotes about battling alongside the likes of Brian Moore or Peter Winterbottom, Dean Richards and Wade Dooley, or some expression of the almost heroic agony involved in taking on ferocious opponents, such as Pascal Ondarts, Olo Brown and scores of others.

People ask you why Jason has been so good. It is not, in essence, an easy question to answer. His game lacks, possibly, a thunderous world-class aspect to it. But he is the ultimate all-round prop. Phil Keith-Roach, the England scrummage coach, once summed it up to something like perfection. 'Jason may not be an explosive scrummager or the most bruising runner. But he is so consistent at all the aspects of the game. Then you factor in the incredible respect in which he is held. It is some package, all that. It's some package.'

Leonard's secret is that he has reinvented himself on several occasions, adapting to the changing needs of his front-row profession as the emphasis of laws and scrummaging have changed. There is something quaint and yet also rather wonderful about his scoring system for off-the-field activities, as well. He ranks his success off the field by the number of props he can persuade to have a drink with him when the fires of battle have died down. It is a tradition that was always scrupulously observed; it is a tradition that, largely, has been lost.

Would rugby really be the worse if every player in every team, even after an international match, were required to spend just ten minutes raising a glass alongside his opposite number? Leonard believes fervently that something is lost when the teams shower and disappear.

What was his recent scoring rate? 'I can't remember the last guy who said: "No, not now, Jase." You have to be careful bursting in and suggesting a drink if you've won, because it could be seen as gloating. They might be on the floor. But I suppose they respect the fact that I'll still be up for it if we lose, however much I am hurting.'

His record in the recent autumn Tests, satisfyingly, had been three out of three. 'I know Patricio Noriega [the Australian prop] very well and caught him for a beer. I sought out Deon Carstens [the South African prop] – he had his mum and dad with him, so I said hello to them too. They were made up. Then Kees Meeuws [the New Zealand prop] and I had a beer after that game. It's not the same as it was, but I still try to catch them.'

How on earth was he going to catch fleet-footed Wallabies and the other racing beasts on fast fields in the forthcoming World Cup? Well, perhaps he did not have burning pace at his disposal, but he clearly had all the wisdom of vast experience, seemed to retain the pain of defeat, and even though he was about to reach three figures in terms of caps, possibly with a later shot at becoming the most capped player of all time, then he was impossible to bet against.

Towards the end of our meeting, I had intended to ask him about his retirement – when would it come, and what were his future plans. But that brightness in his expression and demeanour suggested that nothing of the kind was imminent. I forgot about the retirement questions, and contemplated instead a career still boiling merrily along.

15 February 2003 – England 25, France 17 (Twickenham)

Jason was ready to rumble. It was the evening before the game and all the England players were in suites at the palatial Pennyhill Park in Bagshot. All the coaches had chipped in; the less experienced England players were anxiously trying to absorb every item and every nuance with which they had been fed while the more experienced players trusted that the new information was safely embedded in their subconscious, and that it would leap to mind, without them worrying about it, when the time came.

However, news reached the team hotel that dampened the centenary celebrations to come in the most profound way and even reduced in significance what was going to be the biggest match England had played at home in the whole year.

News came through to the camp that Nick Duncombe, the 21-year-old Harlequins scrum-half and a firm friend of Leonard and the other Harlequins in the squad, had died of what was later diagnosed as cardiac and respiratory failure brought on by sepsis, or blood poisoning. Duncombe had died in Lanzarote, where he had been on a week's training with a few fellow Quins.

The squad were thunderstruck. Dan Luger had been a special friend of Duncombe's and could hardly bring himself to play at all the next day. Luger was never to rediscover his true form in the year ahead, and there could be little doubt that the loss of Duncombe was a factor. The players asked themselves if it was difficult for them to accept the death of a 21-year-old colleague, then how on earth were Duncombe's parents and family even going to begin to get over it?

Duncombe was only 21 but he had packed in a fair bit. At 18, he broke his neck in a schools match but, less than two years later, after a piffling 270 minutes as a professional rugby player, won a full England cap as a replacement for England at Murrayfield. Clive Woodward had plucked him from nowhere and this would have become known, with some affection, as a Woodie-ism – that is, if Woodward had not plucked another unknown called Jonny Wilkinson from thin air two years before, proving that it was the world that was out of step, not Woodward.

Duncombe was a tiny figure, small in terms of height and of physique. He had the whippet features of a jockey. At the *Sunday Times*, when we were having a little fun after the RFU announced as part of a strategic plan that England would win the 2007 World Cup, we chose Duncombe as our number 9 in a putative team.

Leonard, next day, had to be persuaded to go out first so that the crowd could pay homage. He jogged on, expressionless. Those who ran on after him embraced him. Then, he turned towards the halfway line and got on with it.

The French know how to take the field. If I compiled a list of the ten top run-ons of all time, then French teams would fill all ten positions. Perhaps the greatest and most gladiatorial entry was the rampage of the French team on to the field of the Beaujoire Stadium, Nantes, in 1986 – on a day when they went on to play with a blind fury, beating New Zealand in a match that will remain amongst the most striking I have ever seen.

In second place would come the awesome, barrelling sprint of the Begles/Bordeaux team at the Parc des Princes for the French championship final of 1989. All three of the terrifying Begles front row of that era – Serge Simon, Vincent Moscato and Philippe Gimbert – had their heads shaved for the match. They came sprinting on to the pitch like a gang of crazed bouncers, raced across the centre-spot and at one stage it looked as if they intended to sprint clean across the far touchline, through the retaining concrete on the far side and out into the peripherique and beyond.

To judge the state of mind of any team from the way they conduct themselves as they take the field may be a rudimentary notion. But when France ran on to the field at Twickenham on 15 February 2003, apparently for the most important match of their domestic season, they ambled and pranced, rolled a few shoulders, stretched a few hamstrings and, all in all, looked as drained as if they had just played a match.

Certainly, the often-fragile mental state of French teams had been stiffened under Bernard Laporte. His team, to his eternal credit, now gave away fewer silly penalties and were less inclined to blame defeats on Anglo-Saxon refereeing conspiracies (though I often felt that there was substance to those conspiracy theories). However, those of us who deem ourselves fluent in the language of the body remarked before the anthems that they were not conducting themselves like a team who felt that they could win at Twickenham, traditionally a ground that robs them of heart and confidence. So it proved.

Nor was it a momentous day for England. They were always going to win, even enough they allowed France to come close to them towards the end – the classic example of a team lacking self-belief which finally settles and begins to play only when the game is safely lost.

It was also a day when English ambition too often became English incoherence. Indeed, you could wonder again at this new England. For English teams of the past to be deemed too ambitious was a rare accusation. Yet Woodward had been harping for months on the theme of interchangeability.

He had been asking the media and public not to worry about numbers on the backs of the players. He wore a pained expression when anyone tried to clarify, for example, if Jason Robinson would be wearing the number 14 jersey.

'What does it matter?' he would ask.

Charlie Hodgson was playing alongside Jonny Wilkinson as a second five-eighth. In part, considering that the estimable Hodgson had so little experience in the position, it worked reasonably well. But sometimes it was Wilkinson who was first receiver; sometimes it was Hodgson. Sometimes, Robinson came scuttling in to become temporary fly-half. Ben Kay and Steve Thompson often took the ball up in the centre positions.

Fair enough, it was a fluid approach. But too often, it simply became confusing for the crowd and the team. I am firmly of the opinion that a team needs reference points and that any back division needs at least one port in a storm, someone who can grab the ball, bash it up and allow everyone to take a breath and filter back to their proper positions. To put it another way, I have always admired Steve Thompson's impersonation of a centre. But it has never been quite as convincing as the impersonation done by Will Greenwood. It seemed the balance was wrong, and it was no coincidence, and a source of some comfort to England's supporters, that the giant figure of Mike Tindall, missing from this game, was to become ever more influential as the year progressed.

France had more of the game in the first half, for all their lack of inner steel, and they scored through Olivier Magne after Robinson had put England under pressure by choosing wrongly his moment to attack from the back. England did go in 12–7 ahead with four penalties from Wilkinson. It seemed that he would lead a charmed afternoon when he mishit his first kick and the crowd gave a groan, only for the ball to veer unerringly back on course and plop safely over.

England killed off the French in the final quarter, scoring a superb try after runs from Johnson, Kay and Thompson, with Robinson running the perfect crosscut angle on a run from Greenwood, to carry on and score. A few more kicks from Wilkinson and England had dispatched the team that was meant to cause them most problems on their route towards a Grand Slam.

By now, England was good enough to win games when they were not playing well. There was also a striking effort from Lawrence Dallaglio. The angular Dallaglio had not wholly been in favour with Woodward during the autumn matches. Woodward read a column by Dallaglio looking forward to the World Cup and was able, with some glee, to pointedly warn Dallaglio against making any assumptions about the future. But against the French, Dallaglio was much more like his old self. In fact, considering that he had undergone a serious operation on his knee, there were even signs of a little gas returning under his pedal.

There was another item of interest. The French scrum at this stage was regarded as one of the best in the world. In Jean-Jacques Crenca, the French enforcer, France had one of the most respected scrummagers in the game. Yet Paul Honiss, the New Zealand referee, was on the French case all afternoon and penalised France unmercifully. Crenca was livid, as he reflected months later: 'We thought that day that it was the end of the scrum, that the whole phase was no longer of importance in the game. It was as if the referee wanted it to be unopposed.'

The performance of Honiss profoundly gave the lie to suggestions that all southern hemisphere referees were on-message when it came to the essential refereeing task of allowing the superior scrum to make a killing. It was a difference in philosophy which approached the realms of scandal. And, before the year was out, we were to be reminded of such scandal in forcible fashion.

9. SIGNS OF LIFE

14 February 2003 – Llanelli

The next stop was Cardiff, once an impregnable fortress, somewhere England could not win even if they came down with what was, in essence, a superior team. Some time before the 2003 game I'd made what felt, in a way, like a pilgrimage, to talk to Gareth Jenkins, the coach of Llanelli.

Jenkins, a brilliant footballing flanker, had played for and coached Llanelli for centuries; even though he was competing against teams with twice the budget of his Scarlets, he had driven them superbly towards Heineken Cup glory – in 2003, they could, improbably, have won the Cup. Llanelli lost a magnificent semi-final at Nottingham Forest football ground to Leicester when, so it seemed to me and to Jenkins, the referee had penalised the wrong scrum entirely, giving Leicester's Tim Stimpson the chance to kick a stunning late goal. A victory would have put Llanelli through to the final against Munster, and considering that it was to take place at the Millennium Stadium, who would not have backed them?

Jenkins was worth talking to because he was still operating at a proud level. He was the only person operating to that level. In the run-in to the crucial match against England, the Welsh Rugby Union were helplessly in the grip of amateurish officials; the major clubs, abandoned by the Union, were waning; there seemed dramatically few real class players in the country. 'It makes you want to run outside into the road and scream. I am not sure at present if we are capable of ever resurrecting ourselves,' Jenkins said.

He has two views from his home in Llanelli – he overlooks a grassy area of lawns and fields and trees and paths, ideal for tranquillity and for walking the dog. But it is precisely the same patch of ground where he once worked in Llanelli's steelworks. Clearly, as he looked out, he could see, even smell and taste, how it had once been. He drove me around some of the reclamation projects and was obviously proud as punch of the revival, the greening up, of his beloved town. There was even a golf course being built that had been designed by Jack Nicklaus, though no one really knew if the Golden Bear had designed it via e-mail and post, or whether he had indeed come west and supped his pint of Felinfoel Ale as he drew up his West Walian 18 holes.

I wanted reassurance from someone as positive as Jenkins that the whole thing was not simply fading out. Clearly, if even he was pessimistic then there was no hope left. Recently, the once-mighty Swansea had played Leinster at home in the European Cup and lost by 50 points while hardly trying. Even worse, the pathetic WRU had just announced the setting up of a working party, the traditional cop-out when they had run out of ideas, on the future domestic rugby structure.

As I asked at the time – if Welsh rugby is not in your heart, then why care about all this? Australia cricket followers laugh at England cricketers. It's just sport. Why care about a rugby nation that arrogantly lorded it over all in its heyday of the 1970s? The answer is that many people, including many Englishmen, love rugby because they came upon it in the 1970s and saw how Wales played it. Furthermore, the general commercial well-being of European rugby will be catastrophically affected if Wales remain feeble in the European Cup and Six Nations championship. But it's more than that. Rugby is a global brotherhood, and, in sporting terms, one of the family is dying. Dying.

Llanelli has escaped its past, realised that there was no point pining for old structures and an old way of life. Is there a parallel? Of course there is.

Jenkins retains his remarkable energy even now, 'I realise that I am the custodian of something here,' he said of his role at Stradey Park. 'When people come here, they have to buy into what we do at Stradey. You cannot use it as a vehicle for yourself. We are not switching on a whim or trying to follow a fashion. The word is not fashion. It is passion.'

The news from Llanelli was that professional rugby is in good hands. 'I refuse to believe that the Welsh love of the game has gone for good,' says Jenkins. 'But we cannot keep expecting it to remain if we keep denting it, if the custodians of the game are failing.' The news was also that major club rugby could be made to work.

High Speed Train at Bridgend

I had been late for my appointment in the downcast land and Gareth had to wait for me in his car outside the station. Just after Bridgend, the train had braked suddenly and hard, and I'd travelled enough on the High Speed Train to know an emergency stop when I felt one. After less than a minute, when the train had only just come to a halt, the guard's voice came over the tannoy.

'We are sorry for the delay but there has been a fatality on the line,' he said. Obviously, a suicide. Briefly, I wondered how they knew that it was a fatality. There had been no time even to call the paramedics, let alone to pronounce any poor devil dead. Then I realised that the driver, poor bloke, had probably been there before, or knew someone who had. I considered the thunderous power of a train at 100mph and the fragility of the human frame. And then I thought of the police scouring bushes by the side of the track outside Bridgend, hoping that it was a colleague who first found the remains.

Eventually, we limped into Swansea. There was a sizeable dent in the front fender of the engine. I walked through the barrier remembering my dear friend and colleague, Cliff Temple, a brilliant athletics writer, who'd chosen the same horrific route to end a black depression. I always wish, fervently, that someone had been beside the track to do something as Cliff walked the line, waiting to make a choice of oncoming trains; or beside a fence next to the London–West Wales line, to drag back someone whose state of mind held rugby results to be an utter inconsequence.

10. THE HISSING CATHEDRAL

21 February 2003 – Millennium Stadium

On the Friday night before England played Wales, I went to the Millennium Stadium. There was a live television interview to do for *Wales Today*, on pitch-side. My mum was thrilled to see me addressing the nation, although she failed to grasp the essential nature and brevity of modern-day soundbites. She rang 27 members of my family and neighbours and was amazed to find that when she returned to her television set an hour later, I was no longer spouting.

The appearance was somewhat less thrilling for an old college friend who had told his wife that he was with me in London that evening, to cover his departure for, shall we say, different pastures. His wife saw me standing in front of one of the most recognisable backdrops in sport and with the enormous caption 'Live from the Millennium Stadium' plastered on the screen. Apparently, immediately after the interview I sprinted to a helicopter, which whisked me to London.

While the television crew set up their equipment, I walked around the track on the periphery of the pitch. I had stood in the Welsh team dressing-room in 1998, when it was an unplastered shell and with only the giant bent arms of the main girders erected outside. On the opening day of the stadium during the 1999 World Cup, I had tears in my eyes when experiencing its completed state, with all its towering and atmospheric magic, with every seat a good view and with an astonishing soaring homeliness. Even the notably unemotional Sean Fitzpatrick, the former New Zealand captain, admitted to me that he shed a tear when he first took his seat.

That night, the roof was shutting – the two giant flaps gliding inwards and clanging together. So the edifice was now powerful enough even to keep out the elements. The stadium electronics hummed, various unseen compressors hissed and groaned. The stadium that night was like a living thing – a giant, daunting and yet benevolent breathing beast. I have been in some wonderful stadiums in my time and possibly only the revamped Suncorp Stadium in Brisbane (Lang Park if you detest the ambush sponsorship by companies) at least gives the Millennium a run. But it remains a distant rival. Perhaps the Stade de France is more beautiful, but it does lack that essential homeliness and, therefore, that essential bite in the atmosphere.

The Millennium Stadium is a building that convinces and, perhaps ironically, it is a statement of intent and of confidence which, frankly, Wales did not feel when it was being designed and built, and does not feel now that it is in operation. In that sense, its magnificence is a complete accident. The next day, it would be full of people, most of them dressed in red. It would also be full of noise, but because of that lack of confidence, the travelling, expectant English supporters would make much of that noise. How wonderful to find that you have the stadium, but how dreadful to discover that you no longer have the team to play in it.

As I completed my lap and as the TV lights flicked on, it was not easy for a Welsh heart to be sanguine. England was light-years ahead of Wales, on and off the rugby field. It was easy to imagine them scoring 70 points next day without even breaking sweat. And easy to imagine that the second half could be even worse.

22 February 2003 – Wales 9, England 26 (Millennium Stadium)

Perhaps the true value of a performance can only be discovered when it is measured against expectations. Victory for Wales was always out of the question, so was any notion that England would still be sweating deep into the final quarter. All in all, a defeat by merely 9–26 was acceptable. England scored only two tries; Wales could easily have scored one, had not the otherwise excellent Mark Taylor ignored a Welshman running free outside him as the line approached.

However, perhaps in the England camp there were just the first stirrings of something approaching alarm. It was the day when, with Ireland hammering along nicely, at least the more optimistic Irish began to believe that they could stop England in their tracks in Dublin on the last day of the event.

Again, England played with shapelessness. Charlie Hodgson, the Sale fly-half, was once more installed out of position and his kicking game took pressure from the shoulders of Wilkinson. But the experiment was, again, less than a total success. To criticise Hodgson would be like attacking a master carpenter because you didn't like the way he had styled your hair. But I felt with some conviction that Woodward's interchanging, should it become even more prevalent, was producing a team that was in some danger of disappearing up its own backside.

The grizzled forwards, Lawrence Dallaglio and Martin Johnson, were again excellent. Will Greenwood scored the first England try after Luger had made a convincing run; later, a typical burst from Dallaglio led to a try by Joe Worsley. It was easy enough, although the ragged rota of England receivers in the backs tended to confuse the English, as well as the Welsh defence. Wales fielded a small pack, outweighed at least partly because of coach Steve Hansen's devotion to a Kiwi-style fast-moving game.

But most of his selections for that match and during this season indicated that he had forgotten that racehorses win the Derby but are hopeless at pulling the milk float. His team simply did not have the physical authority necessary. They did have Robert Sidoli, a tall and dark-haired grafter from Pontypridd. He was no great shakes as an athlete when you compared him to, say, Dallaglio. He was not as powerful as Johnson. But he was heir to a wondrous Welsh tradition of locks whose sinewy persistence and cussedness caused problems. Good on him and more power to his elbow – not to mention his biceps.

England motored on, happy that Dallaglio was now approaching the top of his game. But if the match was flowing, then, ultimately, it did not satisfy. It did not satisfy Wales because for all their courage and resistance and tackling they were never going to win. It did not satisfy England because they approached true world-class form in none of the key departments. At that stage of the season, it seemed that a rather muted English Lion was merely snacking on easy meat, biding his time till that day when he would be more desperate to make a killing.

23 February 2003 – Extraordinary Meeting, Port Talbot

Wales lost the battle. And the war. On the day after the match, representatives of the 239 member clubs of the Welsh Rugby Union filed into a hall in Port Talbot. It is difficult to measure these things, but it is doubtful if so many tin-pot local dictators, unctuous sporting lay-preachers and dealers in the currency of international rugby tickets had even been confined within the same four walls.

They were there to vote on a new structure for professional rugby in

Wales. The old structure was failing. It was based on the great town clubs of Wales, including some of the most powerful brand names in British sport. But the Welsh Rugby Union, always terrified of professionalism in rugby, had made not a single plan to help the clubs establish a sound structure. At many clubs, benefactors arrived. Without them, there would have been no professional sport in Wales whatsoever and scores and scores of Welsh players would have been forced to make a living in other countries – in England, Scotland, Ireland, France, Italy and Japan.

They gave the structure a fighting chance. Some of them thrived – notably Tony Brown, an English businessman who so revitalised Newport that a moribund dying club became a hive of teeming activity, drawing crowds of nearly 12,000 to matches and running powerful community programmes. In one season, they beat Bath, Newcastle Falcons and Toulouse. Most of the other benefactors tried to drive forward similar schemes. But none of the benefactors, as a group or as individuals, were ever asked to the WRU for a sympathetic hearing and to find out what the Union could do about at least minimising their losses. The criminal indolence and stupidity of the Union reduced the whole scene to a travesty, stopped investment and caused utter confusion just when the clubs wanted assurance and leadership.

It was not working. It was not working because the WRU did not want it to work. It wanted professional rugby, but, like so many people in Wales, it was suspicious of new people coming into rugby, suspicious (not welcoming) of new investment and jealous of successful people coming into the sport who hadn't necessarily paid their boring dues by sitting through 30 years of the strangling Welsh rugby committee system. I remember asking one WRU grandee why he had not thought to ask the great Gerald Davies to become a member of the Union – Davies is an icon, a clear thinker, a giant of a man, a man who cared, passionately, about the sorry state of the Welsh game. 'But he's never been an administrator, he's never held a position in the Union.' Was it really so difficult for my grandee to accept that this was precisely why Gerald had to be drawn in?

Because the system was not working, some fools had occasionally come up with the idea of running provincial teams – no matter that the idea had been a disaster in Scotland and England. David Moffett, an administrator from Down Under who arrived as WRU chief executive to knock heads together, instead buried his in the sand. He came up with an idea to split the country into four, and so crude was the split that it seemed for all the world that he had seen a map of Wales on his desk, drawn a line down the middle to cut the map in half, another crossways to cut it into four, and declared those four lumps the new pro teams.

The delegates were to vote on the future of professional rugby in Wales. Only the tiniest fraction of these delegates, however, were involved in professional rugby and knew anything about it. I would guess that a majority actually disliked it, held to the fatuous, discredited and unctuous notion that rugby as an activity was somehow violated if those who did it best were paid to do so. Many saw pro rugby as a modern-day King Herod. Just as Cliff Brittle, an appalling past chairman of the RFU, had portrayed the major clubs as money-grabbing, power-crazed institutions, then so the ranks of the unctuous did the same in Wales.

The final vote in favour of the new pro structure, a vote by people who had nothing to do with it, was 415 to 7. So for season 2003–04, five professional rugby lumps drew their first breath – they were Neath/Swansea Ospreys, Cardiff Blues, Llanelli Scarlets, Celtic Warriors and Gwent Dragons. It had risen from four lumps to five under pressure from clubs who did not want 100 years of existence to be entirely wasted, though the disastrous first season soon had the Blues and the Warriors contemplating a merger. Three of the teams, because they were crude amalgamations, betrayed Welsh rugby's power and heritage, and its founding on town and community. Three of the five were in receivership by the end of 2003; as feeble crowds rolled up, around 30,000 paying spectators per week simply melted away, went to do other things.

Glanmor Griffiths, the chairman of the Welsh Rugby Union, presided over the meeting. He had never made a serious attempt to engage in fruitful discussion with any of the benefactors. His Union set up an inquiry into the disaster under the chairmanship of Sir Tasker Watkins, the members of which included the likes of Gerald Davies, as respected as ever, and the inquiry team produced a fine, deep, well-researched and well-thought-out document. However, Mr Griffiths immediately realised that if it was adopted as policy then he would lose some of his powerbase. He mounted a rearguard action to effectively tear up the report rather than do as he was morally obliged and put the whole thing to a general meeting, unadorned by his personal stamp.

At no time did he show initiative in the fields of marketing, public relations or technical matters. At no time did he express in public what must have been blindingly obvious – that the WRU was moribund and was knifing through the heart its own professional clubs and national team because the Union was set up to run rugby as it was in 1900 and, a few powerless committees apart, had not changed substantively at all, ever. He could not demand those changes because his powerbase, those who voted him in, were from the ranks of the frightened and the unctuous. They were the amateurs.

Later in the year, he left his post as WRU treasurer. When he left, the Union was £66 million in debt. At no time had the WRU's voice been so muted in the game at large – no one, frankly, gave a monkey's what the WRU felt on any subject. It had helped stage, in 1999, what history will judge as the worst World Cup ever, letting down the nation. Geoff Evans, the IRB game development officer, apart, the Union had failed to produce an administrator of any significance for ten years.

When Griffiths announced his retirement later in 2003, there were paeans of praise for his wonderful service to the game. He announced that he was intending to move, at least temporarily, to Australia, where he had family.

Gerald Davies and I met often around the circuit when he was on his *Times* reporting assignments. He must have been nearly 60 but looked so fit that it was easy to imagine him donning the red jersey and unleashing those side-steps to the same old effect. We'd promise not to bring up the topic of the sport in our country, because all too soon two hours would have passed and we'd both be even more bitterly frustrated than ever and the rest of our dinner companions would be asleep.

My father first took me to watch Newport in the 1960s. When my friends and I went round the country to watch them we didn't really grasp why. They were our team. We liked them through thick and thin. Later, I realised that they were our team because we owned them: they represented us in our town and, before the game went pro, they worked alongside us in factories and schools. People in the Old Globe Inn claimed ownership. They'd sit reading their Sunday papers chipping away, complaining about the scrum-half we had, or lauding the new prop or wishing well the young lad from the next street who'd joined. Even non-rugby fans would know that our team had won, or lost, the day before. But there can be no sense of belonging to something that does not exist as a geographical entity, to some combination of communities. As I say, the scared rabbits propounding the amalgamated clubs confused parochialism with community.

This was the catastrophic error made by Moffett, and all the others who savaged Welsh narrow-minded parochialism. Wales is a place where community figures strongly and provides powerful, useful bonds for sport and life. Rugby teams and the buildings they have owned, or rented, have always been in the centre of the communities. Suddenly, Moffett, barking and shouting, and Steve Hansen, the coach who could never see beyond the end of his Kiwi nose, were inflicting something alien and uncomfortable on the country.

And 415 desperate men voted in favour, inflicted disaster on a world of which they knew nothing and cared even less. It's hard to admit this, and I will have to answer to my friends for it, but the whole episode makes me think less of Wales, and of being Welsh. Professional rugby is elite, something to be admitted, supported, wondered at, funded. Something to look up to. Except in Wales. Elitism in Wales means something different. It means, in the perception of Welsh people, that people are becoming jumped-up, forgetting their own, taking on airs and graces, becoming too good for everyone. We expect everyone to move at the same pace – that of a snail.

'When are you going to lay off this new structure?' an angry and legless WRU official bawled at me across Paddington Station one day in July 2003.

I walked on and sat on my train. 'I'll tell you when,' I thought to myself. 'I'll support it when I no longer care about Welsh rugby, when I no longer care about the lead and encouragement my late father gave me in rugby and life, and I'll support it when I am convinced that Wales is really happy to be slashed crudely into bits because some Kiwis want it like that, and because 415 Welsh fools are too terrified to have it any other way.'

The Gwent Dragons took the field at Rodney Parade for the first time. 'New-port, New-port, New-port,' the skeleton crowd shouted.

11. RUNNING THE WIDE ANGLE

9 March 2003 – England 40, Italy 5 (Twickenham)

It is a satisfying moment, so they tell me, when you realise that a key piece of a jigsaw is falling into place, and it is especially sweet if you have been bloody well telling the person with the pieces scattered in front which the key piece is and where it fits. Clive Woodward never actually said: 'Look, whose team is this?' or threatened to take his jigsaw home, but it had seemed to me for some time that Josh Lewsey, the blond powerhouse full-back from Wasps, was his man for the World Cup. In any case, neither of us were feeling much miffed after 22 minutes of this match because not only had England scored five excellent tries already, having taken Italy to the cleaners, but Lewsey, making his first Six Nations start, had fallen into place with a satisfying click. After Steve Thompson had opened the scoring, a wide burst from Lewsey sent James Simpson-Daniel over to score. Then came the individual moment of the match. Lewsey threw a flourishing dummy, turned on his after-burners and raced between Carlo Festuccia and Giovanni Raineri, and sprinted 70 metres to score, leaving Mirco Bergamasco grasping at air. Soon afterwards, Lewsey again ran a lovely angle on to a Matt Dawson run, to set up a try for Mike Tindall.

Lewsey had always been a player of vast ability. It seemed, however, that there was something in his make-up or his game that Woodward did not absolutely take to because for a season or two it seemed that he would always come up just short, would win a gold watch for long service to the England A team. He even appeared to, at least partially, give up on the full international scene by enlisting in the Army; as far as Woodward was later concerned, a case of premature ejection. But while Woodward was quietly shuffling his backs in the Six Nations, perhaps admitting that too many players were switching too madly between too many roles, he decided to give Lewsey his head.

Jason Robinson was obviously part of the calculations. Robinson had normally been Woodward's full-back, and had been impressive ever since he scuttled on to the field as an England replacement in 1999 – still raw as hell as a rugby union player. Robinson's dazzling running has never quite been shut down, even in this age of video analysis. His professionalism has meant that he has performed the arcane duties with a deliberate but outstanding facility. He has most things, including the kind of almost mystical finishing burst which took him past the gigantic figure of Chris Latham, the Australian full-back, on his way to a try in the first Test in 2001. You can watch the video 50 times and still not quite work out how he did it, where he went, how he managed to whiz past Latham on the outside with only, so it seemed, millimetres of space between Latham and the touchline.

But, as the endless season wore on, it became increasingly apparent, and the subject of a good few column inches, that something was missing. Robinson is not quite of such devastating speed over longer distances, and his natural running lines are short and sharp and staccato and ever-changing. He is a jinker. England appeared to lack a man who ran long and fast arcs out wide, who could cash in on the half-breaks of Will Greenwood and Robinson by taking the ball on into open country. Lewsey runs beautiful arcs at high pace, with the added bonus of a power incredible in one with a relatively small frame. And there he was, arcing past Italy, spreading himself, so it seemed, in the England full-back jersey for months, and even years, to come.

The rest of the game was decidedly odd. Italy, devastated by Lewsey and company, suddenly began to play. Indeed, for the rest of the match – bizarrely – they probably played as well against England, and retained the ball as hungrily as any opposition England were to meet in the whole of the year. It was almost as if England had declared and fallen back to the defensive line to see how much punishment they could soak up – a kind of rope-a-dope in reverse order. Except that they made no such choice: they were simply outplayed. All that Italy managed was one try, through Mirco Bergamasco, this after wonderful and patient retention of the ball.

Naturally, it is one thing to play with such passion and organisation when the match has already been lost. The acid test for Italy is that they should play with such excellence when the match is still in the balance. That calls for inner power. However, since they had already devastated Wales in Rome, their Six Nations season could already be deemed to be in some kind of credit. And if the whole day, played in the absence of Johnson and Dallaglio, was disappointing in some aspects, then the unveiling of Josh Lewsey seemed to make it all worthwhile.

12. WIND UP THE KILTED KIWIS

22 March 2003 – England 40, Scotland 9 (Twickenham)

Dunedin. Edinburgh. One's almost the other backwards, but not quite. But Dunedin's meant to be the Edinburgh of the southern hemisphere, and all of us who've been there many times and find it a friendly place sincerely hope that the citizens of the glorious, brooding, imposing Auld Reekie won't sue. Dunedin's rugby stadium, Carisbrook, is called 'the House of Pain' because of the truly hostile reception visiting teams get there from the crowds (whisper it quietly, which is all you have to do there to be heard, but it's such a genteel arena that it's like popping in to Sunday School where the Good Lord punished minor transgressions of the little worshippers by giving them laryngitis).

There's an affinity. Streets in Dunedin are called Montgomery, Heriots, Melrose, Dunblane, Selkirk and Leith. But of late, who's really been imitating whom? For so long, Scottish rugby has been so in thrall to everything Kiwi that it's as if they want not to emulate them but to be them. The fascination began, no doubt, in 1966. In that year, a hopelessly outgunned British Lions team were thrashed and beaten up around the country. Jim Telfer, a young, aggressive and courageous Scotland back-row forward, toured with his eyes open. The tour nurtured in him respect for Kiwi rugby culture and models which, if anything, grew and grew.

Telfer has dominated Scotland rugby ever since, as player, driving force, as a fine coach and more lately and until his exit after the 2003 World Cup, director of rugby. If anyone was the man for all those jobs, it was he. When you look at the Scotland rugby scene, you see Jim everywhere, and, through him, New Zealand. The country is split into big lumps for its domestic teams; Telfer saw the Kiwi model as the way forward, even though it appeared to have little relevance to Scotland.

To be brutal, none of it has helped very much. Scotland's record over the past decade has been largely lamentable, and in that time the number of world-class players and coaches produced by the country has been disastrously low, even minuscule. When did we see the last truly great Scotland tight-head prop, full-back and centre?

There has been absolutely no dearth of New Zealanders and other outsiders playing for the national team. Sean Lineen, a New Zealander, played splendidly for Scotland between 1989 and '92, went to coach Boroughmuir and, generally, became as useful as any Scot. But he opened the floodgates. Telfer and others realised that the large number of families of Scottish descent in New Zealand meant that there must be a large number of players there with distant but provable qualifications to play for Scotland. They also realised that it was easier to make the Scotland team than their own, they might fancy a blast at international rugby, would be prepared to wear a kilt for any silly publicity shot at Edinburgh airport and, even more magnanimously, would be prepared to accept contracts of considerably higher value than those on offer in New Zealand.

The Kilted Kiwis – and other non-Scots – began to arrive in droves. John Leslie, a fine centre, played for Scotland with one single domestic rugby game under his belt. Brendan Laney, a centre of no special finery, went straight from the airport into the national squad. There has been a steady flow of players who paid no dues to Scottish rugby – Gordon Simpson, Martin Leslie, Glenn Metcalfe, Nathan Hines.

There has also been a stream of coaches. Telfer could not, it seems, conceive that a home-bred coach could possibly be entrusted with one of his pro teams – so Kevin Greene and Keith Robertson were imported, then Kiwi Searancke (disastrously) came and went as Glasgow coach; Tony Gilbert is no longer trying to persuade the new Borders team that rugby life is worth living. The national team now has coach Matt Williams, an Aussie whose track record is not exactly touched by glory, and assistant coach Todd Blackadder, a mediocre All Black captain with no coaching pedigree whatsoever and chosen in large part, so it seemed, because he had a Kiwi gargle to his accent. Which comes first? The Scottish-born chicken or the Down Under egg? Why would any young Scottish coach making his way up possibly give up his day job and move into rugby when the chances of someone from the southern hemisphere being promoted over his head out of the blue are as great as 4–1 on?

Most, but not all, of the kilted Kiwis have been decent chaps and players. But I wonder if the chemistry of an international dressing-room is as strong as some people seem to think. International rugby is a deeply passionate and ferociously patriotic arena. I wonder how much Scotland have lost in terms of that extra, indescribable, soul-deep surge and togetherness that common nationality brings?

Budge Pountney, that magnificent flanker and captain, qualified for Scotland – as far as anyone could ever work out – because an antecedent came from the Channel Islands and if you have a Channel Islands connection and wish to play Test rugby (and because Alderney and Sark are still bubbling under the top international scene) then you can choose any of the four home nations. Pountney played with the relentless passions of a Scot whose antecedents had fought at Drumossie Moor. Exceptional man. Not all the non-Scot Scots were of that ilk; frankly, some simply had taken professional contracts that would have been better invested in young Scots lads.

As Alastair Reid, one of the finest sportswriters, said in 2003:

> The number 7 jersey especially, something that was once, above all others, the signature of Scottish forward play, passionately epitomised by players like Finlay Calder and David Leslie, has become an international lottery and an international joke, taken on a grand tour by an Australian (Andrew Mower), two New Zealanders (Martin Leslie and Cameron Mather) and an Englishman (Budge Pountney) in the last two seasons alone.

Non-Scots were dotted about in the team that came south in 2003 to Twickenham. Is it time to stop such slavish copying? Is it time for Scotland's jersey to be returned to the Scots? As later events were to show, anyone still backing the southern hemisphere against the north may be investing in entirely the wrong horse, in any case.

Four legs good. England advanced towards the Grand Slam shoot-out and it is one of those unwanted but guaranteed facts of life of being a successful team that after they hammered Scotland, scored four sizzling tries in a passably fine performance, everyone at Twickers rose on the final whistle, turned to the person next to them and said a collective 'Ho-hum'. That's the problem with playing well. People feel cheated if there are no diamonds being scattered. We'd feel the same walking back to Cardiff bus station after Welsh matches in the '70s. Yawn. Gareth only scored one brilliant try today. Bob Beamon hated long jumping after his extraordinary world record in Mexico in 1968. After that, people felt cheated when they went to see him and he didn't jump clean out of the stadium. Literally.

Before this Calcutta Cup match we'd watched the Wales–Ireland game on the press box televisions, eating our normal pre-match fare brought up from the kitchens. As ever, there was healthy debate as to what animal the slab of meat had once been and whether the vegetables were meant to be al dente or some halfwit had forgotten to cook them. We watched Ronan O'Gara dropping a dramatic last-gasp goal to win the match after Stephen Jones, the only man of that name ever to play for Wales, had dropped a dramatic next-to-last-gasp goal. Shame for Wales that there hadn't been time for a next-to-next-to. Forget it.

By the end, everyone was gasping. But Ireland were four-for-four and had answered the invitation to a Grand Slam shoot-out at High Noon in the Wild West town of Dublin with six guns blazing. Not that hyperbole and excruciating mixed metaphors were to have any part in the build-up.

Ah. Focal points. England had the helter in dismissing the Scots. But not the skelter of their previous Six Nations matches. Steve Thompson, the giant hooker who used to be a flanker and used to be Steve Walter (until he changed his name as part of a disagreement with his mother and stepfather), and Mike Tindall, who used to be a heavy-footed basher now on the verge of completeness as a Test-centre, drove deep wedges in Scotland, drew in defenders, cleared the field. In that space they created, England scored four tries. Some of the play recalled the late Carwyn James's philosophy on what a rugby team was trying to achieve – 14 men working their nuts off to make a yard of space for the 15th.

England's first try was a smasher. Thompson and Graham Rowntree did the spadework. Rowntree is the kind of player who infuriates other nations. There's poor old us struggling with mediocre props and that ruddy Rowntree is about fifth choice. They'd have him any day, the crop-haired, cauliflower-lugged, short-sighted Midlands marvel. When that pair sent the ball back, with gas safely on it, Wilkinson set the backs running, a delightful short pass from Greenwood sending Cohen and Tindall away, and Lewsey scored in the corner. Scotland, calling on the national pride (of about six nations), defended well, but after half-time it was curtains. Ben Cohen, who had just knocked the ball on in the act of diving to score when Wilkinson chipped diagonally and inch perfect, scored anyway a minute later. The artful Dawson dived and clipped the heels of Bryan Redpath – one of the few Scots of real pedigree – the ball came loose and Cohen fell on it.

Then came Jason time. Robinson, shifted to wing, was in prime form. He had scorched his way to two tries for Sale Sharks in their most recent match. Here, he stepped into first receiver, took a pass from Dawson, made the initial cut with that familiar zipping-led cadence, went round Metcalfe and scored; soon after, he took full advantage of the epic match that Matt

Dawson was having on the fringes – Dawson got off on a Matt-like snipe, made inroads, rode a heavy tackle, worked his shoulders free from it and popped the ball deliciously to Robinson for the try. It was England's 21st consecutive home win, a magnificent record.

And as soon as the noise died, thoughts turned across the Irish Sea, to Dublin, and to yet another appointment with that rather annoying Fate which doled out Grand Slams, or, in England's case, didn't.

It had been a memorable match for Ben Kay, the lock. He had been quiet for Leicester and by all accounts his coaches and fellow Tigers had told him so. When lineout lifting was first brought into rugby four seasons ago, the first season had been horrible – easy skyhook catches by players lifting in isolation with no opposing lift from the opposition. Lineout play had become the most boring foregone conclusion in sport. But Kay was one of the first players in the game to realise that there were ways of stealing the ball and increasing again the element of contest. Players like Kay and John Tait of Cardiff, and a very few others with real sleight of hand and foot, were cunning and skilful. They gradually persuaded coaches that teams could compete against the throw. I spent a pleasant ten minutes talking to Kay about the art of being, well, artful in the lineout. 'You watch their feet to see where they might be going, otherwise it's a question of putting your jumper up where you think the ball is going and being good enough with your lifters, and with your own reach and handling, to try to sneak a few.'

'He's probably one of the best, if not *the* best, lineout forwards in the UK today. He's a sound scrummager and he offers a lot in the loose, too. He's got athleticism and brains and there's a lot more to come from him as well.' Dean Richards seemed to be forgiving him a rather slow spell in the Tiger stripes. Woodward, watching the giant hammering around Twickenham with bits of Scotland hanging from him, was not exactly ill disposed, either.

It was the end of another triumphant week. At around 10 p.m. the three-man *Sunday Times* reporting squad staggered out of Twickenham just before the janitor locked us in. Between us we reckoned we'd turned over 16,000 words of copy in three editions of that week's paper, including reports, analysis, ghosted columns, throws-forward and the like.

We ordered three pints and sat, exhausted and unspeaking, in a pub off Kew Green.

'On the piss again, lads,' said someone, walking past our table. 'Bloody press.'

Next night, there was no pub quiz at The Pickwick Arms in Eton Wick. A public house had stood on the site for over 300 years. Youngs, the brewers, wanted to shut it and evict the landlord. When we arrived to do battle, it was all boarded up. When I first came to London, my friends used to demand that we passed pub after pub until we found a Youngs pub. Their beer, in a bewildering array of choice (Youngs or Youngs Special), was as watery as, well, water. I wouldn't miss the beer. Not that there ever was much. The landlord, clearly not in a pecuniary heaven, would sometimes say 'Sorry, lads, there's no bitter' in a matter-of-fact tone, as if it were not an essential, as if he was saying: 'Sorry, lads, there's no Green Chartreuse.' Bit like the barber determined to keep open even though he didn't do haircuts.

But I would miss the quiz.

13. GRANDEST SLAM, FINEST HOUR

29 March 2003 – France 33, Wales 5 (Stade de France)

The Slam was set for a Sunday. Have you ever met anyone who said that he or she liked Sunday rugby and that they wanted to arrive home drunk on Sunday after a Six Nations match? Nor me. However, the BBC had spoken and, as ever, the home unions had caved in.

The Saturday match on that remarkable weekend was in Paris, where France was sulking because the prospect of a Slam had long gone. There's a moment on the train up from the Gare du Nord when you finally set eyes on the Stade and are reminded of the mother ship in *Close Encounters of the Third Kind* making its dazzling descent and landing. The Stade is beautiful and, with the pressure off both sides because the real business match was in Dublin next day, the prospect was sumptuous.

And the feeling at the end was one of betrayal. Wales subsided to a 33–5 defeat and won a richly deserved first Six Nations whitewash wooden spoon. They were hopeless, wove what they hoped were pretty patterns way behind the advantage line and struggled only when those shifty French actually came up and tried to tackle them.

France, who won easily, were a disgrace. They were clearly not bothered, not focused. They played in dribs and drabs; their intensity was way down. It was a dispiriting occasion. The whole point about the Six Nations is that every game has always been a stupendous one-off. Bad game, great game – it has always meant something. If the result sends you racing up from last in the table to last but one, fantastic. Some of the best Five or Six Nations games ever played have been those which were, in the context of the table, dead rubbers. Here were France too miffed that they'd missed out on the big prize, too snooty to dirty their gleaming shorts in a match which – to them – meant nothing. Horrible. Say what you like about England, in the regime of Clive Woodward every international match has been, to quote our Clive, full on. Respect is always due to the opposition, to the crowd, to the television companies and to the spirit of the game. France showed an utter disdain for everything.

I felt better when I'd filed. Some of the hurt I felt was off my chest. Mark Souster of *The Times*, Nick Cain and myself raced out of the Stade to find a taxi. We had a plane to catch to Dublin, where the next day we would watch two teams who would play for keeps, for hell.

There were no taxis. Eventually, parked precariously by the side of a dual carriageway, we found a taxi, warning lights flashing, clearly waiting for a pre-arranged fare.

'*Aeroport Charles de Gaulle, s'il vous plait*,' we said.

'*Ce taxi est pour M. Hertzog.*'

'*Nous sommes tout M. Hertzog.*'

So we jumped in and set off for the airport, now in good time. As we approached the terminal, the radio crackled into life. The taxi central controller delivered the most ferocious attack in the history of taxis. He ranted and raved on for around five minutes. We didn't have quite enough French to capture all the nuances. Or perhaps there had been no nuances.

As he pulled up, the driver turned to us. '*Vous sont sûr vous êtes tout M. Hertzog?*'

30 March 2003 – Ireland 6, England 42 (Lansdowne Road)

The city was boiling all weekend, engrossed, taken over, by the match. Ireland sniffed their chances and liked the scent.

Pity about the backdrop. Where does charming simply mean rickety? Where does traditional really mean dangerous? Where does weathered really mean dirty? Where does history stand in the way of proper progress, and improvement? Which edifice must be demolished? The answer to all these questions: Lansdowne Road.

It started in injury time when Shane Byrne, Ireland's hooker with a hairstyle that would have embarrassed the lead singer of Showaddywaddy in about 1971, overthrew a lineout. The England back row set off upfield and initiated a series of attacks. It is considered unprofessional to make any show of support in the press box. And a hanging offence in Wales for one of our own to show support for England. I was also sitting by a fervent son of Munster in my colleague Tom English, one of the finest sporting hacks, once physically assaulted in a bar by Pat Whelan, former Ireland coach – no consolation to Tom at first when I said he should regard that kind of moronic reaction as vindication of all he stands for.

But I could not help, just under my breath, hissing 'go on, go on', as England attacked. The match as a contest was over. The Grand Slam was won, England were in the middle-30s on the board, and this against what was unquestionably one of the finest Irish performances I had seen. I wanted England to show us something extra at the end, something for the neutral rugby lover, to produce some kind of brilliance to seal it. That day, I had decided that not even the great Welsh teams of my youth had played to such a level, and that this was rugby as the modern era demands it should be played. It was also the last play of the match and, clearly, England knew it. They could have hoofed the ball out of play and thrown their arms in the air. They did not. Yet.

After the back row drove the ball on, a long pass from Will Greenwood whizzed out to Ben Cohen. After a ruck, Jason Robinson came infield and made a burst; Trevor Woodman almost sniped through; Dan Luger, as replacement, took the move down a midfield channel; Dawson, Dallaglio and Josh Lewsey attacked from the next ruck; Ireland held out, full of pride; the move rumbled on.

Steve Thompson made the next dent, and then Dawson and Wilkinson, running late on to the ball, made a half-break. England blasted away on the Irish right-hand corner, twice Ireland infringed trying to kill the ball. Twice, England took tap penalties. From the second, after Thompson had taken the tap, Dawson sent Dallaglio hurtling towards the posts. Dawson found Robinson after the umpteenth recycle; Wilkinson flipped the ball on without ever gathering it, found outside him Jason Leonard (100 caps, after hard scrummaging, 90 minutes of elapsed play, daisy-fresh). Leonard found Lewsey. All that play, that whole sweeping, sustained attack, had made just one yard of space – and given England one man over. That man, in that yard, was Dan Luger. Lewsey gave him the ball, and Luger scored.

Grand Slam. This was the day when you realised that England's upper limit of performance now, definitely, included the winning of the Rugby World Cup. That didn't mean that it was suddenly a foregone conclusion, or even as much as a 50–50 chance. But it was the day when you realised that they had it in them. I'll tell you how good it was. Ireland gave an excellent performance and throughout a first half of fierce contest and yet lung-bursting pace, they stayed almost level.

The margins had been tiny as the week hurtled on in its preview phase.

I suppose in their hearts, everyone knew that England were in essence the superior team, but no one who had lived through the annual non-Slam catastrophe, and anyone who had sensed the rising tide of expectation in Ireland become a raging torrent, would be so gauche as to suppose that anything depended on a supposed technical superiority. There were 101 sub-plots to go through before England could even think of bringing to bear the fact that, on paper, they were the better rugby team.

The match broke open when Richard Hill snaffled a ball after the England scrum juddered forward, disrupting Ireland. Matt Dawson ran on and Lawrence Dallaglio, playing a magnificent game, banishing all doubts that he was no longer a player of the highest influence, scored the try.

Wilkinson dropped two goals before half-time but, ironically, it was while Wilkinson was off the field at the end that England clinched it; Paul Grayson made an inside pass to Mike Tindall after a forward drive, and Tindall, the man told 19 months before by Woodward to go away and come back with lighter feet and different angles, veered in and veered out, split the Irish defence and scored. 'It was the most important and the best try of my international career,' Tindall said afterwards. 'In the context of the game, it was massive.'

Will Greenwood was driven over for another try and scored his second on the intercept. In his moment of joy, he did the opposite of what scorers are meant to do. He veered outwards, away from the posts, and touched down about a foot from the touch in goal. 'Thanks, mate,' Wilkinson said as he passed Greenwood. Wilkinson made his point; he placed the ball even wider, millimetres away from the touchline, and sent the kick soaring over. It ended 42–6. In amongst these tries, Wilkinson had kicked a penalty when Johnson refused to allow any levity to creep in and, to jeers from the home crowd, called Wilkinson up. 'We were not going to waste the chance of scoring points,' Wilkinson said. 'It was an example of how hard-nosed, ruthless and professional we've become.'

Woodward, who had jumped to his feet for a jig every time England scored (by the end, he must have been jigged out), rounded sweetly on his attackers. 'Had we lost this game the ramifications would have been huge. People would have said again that this is a team that cannot win the big games. If we hadn't nailed this one, it would have been tough to recover and it would have made the months going into the World Cup even harder. We responded with a colossal performance.'

Greenwood agreed. The tall Harlequin, quixotic in his wide try, affectionate in his traditional wave to his father in the stand, had decided where the true glory lay. 'The forwards were awesome. Afterwards, I went around and shook hands with them all, one to eight.'

Heavy times, heady times. And England would go South, as thumping great Champions of the North.

On that Sunday evening, there was a quiz after all. The denizens refused to let it die so they moved round the corner to The Greyhound. They rang me in Dublin to tell me the good news. There was a lady landlord as quiz-mistress, so at least the traditional foul language would be a thing of the past. They briefed me later on their finish in a poor second place.

'Question one,' Julie, the landlady, had begun.

'Speak up, Julie. Can't hear you.'

'Fuck off!' said Julie.

14. OLD JERSEYS

11 June 2003 – New Zealand Rugby Union, CentrePort, Wellington

If a wall, and pillars, can be evocative, then the offices of the New Zealand Rugby Union down on a rather scruffy dockside area in downtown Wellington are stunningly so.

A large part of one wall of the cavernous meeting room is taken up by jerseys, mounted on headless busts, of all the competing teams in the National Provincial Championship. In other words, no logo-plastered Super 12 marketing clothes-horses; in other words, all the famous names of New Zealand rugby history. In other words, all those wonderfully evocative names of teams the British Lions, and other touring teams, would play when tours were tours, men were men, when we listened to transistors in the early hours and only the sheep were nervous.

They were all there – the jerseys of Manawatu, Horowhenua, Southland, Marlborough, Nelson Bays, King Country, Mid-Canterbury, North Otago, Wairarapa-Bush, Wanganui, Bay of Plenty. And the teams who would always combine against the touring teams – West Coast & Buller, Poverty Bay & East Coast.

We were with England on a 'tour'. England had come 12,000 miles to play two games and would go on to Australia to play one. Fatuous.

The great fount of all wisdom regarding rugby tours used to be Terry O'Connor, the rumbustious former *Daily Mail* writer. On my early tours, O'Connor would regale us whippersnappers with touring tales, characters, disasters and triumphs. It was like a particularly spiky apprenticeship. 'Senior journalists,' he once said, 'must pass on the baton to junior journalists.'

But as I walked down the wall, revelling in the colour of the kit and the vividness of history and personal memory, regaling my current colleagues ('I remember when we went to Greymouth in '83, Gisborne in '85,

Invercargill in '87'), I suddenly had a shock of recognition. Now, I was no longer the whippersnapper. He was short, bald, tabloid, stroppy, Irish and way past 70; I was tall, own hair, broadsheet, Welsh and not yet 50. But I had become O'Connor.

On the pillars, more wondrous evocation. On them had been carved the names of every All Black, in order. Fascinating. You could see how far Maori and Island names have burst into the scene recently, dominating more recent teams; you could pick out old-time greats, and you could wonder at the characters, the comradeships and pride in the jersey of Angry Cross, Moke Belliss, Circus Hayward, Bonzo Seeling, Carbine Wallace and generations of splendid men.

14 June 2003 – The Stand of the Super Six, New Zealand 13, England 15 (WestpacTrust Stadium, Wellington)

It is deeply incongruous to speak of seeking vengeance in a place called the 'Cake Tin'. Citizens of Wellington, New Zealand, detest it when outsiders use that nickname for their brand-new stadium just out from the centre of the city. On the other hand, traditionalists all over the world dislike the ambush marketeers who rename famous stadiums after companies, so it was a toss-up which label was most disliked – Cake Tin or Westpac Stadium.

For goodness' sake, seeing the new edifice standing there on a wet Wellington night almost made me nostalgic for the recently demolished Athletic Park, scene of so many New Zealand matches over the decades and of so many cases of hypothermia. The gaunt old place stood at the top of a valley and the tempests would sweep in, roaring through the steep open stands. I still cannot believe that no one ever died there.

The new place even looks like a cake tin, with its outer binding of corrugated material, just like the ridged wrapping my mother used to put around her cakes as they cooled. But never mind the incongruity. New Zealand was boiling for revenge all right. This was the day when England would receive their comeuppance. This was the day when a new All Black team, highly rated in the papers and websites and bars of the country, burst into global consciousness. It was the day when first evidence would be provided that the ever-dull Poms would once again peak between World Cups, and disappear during them. Lovers of conflict craned forward.

Even though there was a hostility around which completely astonished colleagues of mine making their first trip to the country, the days before the match brought little in the way of truly vivid verbal or written barneys.

John Mitchell, then New Zealand coach, is far too gracious and controlled a man to start the kind of infantile England-bashing so favoured by other coaches. All the New Zealand local press could drum up was an assault on England for what they said was a boring effort in victory over the New Zealand Maori in New Plymouth in a mid-week game. They forgot to mention that the match took place in a tempest and against a Maori team that could only win the ball when England dropped it.

'So after days of hearing what the Maori were going to do to us, we see them off big time, then we are criticised for being hard on them and for doing a professional job. What is it with this place?' Clive Woodward said before he left for the Tin.

Indeed. New Zealand is a funny old place – still my favourite rugby venue, still with an essential welcoming magnificence in its population, still with enough wondrous sights to delight the eye. But it seemed to many of us who had toured there on many occasions since the Ark that it had drifted even further away from the centre of the world. I remember regarding Wellington, at the start of the 1990s, as the flagship for the arrival of a new and modern New Zealand. I hardly saw a single Ford Anglia at all on that 1993 trip.

Somehow, however, the place seemed to have got stuck. No historian or sociologist would dream of drawing conclusions from a mere two weeks in a country, so all the evidence was circumstantial. But the bright new strip of bold new restaurants, which had enlivened the harbour area in Wellington, had changed. Their self-confidence was still there, it was just that their decent food had hightailed it out of town. There was even an indication in the rugby community that New Zealand had got itself detached.

In the event, despite the closeness of the scoreline, it was the worst night for Pom haters. It was, in particular, a ghastly experience for anyone who had always treasured the hardness and nobility of New Zealand forward play. The truth is that history will unquestionably see England's performance against New Zealand in Wellington as the worst given in all the 20 matches they were to play between the autumn of 2002 and the end of their World Cup campaign. 'The dressing-room was like a morgue afterwards,' Martin Johnson said. 'I had to remind everyone that winning away in New Zealand is a great achievement.'

The ghastly bit came when both Neil Back and Lawrence Dallaglio were in the sin bin in the third quarter. New Zealand's eight forwards gathered themselves from an attacking five-metre scrum, against an England pack reduced to only six. It seemed that the only pointed issue was which of around 27 routes New Zealand would take to make the try that was beckoning. Four times, the All Black forwards went down for the pushover try. Three times, Phil Vickery and the super six held their ground. Afterwards, one commentator complained that England had fiddled around, not scrummed down properly, gone for the wheel. Quite apart from the fact that it was fabulously rich that a New Zealander was complaining about England failing to scrum, there was also the thought that no self-respecting rugby team in an international was simply going to stand square and allow themselves to be knocked out. England duly fiddled and wheeled. After the fourth scrum, Rodney So'oialo drove for the line, was held short, and England cleared. In the battle of 15 versus 13, England won an amazing 3–0 victory when Wilkinson kicked a penalty. It was surely the most humiliating moment in the history of New Zealand forward play.

After that, England could hardly fail to win. All their points came from Wilkinson and New Zealand scored a try through Doug Howlett, who was palpably offside when he chased a kick from Carlos Spencer. Alan Lewis, an Irish touch judge, was almost dead level with Howlett, almost within touching distance. He merely waved play on.

England were satisfied, but not more than that. Once again, Tindall had been influential. Once again, the indomitable Rowntree had been splendid and Vickery had made a successful return from long-term injury, appearing for the second half to hold out in the famous goal-line stand. England's defence calmly regrouped; there was very little sign of the vaunted New Zealand backs and, instead of revenge, instead of Pom bashing, it was the Poms who had bashed.

Mike Tindall had his feet on the ground. 'In the grand scheme of things, it doesn't have a lot of impact on what happens in October.' True, I suppose. New Zealand followers reckoned their team would improve massively throughout the Tri-Nations. Woodward, keeping his counsel, was positive his team was nowhere remotely near a peak as it rifled the Cake Tin.

Lawrence Dallaglio held forth in a quiet moment after the Test match. He was not being in the least insulting to his New Zealand hosts, just realistic. But his clear impression was that New Zealand's technical thinkers and individual players knew next to nothing about the England team, as individuals or personalities, or about their strengths and weaknesses. Dallaglio had never played before against So'oialo, the young New Zealand number 8. But he and England's video masters had made it their business to eke out every detail of what So'oialo did and didn't do, and the information was put to excellent use on the night. Dallaglio felt that from their public pronouncements, and in the way they played, New Zealand had heard of Jonny Wilkinson and Martin Johnson, but that all the others were a mystery to them.

Frankly, I was absolutely fascinated to watch the All Blacks in training and in their media conferences, and in the match. As ever, they lauded their backs and especially their Polynesians and their Maoris. So many people went around calling each other 'bro' that it seemed that the whole team had the same mum and dad.

There were exciting new faces, notably in the electric Fijian wing, Joe Rokocoko, who had created such an impression in recent domestic matches. Rokocoko was a nice guy. He related the story to the encircling British media hordes about a recent visit to his home village in Fiji. 'People came out to congratulate me, they seemed really happy.' Our Joe's natural charm prevented us from stating the obvious – that for every ten people wishing him well in his new career as the wing for a foreign country, there would be around a hundred who wished that he had stayed and played for Fiji.

Even more fascinating was the composition of the forwards. No one in the world game rated New Zealand's forward play, ruined as it had been by years of neglect in the Super 12. But there were a couple of newish faces. The fresh-faced Chris Jack had already made an impression, performing notably on an earlier trip to play Ireland in Dublin. Ali Williams, the other lock, was similarly unmarked. Williams was more voluble, prone to dodgy haircuts and gestures, talking a talk. Jack seemed the real thing, but was Williams all mouth and trousers? Amazingly, months after that Wellington match, the question was still being posed, with voting split at 50–50, and the casting vote going in favour of the trousers.

In the past, any win over New Zealand in New Zealand would have been enough for at least an invitation to a garden party at Buckingham Palace. This time, this group of young English sportsmen was more intent on winning in Australia the next Saturday.

15 June 2003 – New Jersey; New Zealand Rugby Union, CentrePort, Wellington

Icon. The All Black jersey is an icon comparable with any in the sporting world – with the striped pyjamas of the New York Yankees or with red Ferrari F1 cars. Or the Ashes urn. But the All Blacks don't just stick their heads through the hole any more and take it from there. They have to buy into a Dynamic Layering Concept. They take the field trussed up in technology.

The top bit once called a rugby jersey, now comes in three layers. The under-jersey is a wet-look slipover 'fabricated with . . . stretch micro-fibre', which, according to Adidas – the maker and massive All Black sponsor – 'works in harmony with the other layers'. Good, can't have those layers bickering amongst each other while you're trying to win a Test match.

Then comes an 'active layer', 'followed by a uniform layer'. The active layer offers 'body empowerment' which sounds vaguely like Viagra. It offers 'compression of skin receptors optimising muscular control'. And we don't want the All Blacks to play in any old socks. Their Adidas socks 'compress the calf muscles to reduce vibration and oscillation and therefore reduce muscle fatigue'. I assume that you can easily beat defenders who are oscillating away as they try to tackle you. The shorts are a 'polyester twill fabrication which give moisture management technology'. I presume that means it deals with the problem if you wet yourself laughing at all the marketing topspin.

I'd give a lot to beam Colin Meads into a modern-day All Black dressing-room, sit him down for the ritual of handing out the Holy Grail for the nation's manhood – normally a cotton affair with a plain silver fern. 'Mr Pinetree, here's your number 4 jersey with micro-fibre fabrication and an ergonomically shaped collar, and here are your moisture management technology shorts.' Might just get a dusty reply.

The All Blacks would give anything to have Colin Meads in their dressing-room. He is still revered the length and breadth of the country; he's on the platform at dinner and product launches; he's usually grunting words of common sense and volcanic effect here and there. A great pal of his told me that while there's no fortune to be made in farming these days (Meads farms at Te Kuiti), Meads still hands back a chunk of his fee if he thinks it's on the generous side. His presence alone could intimidate. But if they revere him, why do they forget what he was and what he did?

The jersey-marketing spiel reminds you that New Zealand, perhaps not always a cutting-edge country in terms of a lead to the world, is desperately, anxiously modern when it comes to rugby, to rugby marketing, to the latest concept and fad. It wants to sell itself and to entertain, and wants its team to become All Blacks Inc. It's a frantic, relentlessly modern operation. In so many ways, they lead the rugby world, and always have.

Fine. Maybe the new kit gives them a ten-point start, too. I admit that, at the very top level, most of the time is spent trying to find ways of eking out tiny advantages here and there. But in their drive to modernity they are in danger of losing themselves. Yesterday, the country which gave us the most intimidating forwards in history, and some of the hardest men in any sport, packed down a full eight forwards against six of England, and the six won. Four times. Incredible. I have no doubt whatsoever that, as England held out and as his successors in the Black jersey pussyfooted around, Meads felt a physical pain, and the rape of a magnificent culture, which he helped to create. A culture which, in fact, he personifies.

The drive for technology is, in the end, harmless. Maybe even beneficial. Maybe the kick-off time has to be postponed so that the team can get all their kit on, but fine. The television people show more advertisements. But in their drive to find entertainment they are in danger of bastardising the sport. Many of our New Zealand readers get shirty when I suggest that the Super 12 event is not producing great forwards. That New Zealand is mistaking fast and fresh-faced forwards for the real thing they need in real tests; that they are mistaking action with entertainment. They have been fooled by foolish Aussies into buying into a gushing game with no forward reference points, which suits only Australia. I shall rest my case for ever more on the video of four scrums against six Englishmen at the Westpac Stadium, Wellington, 14 June 2003.

So in the place of Meads, they have fit and lithe young lads who run like the wind – and who cannot push a proper scrum back even when they outnumber by two the other team. Maybe it's my age, but not only the New Zealand policemen look younger and fresh-faced these days, so do the All Black locks.

Of course, another feature of New Zealand rugby is the rapid and selfless way they make good their deficiencies. If they have a weakness they usually eradicate it in time for the next match. It was still possible that they might improve so rapidly in the young southern hemisphere season ahead that they would win the World Cup. But it would take a lightning-quick advancement in their forward play; indeed, it would take a sea change in attitudes. England had seen off, in the matches against the New Zealand Maori in New Plymouth and in the Test match, the best forwards the country had to offer. And they had done so with ridiculous ease. New Zealand's arrogance in its rugby now extended, apparently, to a belief that they can win rugby matches without the ball.

Maybe the old cotton jersey is indeed outmoded, a relic of the bygone era. But it was England, not New Zealand, who was playing the modern style this season. Modern-day rugby is a forward contest again, a grunt, a compelling affair because strong men clash in an elemental battle, as well as in short sprints and dextrous passing. The grunt is needed to clear the field for the real talents behind the scrum. And in a contact sport, in a physical beasting arena such as international rugby, it's not the jersey that counts, however multi-layered and well fabricated. It's the power and experience and animal ferocity of the men wearing it.

15. BODYLINE. AUSSIES DUCK

21 June 2003 – Australia 14, England 25
(Telstra Dome, Melbourne)

It happened on this day. No caveats, no qualification. For the first time in my life I made England firm favourites to win the World Cup. Incredibly, this was the tenth successive victory by Woodward's England over one of the three southern hemisphere giants; the last time they lost was, narrowly, against South Africa in Pretoria, when that nice Mr Wilkinson withdrew on the morning of the match and that, er, relatively nice Mr Healey stepped in at the last minute.

Two scores summed up England's all-court, all-action game, in what was by a street a better game than the previous week's in the Tin. The first was a try by Will Greenwood. The move went through around 14 phases of play, was optimistically and carefully sustained through tackles – the staggering Johnson appeared three times, blasting the ball up, and Wilkinson, Greenwood and Lewsey made dazzling interjections. Greenwood found space to score down the left and, in the land where they revere continuity of play, here was a try to warm Aussie hearts. Strange then that those in the Colonial Stadium, a more glamorous Cake Tin, this time with the lid on to keep everyone inside fresh, rather failed to stand and cheer as Greenwood scored.

Soon after, another try, another style. England brought off a sharp move from a lineout – Johnson peeled around, fed Dallaglio, Dallaglio flipped the ball to the fast-moving Woodman; Back stood at scrum-half for the recycle, sent out a scrappy pass and Wilkinson, Thompson and Greenwood sent Tindall over. One and a half phases – not 13, but still deadly.

England could not quite make all the scores their dominance of forward play and field position dictated. Wilkinson gave England space to breathe with penalties and then England won a lineout. Wilkinson dummied to pass flat outside him and suddenly, on the in-slant, from nowhere, came the giant figure of Cohen. Cohen took the ball, sprinted on his wrong-footing angle check, sizzled past Chris Latham and scored. In the pre-match build up, comprising videotapes of former games, interviews with the greats, and general Oz lauding, there had been no mention of the day's opposition, just fawning over past Aussie achievements. Maybe they were tapped on the shoulder and reminded that another team was on the field. A better team.

Wendell Sailor, one of Australia's rugby league imports, stirred himself superbly towards the end, unleashing a burst through traffic to score, but Wilkinson's boot soon had England two scores ahead again.

Australia had valid excuses. Steve Larkham was unfit and Elton Flatley, the back-up fly-half, had been discarded from the squad after missing a recovery session. The suggestions were that Flatley had taken drink after Australia's victory over Ireland in Perth the previous fortnight. It was a bold move by Jones to exclude him, because Nathan Grey, the reserve centre who stood in at fly-half, was no one's idea of a general or a cutting edge.

Towards the end, Lewsey and Mat Rogers, another league import, had an altercation and had to be separated. Soon after, Rogers tried to attack down the left wing. Lewsey appeared as if from nowhere, hit Rogers with a sensational tackle in the chest, and Rogers, wheezing, took a long time to recover. Australia is not used to being pushed around by the English. For the moment, however, like Rogers trying to unscramble his senses, they had to grin and bear it.

21 June 2003 – Telstra Dome, post-match media conference

The media conference was packed to the gunwales, in a gym under Colonial. The tour was over; one more night's work and we were done for the season. (The next one would begin in about half an hour's time, but who was splitting hairs?)

We waited for Woodward to arrive with his beaming lieutenants for a few platitudes – bad luck, Australia; well done, our brave lads – and off for a drink. Surprisingly, when Woodward walked by the aisle and climbed the podium, he was stone faced. My God, he was going to twist the knife.

First, he attacked Eddie Jones for the traditional Aussie practice of pressuring the referee. Jones had been typically vocal all week. 'I would like to commend the referee. I thought he did an outstanding job considering the amount of hassle and pressure he had been put under all week. I don't believe in coaches putting pressure on referees. It is obviously premeditated. It is not good for the sport. Jones keeps doing it. We will have to wait until October for the next media campaign orchestrated by him. We didn't need any team talk from me. Eddie did one for us.'

Woodward was as relentlessly open in the attack as any of his backs. He then turned back to Jones, who had expressed the view that playing with style in Australia was just as important as victory – admittedly, and to be fair to Woodward, a barrowload of unctuous poppycock. Woodward clearly saw a criticism of the England style in Jones's words. 'Anyone who doesn't think we are good to watch has not been watching us,' he said. 'But it is not about style. It's about winning. When you come down here, it seems the opposition coach is anxious to give you a label. Test rugby is an unforgiving place and it is about winning. I think that one or two people in this part of the world have forgotten that.'

My God, again. Not content with turning history on its head by dominating the southern hemisphere on their own paddocks, he was taking them on now in their old game of verbal, with thunderbolts and propaganda. As he stalked out of the gym, he was ahead by around 50–0.

A few months later, I reflected with Woodward on his tirade and suggested that the spontaneous outbursts against Jones and the media shenanigans were carefully planned.

'I would be telling porky pies if I said I did not work out what I was going to say. I had been copping crap all week and I decided to fire back with a little of my own ammunition. So if we are English, we have to sit quietly and listen to all that kind of stuff?'

If meekness was an English sporting trait, then Woodward had crossed a border to another land. If England rugby teams were always the resigned losers, then his seemed to have left the normal planet entirely. For once, it was dear old Eddie who was ducking the short-pitched stuff.

Walking out of Colonial that night, crossing the Yarra as rain fell, we were aware that something had changed, that the world had shifted on its normal axis. It seemed to us, without any caveats, that England would win the World Cup.

'I read an article that said I was now as unpopular in Australia as Douglas Jardine in the Bodyline series,' Woodward said. He was thrilled.

16. ENGLAND LEVEL, AND FAR AHEAD

23 August 2003 – Wales 9, England 43 (Millennium Stadium)

In a sense, as the warm-up matches began, it was a historic day. This England victory finally, finally, brought them level with Wales in terms of victories won between the two great rugby nations. My teenage son and his pal were amazed. The snapshot of history they had taken in their young lives could not conceive that Wales had ever beaten England before at any time, let alone so frequently through history.

This margin of victory was sizeable as it was, but England missed seven shots at goal, passed up on at least five golden chances to score more tries and barely let Wales across their advantage line, let alone their try-line. At the end, you had to conclude that it was a damn good job that England hadn't brought their first team. None of the run-on team had started in England's previous match, in Melbourne.

Ostensibly, the match was a chance for Woodward to shuffle the last few cards in his pack. Privately, he was now admitting that he was fairly sure of around 23 of his 30-man party for the World Cup. But as ever, Woodward was relentless and perfectly correct. He insisted on a daily basis during the week that it would be a full-on international match, that the preparation and the time put in by his back-room staff would be as intense as ever, that the result of the match was all-important and that anyone showing off and trying to shine as an individual at the expense of the team would be shot. People looked at his expression to see if he really meant that last bit.

It was a philosophy that served Woodward wonderfully well throughout the period of preparation and contrasted with the controversy that enveloped Steve Hansen, his opposite number. Hansen had got himself into considerable trouble with the Welsh media and public before this game by trumpeting the old trash that a performance was as important – even more important – than winning. It is doubtful if he consulted on an individual basis any one of the 40,000 or so Welsh followers in the stadium, who would have told him to a man and woman what he could have done with his concept of performance.

What Wales needed, and have needed ever since Hansen's deeply unsatisfactory reign began, is the inspiration, the lifeblood of finishing first in a rugby match. Victories bring about victories and confidence. It becomes a virtuous circle. Hansen was asking his public to show massive patience until such time as a game came along which he decided had to be won. Trouble was, when it did come along, Wales were so used to losing that they lost that too.

Yes, I may be blue in the mouth. I may be one of those annoying people who rate international coaches on the number of matches that their teams win. But internationals are there to be won, at almost any cost, and in any style appropriate – the idea is not to entertain, but to come home in front.

England came home so far in front that all you could see were their jersey numbers in the far distance. And since Woodward also received the bonus of individual excellence, then no wonder he was grinning like a Cheshire cat afterwards. Julian White, the tight-head prop with the Mr Punch nose, was back from suspension and injury, and absolutely destroyed almost the whole of the left-hand side of the Welsh scrum. When White was replaced, Woodward leapt to his feet high up in the stands and applauded him off.

Joe Worsley was magnificent at number 8 and Andy Gomarsall was effervescent at scrum-half. Yet the chief debate centred around two other Wasps, both of whom had played starring roles in making their club champions of England in the previous season. Alex King had an excellent match, showed some of the tactical nous and variations which make him arguably the most effective fly-half, week in week out, in British domestic rugby. However, drastically for King, he could only put over six of his twelve shots at goal. Clearly, if he was to understudy Wilkinson at the World Cup then he had to do so in as many roles as possible. A 50 per cent kicking rate was not good enough, and so one of English rugby's finest controllers slipped agonisingly down the pecking order.

But surely there would be a compensation for Wasps when the squad was finally announced. Simon Shaw had a history of just missing out on key selections. He was grossly unfortunate, for example, not to appear in any Test match on the 1997 British Lions tour of South Africa, but Shaw, continually reinventing himself to suit the progress of the game and relentlessly effective, had enjoyed a wonderful two seasons with his club, and in the Millennium Stadium his power and athleticism shone through. Wales would have walked across hot coals, any distance you cared to nominate, to recruit a lock one half as effective. Surely, surely, this was the day on which his trip to Australia was sealed.

Wales had no forward base; they had no momentum over the advantage line. England were by no means flattered by a return of five tries, scored by Lewis Moody, Dan Luger, Joe Worsley, Stuart Abbott and Dorian West. England's reserves were easily good enough, taking the victory over a team to which, apparently, performance was everything. Sadly, they were not able to give a performance.

17. TERROR AT THE VÉLODROME

30 August 2003 – France 17, England 16
(Stade Vélodrome, Marseilles)

So you are Bernard Lapasset, president of the French Rugby Federation. You have friends in high Parisian society, including the Government. You are anxious to allow French society peacocks the most convenient opportunity to stare and you are anxious to play where you can charge the maximum for the ticket. So where do you play your home games? The Stade de France is beautiful and genteel, but the crowd will happily make up for lack of rugby knowledge with a Mexican wave.

So you are the French supporters. Most of you live in the south of France anyway and find Parisian prices intolerable. You are the French team. You have never lost in the Stade Vélodrome in Marseilles, the monstrous, hysterical bear-pit where New Zealand and South Africa have both been put to the sword; where they'd no more consider taking part in a Mexican wave than they would applauding politely a try by England.

There was a wonderful moment during the match when Frederic Michalak, the French fly-half, was preparing to kick at goal. He was about to commence his take-off run when a figure scuttled right across in front of him, at that perfect moment to ruin his concentration. It was Dave Tennison, one of the England baggage men. Michalak missed. Mentally, after that, he was carrying more baggage than Tennison. The crowd went lunatic. Let's give Tennison the benefit of the doubt, though so much sharp practice goes on these days amongst the hordes spilling round the trainers' benches that you can never be sure.

This was, according to the match ticket, '*Un match amical*'. You'd have burst out laughing if you'd ever been to the Stade Vélodrome, to read that. It has an edge of anti-Englishness far removed from the air of Parisian gentility.

In the Stade, in high August humidity, and with many of us salmon-pink from an hour on the beach, England's run of 14 consecutive victories came to an end; it was mostly their second team, it was almost all the French first XV, England lost by only a point and could easily have won had not inexperience seen them botch the creation of field position for Paul Grayson to attempt the winning drop-goal near the end.

Was it another indication of the high standards that Woodward and his men now set that they sulked and moaned all throughout the next week – at themselves? Harshly, Andy Robinson attacked Alex Sanderson for transfer of the ball at the back of the scrum, even though it was he who had picked the Sale openside out of position.

France celebrated with a lap of honour. There seemed to be two different perceptions there: England furious when they could have been tolerably happy; France, despite the impression that they were dangerous contenders for the World Cup, were thrilled to beat England's second team. Deep down, did they still feel inferior to Les Rosbifs? We'd find out, perhaps, later in the year.

It was the evening when Austin Healey probably realised that he'd have to make his own arrangements. He had done his best to get fit and in form after injury and operations, and the Stade Vélodrome was his first and only start. Realistically, he was contending with Andy Gomarsall for the third scrum-half position.

Healey, at his best, is wonderful. He, like Clive Woodward, has yet to work out why Australians are allowed to make fun of the English, belittle their country and their sport, and yet when our Ozzer gives a bit back, he is castigated. God bless him. When Healey took Stade Francais apart in the 2001 Heineken Cup final, he showed that he was arguably the most extravagant all-round talent that English rugby has ever produced. Ever since then, battling against injury, against himself and against the fact that he could not live that Euro final down because no one could ever be so brilliant again, he has faded.

And Stade Vélodrome was just what he needed. On this occasion, constrained by the media-speak rules of Woodward's England, he could say nothing. But it was easy to guess. There's that lucky so-so Gomarsall playing against a crap Welsh team with England winning all the ball in a soft match in Cardiff; there's me, hot and sweaty, playing against the full French team in front of 65,000 madmen in a Marseilles hell-hole. That's fair?

England had aspects to be cheerful about: Mike Tindall scored a lovely try, hammering on to the perfect pass from Grayson. They could easily have scored again had not Moody tried to finesse a scoring pass, drawing the tackle to him when all he needed was to put Sanderson into open space. Later, Sanderson charged down a clearance by Michalak, sprinted after it and all he had to do was flop on it. But in his understandable excitement, he was too quick. He just needed to steady for a pace or two and swallow dive. He dived off balance and missed. Still, eagerness can't be a felony, can it?

Nicolas Brusque scored for France, and England could not set themselves for a successful late drop. You had the feeling that had one hardhead such as Dallaglio, Johnson or Dawson been out there, then Grayson might have been given a shot from an armchair.

The fly-halves were interesting. Woodward spent most of the year declaring to anyone who would listen that he was not in the least worried about the prospect of Wilkinson being injured before or during the event. Of course he wasn't. What would you lose? Merely a man who kicked more than nine goals out of every ten attempts, who is the greatest pound-for-pound tackler the game has seen, is a fine strategist, a superb passer and runner, a model professional player and a lovely fellow.

It was, of course, the wish fathering the thought. Mike Catt had been way out of contention, struggling with a hamstring injury. Catt had told me that he felt fit and raring to go, was desperate for a try-out, but Woodward, apart from popping in to one of Bath's pre-season warm-up matches, showed no interest. Dave Walder, the Newcastle Falcon, was also not quite restored after an injury layout; Alex King had missed the target in Cardiff a week before. That left Grayson, wonderfully reliable, well liked, with his own talents, composed, courageous in trying to play flat and with about as much chance of closely replicating the talents of a missing Jonny as Gareth Chilcott replicating Dame Margot Fonteyn.

The other fly-half was Michalak. Michalak has been earmarked as European rugby's next superstar since he came into the Toulouse team at 18, with the same facility to swap between 9 and 10 as Healey. He never quite settled, seemed in the previous season's Heineken Cup to be the conductor of a different orchestra than the one before him. But France had a powerful pack in the making, they had a superb set of backs, they had the knowledge that they always grow in stature during World Cups. If they could find themselves a 10, they had it made. In Marseilles, in Michalak, amongst all the tumult, did we really see someone about to shrug off the cloak of flakiness and don the mantle of greatness? Maybe.

18. CATT AND THE LATEST RUN

6 September 2003 – England 45, France 14 (Twickenham)

Who was to blame for Iain Balshaw? Accusations had been freely scattered around. Balshaw – lithe, blond and pacey – played a brilliant season for England in 2000–01, at which time he was regarded as rugby's global meteor. He cruised around fields with pace, assurance and a kind of spare elegance, and at that stage, it seemed likely that he would quickly become one of the best back three players England had ever produced.

That was then. His problems, and what could be called a personal sporting nightmare, began when he had a grave-quiet British Lions tour to Australia in 2001, just when you might have thought that the fast grounds would give him even more momentum.

Quickly, he became a peripheral figure. People inside the squad, speaking behind the backs of Graham Henry, the coach (and there were enough of those disloyal players on the trip to burn Henry's ears clean off), suggested that Henry did not trust Balshaw, did not know how to use him and that Balshaw's stock had certainly plummeted.

It always seemed to me far more likely that Balshaw was suffering from the equivalent of second-season blues. In other words, when he was the new dazzler running all sorts of new lines with which the defences were not familiar, when he had no fear of failure because he did not yet know what failure was, he was unstoppable. But once the video analysts had got their teeth into him or, more accurately, pressed his buttons, he was suddenly found out and needed new impetus and new moves. On that Lions tour it seemed that he had not yet come up with the new moves; he lacked experience to fall back on and the momentum was grinding to a halt.

His rehabilitation was badly afflicted by injury and even though he was clearly desperate to get back into the good books of Woodward, it took him a helluva long time. However, in this thumping victory, it seemed that he had timed his closing sprint to perfection. He was by no means perfect against the French, because on a couple of occasions he carried the ball too far and was caught with men in space alongside him. But a good deal of the old verve and optimism was back and it was clear from Woodward's excited reaction whenever Balshaw was in possession that Woodward was willing his man onto the plane.

There was another remarkable improvement, into the bargain. By 75,000-odd. This, effectively, was England's send-off match. They were not actually to depart for Australia for another month, but there was a festive and vastly encouraging atmosphere at Twickenham, a ground which has so often seemed to take English victories for granted. There was huge support and it was almost as if the crowd realised that their team would never be the same again – they would either return from Australia with their tails between their legs and with England in obvious need of substantial rebuilding; or, for anyone who wanted to dare the devil, there was the possibility that they might come back and be numbered among the greatest sporting heroes of all time. Maybe, just maybe, there was a portent of things to come in a rising sense of excitement. England's first team were far too good for the French shadow team. Wilkinson kicked splendidly in the first half, as ever tiding his team over a sticky patch with the oxygen of penalty goals. He missed a conversion in the second half, when England were clean out of sight. Woodward immediately replaced him with Paul Grayson. Yeah, Jonny's cracked, we thought. Hopeless.

Then, England clicked into gear either side of half-time and looked like a team of world class. They scored three tries in quick succession. First, Wilkinson chipped cleverly and Cohen, in brilliant form, ran on to score. Second, Wilkinson cleverly held the ball up high above the tackle, Greenwood came on the perfect slanting run and Cohen scored again. Third, an absolutely sumptuous show-and-go by Jason Robinson completely bewildered Clement Poitrenaud and Xavier Garbajosa. On he went with that lightning cadence (or scuttle). Finally, with England seeking a definitive statement at the end, Josh Lewsey began a splendid combined movement and popped up to score.

And that was the end of the evidence for the prosecution of England's selection process. Perhaps a certain fitfulness remained in their performance and gave hope to the massed ranks of opposing teams who were desperate for England not to take the world title. But in terms of real rugby matches, the preparation was over and it was by no means avoiding the issue of their defeat in Marseilles to say that the last time their first XV had lost a match was somewhere back in the mists of time.

As Clive Woodward walked up the room and sat at the top table, we knew that at some stage in the previous evening, some players who had slogged and slaved through the whole build-up process, had probably dreamed of standing on the rostrum waiting for their medal, had now had to pack their bags, drive out of Pennyhill Park and, the day after, clock in at their Zurich club for what must have seemed a horrendously humdrum domestic match.

Woodward appeared just a little shaky, no one envied him the tap on various doors. But he was also businesslike and brisk. The key was the 30 names he was announcing, the human interest story surrounding those he was leaving at home was up to the media and those players to whom he had had to break the dreadful news.

And Simon Shaw, the giant from Wasps, and, week-in week-out, one of the best players in the whole Premiership, was indeed discarded, effectively in favour of Martin Corry, the Leicester back-row man who had rediscovered enough of his true form to make it as a kind of utility player covering the back five. It may be true that, as the coaches hinted, the giant Shaw, superbly visible in almost every game he played, did not stand up to the baleful scrutiny of the video quite as well as the other lot. Be that as it may, he was grievously hard done by.

The other major casualties were Graham Rowntree, who had never let England down, was never likely to and had never taken a backward step when England's six forwards held on so marvellously in the Cake Tin; Austin Healey, who never recaptured his dazzling best and was making pessimistic noises for a week before the final selection was announced; and James Simpson-Daniel, once a prospect for outside-centre, once a man who held up the prospect of England rewriting the job description and using a small and yet deadly outside-centre. It had not worked out – Simpson-Daniel, sharp as a tack in the autumn, lost momentum and picked up injuries. In any case, the giant figure of Mike Tindall was preventing Woodward rewriting any job description. He was playing out of his skin.

Balshaw had indeed timed his late run to perfection, but in terms of the fast finish he was actually out-paced. Remarkably, after broad hints from Woodward that no one from outside the operation of the squad really had a chance, in came Mike Catt. Sensationally, after an absence of almost two years, the controversial Catt was back with the cream.

Woodward almost played down his return. 'Quite simply, Mike was the next person in. We'd already lost Charlie Hodgson and Alex King through injury, and once Alex was injured, it was a very simple choice. He has been out for a long time although his kicking game is fantastic.' It hardly seemed an overwhelming welcome to the prodigal son, but there were those of us who believed that Catt would not be in Australia simply to run on with the oranges.

Woodward offered a final word of consolation to Shaw. 'He would be in any other international team in the world and not to pick him is the hardest decision I have had to make in my six years as head coach with England.' No consolation, because Shaw was not eligible for any other international team in the world. He had fought a magnificent campaign to go with England, and he had failed.

The squad Woodward announced was:

Full-backs/Wings: Iain Balshaw (Bath), Ben Cohen (Northampton Saints), Josh Lewsey (London Wasps), Dan Luger (Perpignan), Jason Robinson (Sale Sharks)

Centres: Stuart Abbott (London Wasps), Will Greenwood (NEC Harlequins), Mike Tindall (Bath)

Fly-halves: Mike Catt (Bath), Paul Grayson (Northampton Saints), Jonny Wilkinson (Newcastle Falcons)

Scrum-halves: Kyran Bracken (Saracens), Matt Dawson (Northampton Saints), Andy Gomarsall (Gloucester)

Props: Jason Leonard (NEC Harlequins), Phil Vickery (Gloucester), Julian White (Leicester Tigers), Trevor Woodman (Gloucester)

Hookers: Mark Regan (Leeds Tykes), Steve Thompson (Northampton Saints), Dorian West (Leicester Tigers)

Locks: Danny Grewcock (Bath), Martin Johnson (captain – Leicester Tigers), Ben Kay (Leicester Tigers)

Back Row: Neil Back (Leicester Tigers), Martin Corry, (Leicester Tigers), Lawrence Dallaglio (London Wasps), Richard Hill (Saracens), Lewis Moody (Leicester Tigers), Joe Worsley (London Wasps)

The selection of the back-room was also almost complete. The following were to travel to Australia: Clive Woodward (head coach), Andy Robinson (coach), Phil Larder (defensive coach), Dave Alred (kicking coach), Tony Biscombe (video analysis), Sherylle Calder (visual awareness coach), Dave Campbell (chef), Simon Hardy (specialist coach), Phil Keith-Roach (scrum coach), Simon Kemp (team doctor), Barney Kenny (physio), Steve Lander (referee adviser), Phil Pask (physio), Richard Prescott (media liaison officer), Louise Ramsay (team manager), Dave Reddin (fitness coach), Richard Smith (lawyer), Dave Tennison (kit manager), Richard Wegrzyk (masseur). Uncle Tom Cobleigh, sadly, was unavailable.

PART THREE

Glory – Drop of History

19. A WALK ON GILDED SPLINTERS

2 October 2003 – Taplow, Berkshire

England had flown to Australia on 1 October. It is unrecorded how much a barrage of fervent sighs of relief from the players aided the lift-off at the end of their take-off run. Experienced as they were, fit and confident and seen-it-all, I reckoned that if any of them did not feel a childlike excitement and nervousness, or feel as exalted as Richard the Lionheart departing on a crusade, then they should not have been there.

The fact that they were favourites in the eyes of many, and the number-one ranked team in the world, contributed to a further quickening of the pulse. Nah, they can't win it. Can they? As far as these things can ever be measured, I was in no doubt that they were the best-prepared sporting team ever to leave the country. They had checked out of Pennyhill Park, the palace of sweat where they had given, frankly, everything. And if there was an ounce of excess weight amongst them then it was only because they'd had a forkful of pasta too much the night before. The rigours of the three warm-up games were almost nothing compared to the way they had trained for them, and for the real thing Down Under.

They would be away for eight weeks, to the day. As they drove out of Pennyhill Park, workmen were already dismantling the canvas gym by the side of the training field where they had toiled, and probably dreamed. They had pushed themselves through the heat of one of the country's hottest summers. One day, we went to watch them at it. 'I've been beasted,' said Stuart Abbott, the centre, as he left the field dripping with sweat. The great gladiator, Lawrence Dallaglio, found the vast demands entirely to his liking. He looked enormous, yet lean and fit as a trout. 'It's glorious,' he said of the rigorous regime. 'I am absolutely loving it. Loving it. People are chomping at the bit.'

Most of the fitness work, the planning to hit a peak at the right time, the care for the older players so that they would be left fit yet fresh, was in the hands of David Reddin, slim and elastic and always described by Woodward as 'the best conditioning coach there is'. Players of old would equate fitness training with endless communal running and thrashing around. England, of course, are different. 'Every player is at a different stage with his conditioning, so Dave has an individual plan for each of them,' Woodward said.

The sight of the day that summer was the arrival of the ice lorry, which deposited tons of ice in canvas baths that had been erected on the training field. The players would sit immersed in these for five minutes. It helps recovery, apparently, pumps out the impurities and the lactic acid when the body warms up again. I think I'd rather be tired. English rugby had not seen so much ice since the old-style RFU committee hit the gin and tonic.

Woodward had covered every base. At one conference, he was taken to task about the lack of warm-weather training – rather odd considering that England was consistently hotter than the Costa Brava all summer. As ever, Woodward was ready with the answer because he had asked himself the question months before. 'The experts tell us that to really acclimatise properly means we would have to have spent a long, long time in a hot climate,' he says. 'That wasn't possible. We think we've got things right and the hot English summer days have also been a blessing; we are increasing our knowledge about hydration, about how to produce peak performance in heat, and how to plan rest.

'But we're also talking about the effects of dew. Our games begin at 8 p.m. and dew will be coming down hard. The fields may be quite wet by then.' Dew? When had that even been a factor in rugby? It was an outward sign of a meticulousness that reached the lower registers of some kind of benevolent paranoia.

As the players departed, Neil Back looked back on the hard road of preparation. Don't forget that Back is the most slavish trainer of them all. 'I am not brown-nosing, but this is without doubt the best training camp I have ever been in.' As an exercise in removing the element of chance from rugby, it was all masterful. Admittedly, the element of chance in a game with an oval ball and capricious referees will always be high. But it was likely that the team that would win the World Cup would be the one whose preparations had given them a thin but telling edge.

Their monster squad of players, coaches, cooks and bottlewashers, augmented by a legal eagle, did not, quite, take up the whole of the British Airways 747, though they did fill the business class cabin. They'd been togged up in light grey suits with light brown shoes. No doubt that was up with the latest trends of colour combination, though they looked like a bunch that'd had their black shoes nicked.

It was all aboard, and left wheel. It was not so long ago that Martin Bayfield and Wade Dooley, the England locks of the early 1990s, all 13 ft 6 in. of them combined, had to travel in economy on the long inter-hemisphere legs. Naturally, all the officials turned sharp left on boarding. Good old amateurism. I once chatted to John Kendall-Carpenter, a high-ranking rugby official, at an airport. We boarded together and then parted at the door. 'My goodness, are you going down there?' he said with distaste, gesturing towards the economy seats.

The team arrived in Perth to an ambivalent welcome. All week before their arrival, the Australian media had shown a fascination that was almost morbid with England, all things English, and especially two rugby players. One was Johnson, because if there is one thing Australia hates above most, it is someone in the opposition in a physical contact sport palpably harder than they are. The other was Wilkinson, because if there is one thing they hate above all else, it is the idea that England could be equipped to beat them in sport. Wilkinson had with him a load of that equipment.

The knives were out for England as the country prepared to defend its sporting honour. Preparations were redoubled, tactics honed, the key players were asked to step up and take the fight to England. So much for the Aussie media. Apparently, in the Aussie rugby squad, it was much the same.

Some of the UK media party were to follow the day after the team. It was a charmed time of my life, a walk on air. Naturally, there are mixed feelings. It is always hard to leave your loved ones for two months. How would they cope? 'What am I going to do if one of Rosie's guinea pigs dies?' asked my wife, obviously distraught at my departure. She always smiles when her friends berate their husbands for staying out late once a year. Hers was saying goodbye on an early autumn day and would be back in the winter.

Most of my colleagues had been away for scores of their children's birthdays and Nick Cain, my *Sunday Times* sidekick, left just a week after Martha, his second daughter, had arrived. But I found the sense of suppressed excitement, even after four World Cups and enough tours Down Under to qualify for naturalisation (in the unlikely event I'd want to apply for it), satisfyingly high. I could not sleep the night before departure, as if I was back at home in Wales in the 1960s, willing the clock to tick around so that our holiday to Weymouth would begin.

Everything had seemed touched with gilded fortune. Even the packing went smoothly. No fretting. No throwing items in, out, in, out. For once, we were leaving out the heavy clothing – for the first time, we rugby hacks were touring in someone else's spring and summer. The World Cup was in October and November, while the normal touring slot Down Under is June/July, midwinter. I had been abroad on the longest day of the year in the UK – and therefore, the shortest day of the year where we were in the deep south – for 17 out of the last 18 years, wreathed in wood smoke in dark New Zealand June evenings, quailing spiritually in the face of the sudden and early Highveld violet sunset. I found on cold and shockingly brief Kiwi winter days that even television coverage of Wimbledon made you homesick. I once sat through a five-setter involving Jeremy Bates. This time, we were going where the sun keeps shining. Going where the weather suits my clothes. Pity they didn't suit me.

Even better, Emirates, who were carrying many of the media party, ran a promotion to send a buckshee limo to take you to the airport, providing you lived inside a 50-mile radius. I checked on a computer route planner. I lived 49.8 miles away from Gatwick. I was in, unless the driver turned left down Lake End Road and came round the long way past the Palmer Arms.

I was ready. My dear friend, Steve Bale, of *The Express*, arrived and parked his car in my drive. The limo drew up, all leather seats, and we were about to jump in. Our chauffeur even had a hat. Suddenly, I realised that I didn't have my wallet. I couldn't find it. Despite ransacking the house in a frantic panic like some despairing and peripatetic burglar, throwing things out of drawers, I never found it. I left without a penny to my name, nor a credit card, nor my press card, fuming at fate and myself. All composure gone. Was this a portent?

Ah, but American Express would come to the rescue. Wouldn't they? Remember their comforting advertised promise, to have a replacement card whisked to you so that it is handed to you at hotel check-in, or soon after, even if you are staying in the jungle, or on the moon? I ordered a new card from the back of the limo in a call of monumental proportions, which took almost the whole trip. Ten days after I asked for a card to be sent to Perth and they had promised it, it had not appeared. Ten days after it was solemnly and even smugly promised, after hunting round the wide range of Perth Amex offices (all stupefied) on a daily basis, being promised the card every time, then being told that their people had input the wrong month, or input Perth in Scotland, or that that office had closed, or moved, that it would be there next day, then the next day, then the next day, but never was, I finally received a temporary card. At last, I could start paying back the thousands I had borrowed.

When it came, my phone bill for chasing it up came to over £250 (you had to ring the United Kingdom number, local Amex offices didn't want to know), there was no freephone number, you had to hold through an interminable number of multiple-choice options, some of which directed you through to their cheapskate, unintelligible call centre in India, where you were put on eternal hold while they tried to pass the buck to someone else (no one I ever spoke to ever had a log of my previous calls, so I had to start from scratch with an explanation for every new Amex person who answered) and often, after a wait of, say, 30 minutes, the line would simply go dead.

A little later in the tour, perfectly timed for that very hour when I had to pay for some extremely urgent medical treatment, the card was disconnected. No explanation, no call to suggest I might like to pay in some money or would it be all right to maroon me. Nothing. Suddenly, it stopped working. The reason was that American Express was worried, so they said to their panicky customer, about some 'abnormal expenditure'. Apparently, I'd run up more than they thought I would – even though the proud boast is that there is no credit limit, so technically, you can charge to your card a nuclear submarine.

I asked them to consider that, as I was on a business trip lasting two months on the other side of the world, and obviously so from the record of charges, then it was likely that I might just run up the odd few dollars here and there. I explained that I needed the card within two hours for urgent medical treatment. They had a think. I could make a payment in to restore the account to reasonable proportions using my Switch card, they said. Right. Here's the number, I said.

No, they said, you can only use the Switch card option when paying via their website. It took around an hour to find the site, establish my password, and then I found that the Switch option was temporarily not available. It was less than an hour till I had to go for the treatment.

They would put my card back on line, so they said – if I could get a written bank reference that I was good for the monthly bill. I told them that it was then four in the morning in the UK. They did not budge an inch. They were snotty, condescending, rude and unhelpful. It was only in the formative stages of the World Cup, but already there was one conclusion – American Express were difficult to deal with.

20. WARM WILD WEST

3 October 2003 – Perth International Airport

The doors into the arrivals hall slid back and we were officially in Australia. There was the normal craning mass of intent faces, people desperate to throw their arms around returning loved ones and drivers holding placards bearing the names of arriving middle management.

But behind them all was a giant poster, welcoming everyone to the Rugby World Cup 2003. Such posters lined the hall. All the hire car desks seemed to be running official rugby promotions or rugby-related ambush promotions. I am categorically not numbered amongst those who deem taxi drivers to be an infallible barometer of local feeling. Whenever the Dublin Airport taxi driver asks, inevitably: 'Are ye over fer the match?' as an opening gambit to what would otherwise be his interminable monologue on the likely Irish victory and the whole sociology of the Six Nations itself, I always have ready the conversation-stopping answer.

'No.'

Yet the Perth driver was proud as punch that the tournament was coming to his country (well, his adopted country. In eight weeks I never had a taxi driver with an Aussie accent). He was clued up on the issues, spoke of a buzz in town even though the first game was still over a week away. He confessed to not following rugby union normally, but he had heard of key players ('that Wilkinson fellow'), stuck in his oar by parroting what we found was the ingrained, indoctrinated Aussie view of the England team (the Poms are boring, the Aussies are thrilling).

Whenever I go on an overseas assignment I'm always fascinated to gauge the local interest. Sometimes you might be in a venue that is buzzing because of the event you have come to watch. Sometimes, though less frequently these days, the event feels lost amongst local apathy, you find it mentioned in a tiny footnote of a local paper. As G.K. Chesterton wrote: 'Journalism largely consists in saying "Lord Jones Is Dead" to

116

people who never knew Lord Jones was alive.' True, and nice of him to mention me.

It's a matter of feeling important, I suppose. You can be sure, if the event is playing small in the locality, that the sports desk back at home will add to the sense of letdown you feel about the fact that something you have come 12,000 miles or so to report on with a sense of excitement is not registering even as a local blip.

'It's Steve, I've arrived.'

'Ah, yes. And where are you again, old boy? Oh, really? Send over six paragraphs.'

But what could you judge from a few posters in an arrivals hall? An awful lot. Two days before the Rugby World Cup 1999 began in Cardiff there was hardly a sign that it was impending. There was no recognition at the Severn Bridge, the crossing point into Wales, or at Cardiff Airport, or at Cardiff railway station. This was only the outward manifestation of an almost criminal abrogation of the organisers' responsibilities to inject everyone with World Cup fever.

In Perth, hours and hours and thousands of miles from anywhere in the far west, not a rugby city in any major sense, a week before the Rugby World Cup was to kick off, the tournament was causing a real sense of thrill. I strode into the foyer of the Perth Hyatt in great humour, till they asked to take a swipe of my credit card. The hotel manager was called. In grave tones I explained that I was rugby correspondent of the *Sunday Times*, London, that I and up to 50 of my colleagues would be favouring his fine establishment with our custom for, in some cases, 14 days and would he trust me to bring my card to be swiped when American Express sent it? He would be delighted to wait, he told me, recognising me as a guest of some standing.

That night, it was agreed as official policy that we would employ the normal means of sorting the jet lag – stay up as long as you possibly can so you sleep longer and your body clock adapts to the new zone.

'Right. We'll try to get through till 9 p.m.,' said a bright spark. At 4 a.m. in the morning, with adrenalin and ice-cold fizzy stuff fending off sleep, I sat in the hotel foyer bar. There was a major function on, and men with dinner suits and females in fine fashion were still cramming the area. Many were drunk, and one ended a nasty verbal argument with the line: '*And* I earn more than you.'

One tall, endlessly leggy girl with a minuscule pineapple-yellow and white dress, cut so low at the front and so high at the hem that it was hardly worth bothering with, tottered towards us, leaned over and, miserable and slurring, began to brief us, total strangers, on her view that her boyfriend was boring, didn't love her, men were all the same and she was very upset. She leaned forward too far, sank on top of me, swivelled so she was sitting on my lap with her endless legs in the air, and barely enough left to the imagination to fill a postage stamp. As she writhed helplessly, the manager walked by. He looked, walked over to one of his barmaids, chatted for a little while, looked again and walked away.

'What did the manager say?' I asked the barmaid a few minutes later.

'He said that party of Brit journos are quick workers, that guy with the tall girl's only checked in today.'

Later that long night, a colleague opened his toilet door. It was only when it shut behind him that he realised that he'd left his room through the exit door and was locked out, starkers. He was only on the first floor, so eventually, standing behind a pot plant, he attracted someone's attention by waving down to reception.

6 October 2003 – Scarbrough Beach

England were training that day, but strictly in private. The media diary, however, said that Samoa were training in public, at Scarbrough. When we arrived, across the dunes, the surf was way up, sifting the surfers from the posers. The Samoans were training on a large patch of green underneath the boardwalk of Scarbrough Beach, half an hour by hire car from Perth. They were training for their first match, over a week ahead, against Uruguay. Training. In public. People were seeing World Cup players at first hand.

At first, the Samoans were shambolic. Training stopped every time a swimsuit wandered by. 'Come on, boys, concentrate!' shouted Semo Sititi, the captain. They were concentrating, skipper. Very hard. Just not on rugby. Their lineout lifting drills were rudimentary. They split into small lifting teams, hoisting their big men; the ball went bouncing crazily off fingertips or was overthrown. Some of them clearly were unused to being lifted. The first time they hoist you, and the next 50 times after that, you are usually more interested in whether they are going to return you safely to earth rather than bothering about the ruddy ball.

There was no real hi-tech aura about their kick-off reception drills either – Michael Jones, the saintly former All Black, every Samoan's and every All Black's most inspirational figure, ever, stood up on the boardwalk and hurled the ball down towards the forwards on the grass beneath.

Gradually, however, they switched on. Perceptibly, the focus and the passion of a wondrously proud rugby race shone through. The semi-opposed session brought clattering hits; the urgency became palpable. If something went wrong, 30 faces would turn dutifully to John Boe, the Kiwi coach, or to Michael, in supplication. To watch them go about their business was a splendid way to spend a morning. They even had the perfect simulation for the mighty defences of South Africa and England. They attacked towards a brick wall on the edge of the green patch. Try crossing that gain line.

It has been said before, it is written every time Samoa play a match, but if they had been able to get together all those qualified for Samoa at any point in the last 15 years, if they had been able to train them up using, say, one-third of the budget which England used to prepare their squad, then the World Cup would never have taken place. No point. They'd walk it.

Then you hear that the average income for a medium-grade professional player in the National Provincial competition in New Zealand, home of the raiding parties for Samoan talent, is 25 times the average wage in the Samoan Islands. You hear the Samoan Union predicting that, unless they can get some kind of financial input, then they will have to cease to play international rugby. You hear of all the players who stayed at their professional clubs in England and New Zealand instead of travelling to take part in the World Cup because of the financial hit they would have taken.

Obviously, you admire even more, then, the likes of Terry Fanolua, the Gloucester centre, who took the hit, arrived at the World Cup with Manu Samoa, and had still not recovered his place in the Gloucester team six weeks after he arrived back. What you never hear is any recognition in the rest of the world of their plight. What you never hear is any five-year plan from the IRB to revive them.

Boe, vastly impressive, measured and yet driven, had just lost his paid post with the New Zealand Rugby Union. He could not say whether that was due to the fact that he had recently criticised them for their attitude to Samoan rugby. 'Many great players from Samoa or Samoan extraction have become All Blacks. Maybe some people in New Zealand might be a little more prepared to put something back,' he said, as the waves crashed and the tackles thundered behind him. For God's sake, New Zealand have never played a Test match in Apia. Rape the country, then ignore it.

How bitter was the frustration that the squad he had garnered from abroad, from humble Australian domestic rugby, from anywhere Samoans hung out, was effectively his second team? Did he dream of the team he could have had? 'Sometimes. But that emotion is always forgotten when you deal with these players.' He gestured behind him. 'They are very special people, they are very proud of their country and its traditions. It is such a privilege that I can be allowed to see it all close up and experience it with them. Their big hearts deserve help from the bigger powers.'

And what did the team make of this dedicated, generous (and now unemployed) man? 'John Boe,' said Sititi, 'is a Samoan.' I was determined that I would not get suckered into missing the vividness of the tournament simply by following moneyed teams.

8 October 2003 – Perth High School, behind screens

How could it be marvellous just to watch a training session? Well, it was.

For rugby camp followers and hacks on tour after tour, training would always be the social event of the morning. We'd stand on the sidelines, watch the players go through their paces, catch up on injury news, gossip and hang out. Now, the pompous big teams believe that every unfamiliar face is a spy and they train in strict secret. When England trained on a school ground at Perth, Clive Woodward was given the option of having hessian screens erected as a final counter-espionage measure. Preposterous, of course. Despite what they would have you believe, every team trains in roughly the same way.

Later in the tour, there was bickering and accusations as helicopters hovered over a session. Just to maintain some semblance of the old accessibility (most training sessions used to take place in front of around 300 adoring schoolchildren and local fans), Rugby World Cup officials set down firm rules: teams had to provide media access to either the first 20 minutes of every session or full access to one full session per week. The Samoans rarely minded who came to watch them. Other teams, such as the Romanians, were never really bothered but decided that if they were really serious then they should up their own level of paranoia, so they started private sessions, too.

The 20-minute media segments comprised the team wandering round in a desultory warm-up, before a gang of security guards and media-prevention heavies ejected everyone, usually including the protesting groundsman who was trying to mark out the adjacent pitch. Anyone who refused to leave was brutally tortured.

But Woodward was very far from the only coach who firmly believed that all the other teams were spying on them. The conspiracy theory had gained credence over the years. On the Tour to Hell, the 1998 England disaster Down Under when they lost by 70 to Australia, and both Tests in New Zealand, England had trained using a new combination of players at a shabby park in Dunedin, South Island. Unusually, Tim Stimpson, the full-back, had lined up as a wing.

Less than an hour after that supposedly private session had ended, and on the other side of town, John Hart, the All Black coach, had walked into a press conference and airily called out: 'I see England are going to play Stimpson on the wing, then.' The explanation was that an English travelling hack had joined Hart in a lift, blurted out the nugget of information and the whole thing was forever portrayed as the day that the Blacks sent spies.

Lineout codes are, apparently, a Holy Grail for the spies. In 2001, the rumours were persistent that the Wallabies had broken the Lions' lineout codes. Hardly an exercise needing the bombes, cribs and interceptions of a hut at Bletchley Park's Enigma code-breaking station. One team I played for in Wales had a cunning plan. The signal would be hidden in an apparently innocuous phrase of encouragement that the scrum-half would shout to the forwards as they stood in the lineout.

If he said a phrase with 'high' in it, it would be a front ball. If he said a phrase with 'jump' in it, middle ball. If he said a phrase with 'boys' in it, it would be a throw to the tail. I can still see Richard Beale, our confused scrum-half, contemplating at the first lineout. We all stood waiting for the call, so long that the referee was about to penalise us for delaying the game. 'Right,' he said eventually. 'Let's have a high jump, boys.'

Woodward was serious. 'If a team goes out of its way to watch you and record you, there is not a lot that you can do about it. You take the obvious precautions: the security at training grounds, security guards out there patrolling the fences. It is quite an important part of the game: if I could watch every team we play against, it would be quite an advantage. But we do everything that we can do to stop that, and, considering how huge the tournament is, we think that we have done as much as we can without being neurotic about it.'

As the Samoans trained, we combed the beach area for possible suspects. Let's see – that girl walking by with the tiny bikini. Could she be working for the Uruguayans? The old couple supporting each other arm in arm, along the prom. Look beneath the disguise. Is it really Woody and Robbo?

Neurotic? Perish the thought.

But who cared about the interests of hacks? What was of far more significance was the ever-widening gap between top rugby players and their public. No one expects international players to barge their way into public bars just to prove some redundant point about rugby's egalitarianism. But it would be lovely if the grand old tradition was preserved of allowing kids and locals to come and watch, say, one training session per week, just to touch the hem of the greats, to look in wonder at Jonny or Tana or Fabien or Wendell in close-up.

9 October 2003 – Melbourne International Airport

There was an intonation of some gravity in the voice of the television news anchor people. It was as if the Pope had arrived. 'New Zealand's All Blacks arrived tonight at Melbourne International Airport. Fresh from their triumphs in the Bledisloe Cup and Tri-Nations, the squad flew in full of confidence.' The bookies had New Zealand as favourites to win. Bookies are like that. Prisoners of habit. They still had Red Rum to win the National even after my cat ate him out of a tin.

New Zealand had won the Tri-Nations, but that had been a bizarre event. New Zealand had scored 50 points in both their away matches, in Sydney and Pretoria, almost humiliating their opponents. Yet in the return fixtures in New Zealand, they had struggled to beat South Africa by 19–11 in Dunedin, and Australia by 21–17 in Auckland.

Strange. A possible explanation was that when South Africa and Australia were playing at home, they tried to take New Zealand on in a game that was fast and loose; but when trying to claw back credibility and facing annihilation away from home, attacking New Zealand's game at the forward source, they found weaknesses. However, millions of Kiwis, if websites and phone-in programmes were to be believed, acknowledged no weaknesses. In fact, some of them never appeared to actually realise that there were any other teams in the World Cup at all.

The pictures at the arrivals hall showed a ragbag group of adoring Kiwi fans clapping their men through, showed the intent expression on the face of John Mitchell, concentrated lovingly on the fast backs, showed Doug Howlett's ringlets and Tana Umaga's dreadlocks. And the youthful face of Joe Rokocoko, already a darling.

Also pictured coming through the terminal were a group of more nondescript men, and clearly the voice-over girl had no idea who they were. I was at a loss myself. They were just vaguely familiar. Then, the penny dropped. It was the New Zealand forwards.

21. FLAG OF CONVENIENCE?

9 October 2003 – Georgia Media Day, Perth

England were now preparing to open their campaign. It was time to find Georgian material for the preview. It was a little like the British TV reporter in Edward Behr's book on journalism who, allegedly, approached groups of Belgium refugees fleeing from rebel troops in the Congo in the 1960s with the question: 'Anyone here been raped and speaks English?'

Well, there's no interview if you don't speak the language, especially if you come from Britain, the land of lazy non-linguists. And if the Georgian team, gathering a little shyly for their media free-for-all, were not going to be assaulted by England then something rather nasty in a sporting sense seemed bound to happen to them in a few days' time at the Subiaco Oval.

Already, the Georgians had been wonderful. Perth, alive with embraces for their visitors, had already formed the Georgian Supporters Club, devoted to cheering the Georgians, to embracing all things Georgian, and comprising Georgians, Aussies of Georgian extraction and Aussies with no allegiance to the country whatsoever. There were social nights, fundraising and personal appearances from the players.

In the months leading up to the tournament, persistent rumours had surfaced about the privations the squad had to battle through and the lack of finance. One report held that they had had to hold a training weekend staying in tents; the answer was that it was all a team-building endurance test and was meant to be deprived. There were also rumours of unrest between the Georgian-based players and the French-based players. Frankly, it was impossible to detect anything but unity and strength of purpose by the time they reached Australia.

What were easier to detect were the privations. Georgia's officials told a tale that was repeated by officials of a disturbing number of other nations in Australia. Some of their best players had not come. Their French employers, effectively, banned them. 'The French clubs said it is OK for them to go,' said Zaza Kassachvili, the Georgian Rugby Union's vice-president. 'But when you come back, bye-bye.' The IRB had twice investigated reports that French clubs were not releasing Georgians as they were obligated to under Regulation Nine, the sacred IRB law which gives primacy to international rugby. Twice, the clubs in question issued statements saying that they had asked their players and been told that they no longer wanted to play for Georgia in the tournament. Cravenly, the IRB threw up its hands, helpless and impotent.

Zaza was to become a minor cult figure. Clearly, whatever his official title, he was running the show, was obviously a man of some vast influence back at home, possibly high in business, or high in the Government. I watched him one day as the Georgians were waiting to board a flight. The team, and a long horde of fellow passengers, had been standing impatiently in a vast queue waiting to board, while Zaza had sat to the side, making notes and calls on his mobile. As soon as they called the flight and the queue started to shuffle forward, Zaza rose, walked straight to the front of a line of around 200 passengers, showed his boarding pass and by the time I had boarded he was asleep in his seat. Class, class.

They had no money for proper preparation, diet, warm-up matches, nothing. They had eight rugby fields in the whole of Georgia. Zaza, a charismatic, voluble spokesman, was asked about scrummaging machines.

'We have one,' he said.

Did he mean that they had one with them in Australia? 'No, we have one in the whole of Georgia.' All in all, Georgia's superb scrummaging was to be a marvel of the whole World Cup.

But consider the potential of the place; consider what the International Rugby Board is passing up in their failure to help. Recently, over 45,000 went to the Georgia–Russia match. Interest at home was enormous. Georgians are anxious to break all remaining threads tying them to the dreaded Russia, and a recent poll was conducted in which Georgians had to nominate the sport in which their country could best compete on the international stage. Over 47 per cent chose rugby; wrestling, in which Georgia already has world champions, came in second at 21 per cent; football finished nowhere.

The Georgians at least had a month of reasonable treatment. Kukri, the British-based sporting firm, had made a special set of kit and training and leisurewear, bless them. Half of Perth seemed to be wearing Georgian replica jerseys. If only the world game could ever develop a conscience about them, they would become formidable. As it was, they were facing in their first game a national team that spent more on ice for their special baths than the Georgians spent on food.

But who to interview? Someone did speak some English. Someone called Gregoire Yachvili. The media guide had him down as a 26-year-old flanker and brother of Dimitri Yachvili, the French reserve scrum-half who was in Australia with the French squad. Ah, well. Just a small peg on which to hang something. Two brothers, separate teams.

And another idea germinated as I read through the valiant Georgian media guide. Gregoire Yachvili was born in France, had played all his rugby in France, had lived nowhere but France. He'd never even been to Georgia till relatively recently, when he had played his first game for 'his' country in Tbilisi. I mentally sketched out an attack on the players watering down the nationalistic concept of the Rugby World Cup by playing under flags of convenience.

Yachvili walked up, dead on time and prepared to talk (so putting him two steps ahead already of players from the bigger teams, who were unfailingly late and treated the question 'How's things?' as if you'd begged them to confirm to you that they took performance-enhancing drugs).

'So, Gregoire. Why do you play for Georgia, you have lived all your life in France?' So he told me. It was simple. And yet it wasn't. His grandfather, Charles, was born in Georgia in 1920 as one of eleven. He was conscripted into the Red Army and fought in Leningrad during the siege by the Germans. After months of freezing temperatures and minuscule rations, he was captured and put into a concentration camp. He escaped and was recaptured. He escaped again and managed to reach the town of Brive, in southern France. There, he joined the Resistance, met a Frenchwoman who secretly fed Resistance fighters, married her, and a son, Michel, was conceived just before the Armistice.

There was no future for Charles when the war ended in a Georgia still in the grip of Stalinist Russia and where people who had been captured were seen as culpable. So he stayed. Michel grew into a sportsman. A good one. A very good one. He hooked for France in 1968 when they won their first-ever Grand Slam, had played in Australia himself, in an 11–10 defeat to the Wallabies at the Sydney Cricket Ground. He won 19 caps. He and Germaine, his French wife, had three sons – Dimitri, Gregoire and Charles-Edouard, the last named by all accounts a player of formidable promise.

Gregoire was always ferociously close to his grandfather. 'Dimitri opted for France, and I always respected his decision. But when Claude Saurel [the Georgians' French coach] approached me, I decided immediately I had to do it. It was in my heart. Now, we are at the World Cup. Many great players in France will never have the chance to play in it. But I am here. If my grandfather is looking down, he will be as happy as me.'

His first visit to Georgia had reinforced his loyalty in blocks of concrete. After Saurel had recruited him, he went to play in the European Nations Cup against Portugal. His plane touched down at Tbilisi Airport at 5.30 in the morning. There were 25 members of his family there to meet him, people he had never met before. 'It was very emotional. During the match, they flew the French flag in the stadium. And I learned so much about the Georgian people. The country is very deprived economically. They have problems to face every day, but their generosity is remarkable. They have hardly anything, but whatever they have, they will give to you.'

What of the deprivations, the impossible build-up? Claude Saurel was practically on his own as coach, Woodward had more coaches than Saurel could shake a stick at. Yachvili was unmoved. 'Maybe we would have liked more doctors and physios and attendants. But we don't have them. We have worked hard, we are very proud and we will give everything we have.'

What were the differences between the home-based element and those who played in France? 'Perhaps we have been taught more skill. But those who have come here from Georgia can teach us about fire and passion. To hear their prayer in the dressing-room before we run out is very inspiring.'

Quietly, I yanked down the flag-of-convenience angle. Gregoire's right to play for his country in the World Cup was absolute. His eyes were blazing with a quiet intent. To meet him was a delight. He was looking forward to meeting Michel and Germaine, Mum and Dad, who had fixed a trip so that they could see Dimitri's France in two games, and Greg's Georgia in two. To me, players like him were to give the tournament a heartbeat. A reason for it to take place.

In three days' time, his under-prepared but fierce team would meet England, and Gregoire Yachvili would mark Jonny Wilkinson. I felt sorry for him. Jonny, that is.

22. BRIDGE WITH A WORLD SPAN

9 October 2003 – Sydney Harbour

It is not fair on Sydney to point out that if you took away the harbour area with its Bridge and Opera House and inlets, then it would be just another ho-hum, traffic-ridden and unprepossessing big city. You can't take the Prince out of *Hamlet*. He's there, so take it as a whole.

For some time, work had been proceeding on the side girders of the Harbour Bridge. Clearly, the rugby organisers had commandeered the great landmark to put up some sort of symbol, on that part of the bridge where the Olympic rings shone out in 2000, something which would tell the passengers on the ferries beneath, the people of Sydney still unsuspecting, and the world outside, that rugby had come to Sydney.

The first formality, however, was a capping ceremony. Simultaneous ceremonies took place this evening in all the World Cup venues where teams were based. Every one of the 600 players who had arrived received a World Cup cap. There was an added touch, which was a tribute to the unstuffy Aussie approach. Every player who had originally been chosen for his country's squad but been forced to withdraw through injury also received a cap. In Britain, some parsimonious old official would have stood out against that.

That night, Bob Carr, the New South Wales president, stood near the Opera House and, as half the city craned its head towards the Bridge, he threw the switch. There, illuminated in yellow, was the familiar Rugby World Cup logo, the representation of a rugby ball as if made from scaffolding, or else like the skeleton of a fish that Tom had left on his plate as he took off to chase Jerry.

It was a memorable moment, it was a lovely idea, and we were all given a handout explaining how every rivet and cable and screw had been inserted. The logo stood up there for eight weeks and more, illuminating the bars and cafés and inlets and jetties of the Circular Quay area, presiding as opera-goers wandered the far bank opposite for *Madame Butterfly*, the production of the autumn season; towering over the famous Doyle's fish restaurant. And, figuratively, illuminating everything in a rosy rugby glow.

It was a gesture among gestures and a typical one. Australia did more than rise to the occasion of hosting a World Cup. They *made* the World Cup. Not the team, or the stadiums (good though they were), or the sights, but the people. Figuratively, on this massive island, the tournament was everywhere. The attendances over the next weeks were to be remarkable; the atmosphere created was wondrous, tangible. The people of Australia gave rugby its best party ever, and rugby has had some parties.

There was one root to the unfolding greatness of Rugby World Cup 2003: that it was held in Australia, and Australia only. Previous European World Cups had been scattered around half the continent, and the focus was shattered. The 1999 World Cup, hosted by Wales but scattered all over, was the nearest the game should ever come to staging a bad World Cup.

Australia's tournament, originally, was also to be shared. Till a messy dispute started between the International Rugby Board and the New Zealand Rugby Union, a backward body in what was, in terms of Australia, a backdated country, it was to be split between the two. The effect of the one-host concept was amazing. It was all so simple. Rugby World Cup 2003 was in Australia. Australians are proud of their country. The world would be watching. Australians wanted their country to be seen in a good light. The better the World Cup, the more reflected glory.

Whether male or female, staid or extrovert, young or old, drunk or sober, Aussie rules fans or rugby league fans or rugby union followers or none of these, they came out in gigantic numbers. They came out dressed in garish colours, gloriously willing to make a complete spectacle of themselves. In the early stages in distant Perth, 40,000 came out to watch England play South Africa, and the next day, on a grim Sunday evening, 22,000 came back to watch Samoa play Uruguay. An amazing 47,000 watched France play Fiji at the Suncorp Stadium, Brisbane; 48,000 watched South Africa play Samoa.

At the Telstra Dome in Melbourne, New Zealand versus Italy attracted 40,000, in the Telstra Stadium in Sydney, the 80,000 barrier was broken for five of the seven games, and 78,974 watched France play Scotland. The host team did not even have to be playing. It is not only a comment on Scotland's death as a rugby-watching nation but also on the fervour for the event in Australia, that all Scotland's matches in Australia drew more people than if they had been played 11,000 miles away in Scotland.

What was the most remarkable attendance of all? The final match in Pool C was between Georgia and Uruguay at the (cunningly named) Aussie Stadium, the second arena used in Sydney and formerly the Sydney Football Stadium. For that match, a dead rubber between two teams who had lost all their games, and with Pool games now formalities before the knockout stages started, nearly 29,000 people attended and split themselves between the two teams with a fervency which could not have been bettered if they had all come from Tbilisi or Montevideo. The ovation which the crowd gave to the teams at the end provided moments of the highest emotion.

The Australian Rugby Union's campaign to fill the stadiums and galvanise the people was called 'True Colours'. Every day, there would be True Colours bulletins. They punched out the messages – where the games were that day, which matches had tickets available, where the street parties were, the exhibitions, the official bars, the luncheons, the open training sessions, the silly stunts, the focus of the events, the oddities, the places to take kids. And it was not just the sheer numbers. It was the openhearted demeanour of the people who came to games and, by goodness, of almost everyone you came across outside stadiums too. Yes, long before the end there were around 80,000 travelling fans from outside the country and an army in white had almost taken over. But it was the people of Australia who underpinned it all.

One of many inspired ruses to jazz up the action was the 'adopt a second team' strategy. You could either opt to support the second team of your choice (apart from Australia, your number one) or you could even log on to the Union website and they would allocate one. Distressingly, when I tried it, they gave me Scotland.

When the cameras panned round the crowd, there would always be hundreds (at least) of people dressed up in the national colour or favoured costume of the competing teams – you never knew if, below it all, some of the fans were made-up Aussies, but most of the matches were a riot of fun and vividness and the highest good humour. When Samoa played Georgia in Perth, True Colours designated that all those living north of the Swan River would support Samoa; all those living on the south would support Georgia. When Romania and Namibia, the two bottom teams in Pool C, played what seemed, before the event, to be a god-forsaken match in Launceston, Tasmania, True Colours declared that all those born in an even year would support one team and all those born in an odd year the other.

The match that God was expecting to forsake was, of course, a sell-out.

The island embraced the match and the two teams with such fervency that the Romanian media officer was moved to tears as he tried to issue a formal vote of thanks. To a man, the players in the smaller teams lapped it up.

The business community, too, jumped on board the RWC express with a vast enthusiasm. The country was plastered, on its television commercials, hoardings, banners, local promotions, pubs and restaurants and clubs and tourist attractions and cities and outback, with World Cup material. Qantas, one of the main sponsors, ran World Cup material on a major series of television advertisements, through every airport in the country and had the tournament on their in-flight entertainment programme. Satisfyingly, analysts at the Australian stock exchange said that a rise in their share price in November was caused chiefly by their World Cup investment. Clearly, whatever Qantas had paid RWC Ltd to be an official sponsor, they had at least quadrupled the value to the sport with their own campaigns.

Every sponsor and every ambush marketeer was in a fervour. Visa set up their panel of Visa ambassadors (Francois Pienaar, Zinzan Brooke, Gavin Hastings and John Eales) who toured the country; Heineken designated hundreds of pubs as official RWC outlets; Bundaberg Rum (the famous Bundy) set up a chain of Bundy Ambassador pubs – and still you could find no one who had ever actually tasted that strange, warm, plastic-bottled concoction called Bundy and Coke.

There were Rugby Fever sites all over, each team in every location had its own gathering points (one pub became 'Boktown', another would become 'Official meeting place for England fans' and so on). Every tourist attraction leapt into the rugby schedule. 'Love Rugby, Love Sydney Aquarium,' said the giant posters on Cockle Bay Wharf.

As I say, as early as the walk into Perth Airport the tenor was established. Each media man or woman had to designate which of the main media centres he or she would use to pick up initial accreditation. Those of us chasing England and beginning our trip in Perth nominated the Subiaco Oval centre.

Anyone who'd been on the reporting circuit for long mentally set aside at least three hours to find the right place after being passed around the whole circumference of the stadium three times, to insist that you did wish to cover the tournament even though they didn't have your name anywhere, to spend another age working out where your telephones or modem sockets might be (paid for months ago), where any press conferences might take place and how on earth you worked the internal tournament information system.

We walked into the centre to be greeted with some of the most gigantic sets of beams in the history of the southern hemisphere, gave them our names and within about 20 seconds were standing there incredulous with laminated media passes around our necks, a splendid free red shoulder bag with a variety of media guides and a free battery-operated Field Ears, through which you could hear at each game either the referee, a radio commentary or a combination of both. Glory be, the sound quality was pin sharp, whereas in Europe you have to tolerate people ordering taxis and Chinese takeaways with the ref's voice wailing somewhere in the fuzz of static.

It was another 'We love our Australia' gesture. Thousands of volunteers had put up their hands, wanting to help in Australia's World Cup. The media operation was absolutely outstanding, but, again, it was not so much the technical aspects but the warm demeanour of the people involved which stayed with you.

The first impressions were wonderfully, triumphantly confirmed. Australia came alive for the World Cup. It took over the rugby nuts, it took over rank-and-file Australians and it took over every visitor with rugby or humanity in his or her soul.

People would e-mail me from the UK throughout the tournament, talking about the horrible Pom-bashing Aussie media and the loudmouth Ocker tirades that everyone supposed we were being subjected to. 'Bloody Aussies,' they said. I pointed out in reply that, with some exceptions, I had grown to rather like them.

10 October 2003 – Somewhere in Australia

If there's one thing that offends the spirit of rugby, it's the jaundiced notion held by some at World Cup time that it's only USA v. Fiji today, or Namibia v. Romania, nothing riding on that, can't be bothered to watch, let's go and play golf or have dinner. Who cares? I do. Every Rugby World Cup game is a potential delight, a potential source of joy, or controversy, or of a story, or newness.

I remember looking around the press conference after the match between Argentina and Romania at Aussie Stadium in Sydney later in the tournament and realising that the *Sunday Times*, which did not appear for another four days, had five writers present.

Maybe the bean counters at home would not have deemed it the best use of resources, maybe we'd cocked up our pre-event planning meeting in a big way. But I was proud that so many of my colleagues were keen to wallow in the event. Indeed, it was the Australian public's triumphant rejection of the notion that only a few games between the top teams meant anything that was to become one of the concrete platforms on which the success of the whole event would be based.

The match schedule was perfect for rugby followers (or, in the vivid Australian vernacular, rugby tragics) – unless you were Italian. In previous World Cups, some days would see four or even five matches played, but then there would be long empty days in between. This time, there was a match on almost every day between the opening ceremony and the start of the knockout stages. Smashing. You could focus on one match at a time, read up on it, savour the prospect and your attention span would last the distance, unless one of the boring teams was playing, such as New Zealand or Australia.

The chief casualty was Italy. They had to play their four Pool games inside fourteen days, an itinerary that not one of the major nations would ever have accepted. It was a scandal and, in my opinion, it was to cost Italy a qualification spot, which they deserved at the expense of Wales. But otherwise, smashing. I intended to watch every minute of every game either live or on television.

That was the theory. On the day we reached Perth, we collected posters given away by a Perth newspaper. It gave all the kick-off times and details of television coverage, which was to be shared between the Channel 7 terrestrial station and Fox Sports satellite station. We pored over the poster for hour after hour, hunting down our daily match fix.

But eight weeks later, we were still scratching our heads. We never really understood it. Were the starting times given Perth time, or local time where the match was taking place? Was the match to be shown live, or delayed but in full ('as live', as they call it), or just in highlights form? If it was down in the national paper as definitely live, then was it live in Perth? Australian sport is well known for regionalising live coverage. If it was not live, then we had to go down to the local media centre, which took a closed-circuit feed of every game. If it was live but on the satellite channel, then did our hotel have that channel?

'No, we can't get it in this hotel.'

'Yes, we can. I was watching Fox Sports this morning.'

'Yeah, but that's Fox Sports 1, we need Fox Sports 2. They get that at the bar in that arcade over the road.'

'Yes, but when we went in there the other day there were loads of Aussie pissheads watching that Aussie rules crap.'

But once you'd worked out from the confusing grid on the poster if kick-off time was local, or Perth time, that brought another set of problems with the time differences. Seems that every town in Australia is different.

'Let's see, Perth is three hours ahead. So that match kicks off at 7.30 this evening.'

'But is that local time or Perth time?'

'Local. We're three hours ahead of Sydney.'

'Yes, but the match is in Adelaide.'

'That's two and a half hours ahead of Perth.'

'How can anywhere be sodding half an hour ahead?'

'But, anyway, that's only being shown in the rest of Australia. It's not on here.'

It was a problem some of us never really got our heads round. Just as you were going upstairs to watch a game on television, which you were certain would be starting in five minutes, and you'd ordered six room-service pizzas for the lads, you'd meet in the hotel foyer some cleverdick and wizard of the time differences.

'See that USA–Fiji game this evening?'

'What? Oh, yes, a great game. Really enjoyed it.' You'd wander back to the room-service pizzas and scan the papers to find when the highlights were on. Hmm. At 11.30 tonight – but was that Perth time, or Sydney time? And does this hotel have Fox Sports or not?

On the Gold Coast above Brisbane, there was actually a field which marked the boundary of a time zone – most boundaries are stuck out in the desert or the bush. But while on the Gold Coast I had a medical appointment, which was given on the card in New South Wales time as well as Queensland time. When I got there, the receptionist looked a little stern. 'Mr Jones,' she said. 'You should have been here an hour ago.'

10 October 2003 – Sheraton Hotel, Perth

England announced their team to play Georgia in the opening game, and the pent-up energy could, at last, at bloody last, be released. Lawrence Dallaglio, even walking through the open spaces on the banks of the Swan River, had the air of a caged tiger.

The consistency of Woodward's preparation was obvious when you scanned the media release. Josh Lewsey was at full-back; Jason Robinson and Ben Cohen were on the wings; Will Greenwood and Mike Tindall were in the centre; and Jonny Wilkinson and Matt Dawson at half-back; Trevor Woodman and Phil Vickery were Steve Thompson's props; Ben Kay would partner Captain Fantastic; and Richard Hill, Lawrence Dallaglio and Neil Back were in the back row.

Perhaps one of the last to confirm himself in the starting team had been the mighty Tindall, Bath's 16-stone Yorkshireman. Woodward's hankering for Bobby Dazzler at outside-centre had been strong and he and Andy Robinson had both been on Tindall's case for years. 'They said I should work on my feet movement, pace, running lines and speed off the mark.' So they thought your hairstyle was all right, then, Mike? There were plenty of other reservations – expressed by people like Will Carling and Stuart Barnes, who felt that he was too heavy-footed.

But since then, the change had been profound both in Tindall's game, as he showed with a devastating performance in the Grand Slam match against Ireland in Dublin, and in the perceptions of him.

'He's up there with Jonny, Lawrence and Johnson,' Woodward had told me just before England left Pennyhill. 'He's up there as a senior player.'

'Well, I'm not quite in the back of the bus yet, with the real old-timers of the inner circle. But I think I have made a good progression, though there is always another level you aspire to. I'd still like to be as elusive as Jason Robinson and you'd always like the gas of a Balshaw. But if you are always making progress towards those ideals, then you can be happy. I am stronger and quicker now than I was a year ago, even six months ago.

'It's also important how you interact with the others. Confidence means something inside yourself, but it's also a matter of positioning on the field and being able to read what others are doing. I understand better what Jonny's trying to do and what Jason is up to, and I am running better lines off them. I am also stepping up to the plate more. Some people come in at 20 and immediately start calling their shots. It took me a little longer to feel comfortable doing that.'

Sometimes, I become nervous when rugby teams talk about all-out attack, about dazzling. New Zealand had won two Tri-Nations matches through back-line brilliance. But was it ever enough? Mike Tindall, it seemed to me, brought a priceless set of gifts to the party. He could play rugby; he could really shift. But if it went wrong, he could grab the ball, beast it up and hang on till England regrouped. The last piece of the jigsaw, perhaps. But now he was the full picture.

10 October 2003 – WACA, Perth

From the window of the Perth hotel you could see the floodlight pylons of the WACA, where once the fastest wicket in cricket lay in wait for frightened batsmen. Australia were about to play Zimbabwe in the First Test of a series and both teams were staying in our hotel. The Aussie team, compared to the sleek giants of a national rugby squad, looked like a posse of scrawny posers.

Heath Streak, the Zimbabwe captain, was far more impressive. Streak was still leading out his beloved country even though the desperate regime of Robert Mugabe had driven many of his best colleagues out of the country and overseas to earn a living; he was still leading them out even though the land-grabbers had taken away three-quarters of the land of his father, who had been briefly imprisoned for failing to hand over his farm, his life's work, to the Mugabe mobs. Heath himself had staved off one part of the grab, arriving at the gates in full Zimbabwe kit, eventually signing autographs as the mob, faced by a quiet and impressive gesture, disbanded.

You felt deeply for him, trying to earn a living, trying to make sense of a situation where the country he loved was descending into brutality, battling between opposing extremes. The Zanu PF thugs (some of them actually on the Zimbabwe cricket board) would stamp on any dissent from the cricketers, putting paid to the career of Henry Olonga, the black fast bowler who went public with his contempt for the regime, effectively exiling himself in fear of his life. But Streak was also criticised by anti-government activists for failing to take a strong anti-Mugabe line and for calling for cricket contacts to be maintained – as if his life was worth a few public pronouncements. All very well for them.

On the sporting field, no respite. He had led Zimbabwe up hill and down dale for years, battling through one-sided Test matches and a torrent of one-day internationals, bowling over 3,500 overs, with a team increasingly denuded of top players, with a 20-year-old vice-captain. Earning a living and leading his country with supreme dignity.

On the morning of the first day of the first Test at the WACA, I met him in the newsagents. There was just a suggestion in the early tour games that Zimbabwe were improving. 'Good luck with it,' I said as we both stood at the counter. 'Thanks very much,' he said softly, and walked away.

Two days later, I came across him again. He came staggering into the hotel, grey-faced and vacant. He had bowled for two days. Australia's score was 735–6, and Matthew Hayden had just made the highest score in Test history, 380. Streak's analysis was 0 for 136. It seemed it was a quick wicket – quick off the bat. But despite the weakness of his team, what else was there to do than go out the next day and try to save the game? (They didn't.) He is a cricketer. Given the desperate nature of his country's government, what else was there to do but endure? After all, he is a Zimbabwean, too. Great fellow.

23. THE CEREMONY OF THE SCRUM

10 October – Telstra Stadium, Sydney; Opening Ceremony

If you were comparing the 2003 World Cup with Wales 1999, I suppose you'd say that Wales effectively went into an early lead. The Sydney Opening Ceremony was fine, but not as passionate, acclaimed or as moving as the proceedings in Cardiff. The Telstra Stadium, scene of decent derring-do at the 2000 Olympics (even though the home country had a one-athlete athletics team) is nowhere remotely as imposing as the Millennium Stadium.

At that time, Wales and Welshness was going through a heady time; Welsh rugby, fresh from a victory over England at Wembley, had come roaring back to the newly opened arena on a high after ten successive wins, all over elite teams.

It was also a time when Welsh bands ruled the rock scene. Catatonia played at the ceremony, when they were darlings of all Wales. When Cerys Matthews, the lead singer, took off her black jacket on stage and revealed a red rugby jersey underneath, the roar was louder than for the Welsh tries later in the day. Bryn Terfel and Shirley Bassey may be an unlikely pair, but they gelled passably in a duet.

Aussie 2003 offered us Deborah Cheetham and Jose Cura. Well, was Deb from Tiger Bay? Was she one of the leading middle-of-the-road divas and trouts on the planet? As for Jose, if you want a rather portly bearded baritone then Bryn's your man. But God bless them, even though only their mothers might have known them well, they sang the Australian and Argentine anthems magnificently.

There was one absolutely delightful item. John Eales arrived carrying a ball and around 1,000 children engulfed him – the adoring mass changed shape and, by using the kids in the correct formations wearing the correct colours, they formed a giant rugby player, which, when perceived from above, 'ran' down the field and scored a try.

We then had that household name on the rock front, that answer to the Beatles, Led Zeppelin, U2, Linkin Park and all the others – er, George. Let's hear it! Suit yourself.

Anyway, no sniggering. It was a colourful opening, it was fun, most of it worked, and John Howard, the cheerful Prime Minister (not quite so cheerful eight weeks later, but we will come to that), declared the fifth World Cup up and running.

Next day, True Colours reported sales at the catering outlets in the stadium. In the land of the free and the fit (so the legend of Australia runs) they sold 500 bowls of salad – and 23,000 buckets of chips, 15,000 hot dogs, 15,000 hot pies, 3,500 pizzas and 3,500 hamburgers. Legend? Huh!

10 October 2003 – Australia 24, Argentina 8 (Telstra Stadium, Sydney)

Naturally, no one wanted to see Australia turned over in the opening match of their own World Cup. Well, not more than a few million here and there. All right, every non-Australian on the planet. And England sat bolt upright for this one. When I had last sat down with Woodward we had both agreed that our tips to reach the final were Australia and England, and his five years living in Manly, near Sydney, and the evidence of the cricket, rugby and rugby league teams of the past decade, has given him a fierce respect for the Australian sportsman; if never an affection.

But they won all right, in a match that enthusiastically embraced the proud tradition that the opening game of every World Cup is poor. But some of that old assurance, that relentless ball retention and that incisiveness seemed to be absent. Being saved for another day? Gone for good? Who knew at the time?

They did not seem to be particularly stunning. George Gregan, the lithe captain, had visibly lost his fizz in the season to date. His partner-in-crime around the fringes, Toutai Kefu, had to miss the tournament with injury, and it was a sad blow. Gregan had also crossed swords before the tournament with John O'Neill, the ARU chief executive, over financial rewards for the team. Gregan is always at his best when conspiring with big back row men around the fringes, shouting and then smarming the ref, sledging and sliding. It seemed to me that his shoulders had slightly hunched and that David Lyons, the new number 8, had nothing like Kefu's old ability.

No one in the world of front-row play rated any of the props in the squad. A South African journalist spent the World Cup patiently trying to sell the *Sunday Times* his story 'proving' with diagrams and reactions from opponents that Bill Young was the biggest cheat in the front row union – though Brendan Cannon was bound to become a star of the World Cup as hooker.

They had clearly not yet had a return on their considerable investment in rugby league talent, because Wendell Sailor and Mat Rogers, wing and full-back respectively, who were chosen for the first game, and Lote Tuqiri, who was not, had been no more impressive than, say, the reserve Wallaby players whom the trio had leapfrogged and who came buckshee. It would be fascinating to see if they picked up the union pace.

And the midfield? For the opening, they stationed Elton Flatley and Matt Burke, one a sound but unspectacular footballer and one a bigger, sound and yet unspectacular footballer, and defensive coaches in the tournament simply turned over and went back to peaceful sleep.

Of course they had talents – Larkham, though only fitfully these days, might unblock a defence with a pass; Nathan Sharpe and David Giffin were a giant pair of locks, and the double openside combination of George Smith and Phil Waugh, given lax refereeing, could be wonderfully effective. But unless Eddie Jones, the coach, was holding something back that was explosive, unless a young thruster such as Matt Giteau could come on and revive them, unless they grew massively into their Wallaby jerseys simply by the goad of being the host team, it seemed they would be beatable. Their continuity game was now old hat, especially since the likes of Kefu and Owen Finegan were no longer around to beast the ball up.

Ultimately, Argentina's inner men could not bring themselves to agree with this theory. They played as if they did not really believe they could win; they fiddled around with silly play – Felipe Contepomi missed easy kicks at goal, a disaster. Manuel, his brother, chased a perfect kick falling under the Wallaby posts, needed a gymnastic jump to contest the ball or else to hammer the catcher, Mat Rogers, to try to force a turnover. But stupidly, he took Rogers out in the air, went to the sin bin and the chance was lost.

There is just a slightly panicky air about the Pumas these days. At their best, they can beat anyone, and I mean anyone. When their pack decide that it is prepared to move about the field, when they are hit-hit-hitting on the pick-and-drive up the fringes with Gus Pichot sniping and slithering like an eel, when either Gonzalo Quesada or Felipe Contepomi are organising some back play, when Ignacio Corleto wants to play, rather than pose, they can be deadly.

But there is a point of critical mass that they cannot quite reach. They reached the quarter-finals in 1999, dumping Ireland, and they lost track in a winnable and brilliant quarter-final with France only because, so it seemed, the enormity of what they were about to achieve hit them. They were robbed of a victory they absolutely deserved by horrendous officiating in their away match in South Africa in June 2003, being called back after a try had been scored for a penalty against an Argentina forward who had thrown a punch while retaliating after being attacked when trapped on the floor. But they cannot break through into the clear air of the top five in the world, and a team that has been together for so long will soon begin to break up. A shame, because they are the only contenders from outside the old elite.

Australia scored the first points of the World Cup when Flatley put over a penalty; they scored the first try when the burly Sailor battled his way over with real conviction, through three tackles. They had matters pretty well in hand.

However, the Pumas, maddening at first because of their frailties, then became even more maddening when they showed what they could do. Pichot finally trusted the backs outside him (Argentina backs normally come into the same category as great black swimmers, great Scotland goalkeepers and great All Black props). When he did so, Jose Orengo made a brilliant break, held the ball up and, in millimetres of space, found Corleto outside him for the try.

What happened next threatened to plunge the World Cup into early refereeing controversy. The previous autumn, Woodward had raised the question of illegal blocking runners in front of the ball, and England had also travelled down in a white funk in case referees were going to toe the southern line and not allow teams to scrummage properly. The refereeing authorities claimed, however, that everyone was on the same song sheet; there were no differences in interpretation between the hemispheres. They put themselves to the test immediately by appointing Paul Honiss as referee for the opening match, a New Zealander who seemed to personify the differences that have always existed.

Australia tried to strike back immediately after the Corleto try. Giteau had arrived as a replacement and when he attacked down the right, he dummied to pass to Burke, Burke ran straight on and cleaned up Manuel Contepomi, Giteau ran the ball right behind Burke's blocking run, Joe Roff ran straight through the hole that was cleared for him by the taking out of Contepomi, and ran on to score. Honiss let it go.

He also infuriated the Pumas' tight forwards beyond words. He whistled them to distraction for throwing the ball in crooked to the lineout, and yet allowed the Australians to throw the ball straight down their own line. He allowed Australia to do what Australia always do in the scrum – fuss and fret and collapse, stand off the hit, avoid the confrontation, dissipate. Anything.

In both these two aspects Honiss was clearly betraying the IRB charter to allow fair contest for possession. Honiss had been asked about his sense of anticipation before the match. 'I'm not nervous, although there could be a few butterflies when I run on to this great stadium,' he said. Butterflies when you ran on? We'd seen you referee before, Paul. We were wetting ourselves.

Australia eventually coasted through till the end, their challenge to retain Bill, as they called the William Webb Ellis trophy, well launched. It was a good, if not a spectacular, start. But we were off, and running.

11 October 2003 – Sheraton Hotel, Perth

This afternoon, South Africa were to play Uruguay at the Subiaco. First, Woodward and Robinson faced a breakfast media gathering. I allowed the opening salvoes to pass. 'Clive,' I said. 'There is supposed to be standardisation of laws. But didn't Australia score their vital try from a classic illegal block?'

He was not, quite, up for a barney that early. 'Well, referees have a difficult job and sometimes at ground level it's difficult to get a complete picture of what is going on,' Woodward said. I didn't follow up by pointing out that Honiss did not have to see the block. It was so thunderous he could have heard it.

'Andy,' I said. 'The Pumas were clearly annoyed that they felt they were not allowed to scrum properly. You've come down with a big scrum. Are you worried you will not be allowed to use it?'

'Scrummaging is part of the game; we want to be allowed to scrummage. We certainly expect to be allowed to scrummage against Georgia and South Africa, because they will want to scrummage too.' Robinson was still privately fuming at the refereeing of the scrum on the 2001 Lions tour.

That was their public view. I hope that it is not unethical to point out that they were not remotely so measured in the off-the-record briefing afterwards. In the old disagreements in rugby philosophy, England would suffer if a conspiracy (subconscious, of course, old chap) grew to nullify their strengths. The subject died down with a week or two of reasonable refereeing. But it was to return and at one stage threatened to haunt Woodward and Robinson to their graves.

24. MARCHING FOR GEORGIA

12 October 2003 – England 84, Georgia 6
(Subiaco Oval, Perth)

At last, England were playing a World Cup game. White jerseys in earnest, on the field and around the stadium. The first loud stirrings of what was to become support of magnificent quality throughout England's campaign.

First, what was to become a familiar pre-match tableau unfolded. After raucous pre-match music, after the interaction of wonderfully colourful crowds, the stadium public address system would lapse into quiet. Then, a short riff from the 'World in Union' song would be played, and repeated.

First on to the arena would be the four singers who were to sing the anthems, a duet for each side. The organisers had gone to a deal of trouble to put together the World in Union choir, which supplied the four singers for each game. They were all decked out in a colourful cod national costume, almost surreal in its gaudy representations and dazzling colours.

The referee and match officials would have to walk with them in formation towards the centre of the field. Fancy having to walk alongside those clowns. The singers must have been really embarrassed.

Frankly, all the anthems seemed secretly to have been rewritten especially. Every one now had a lead-in coda of whoo-whoos and mock ethereal strains before it even plunged into something we knew and loved as 'God Save the Queen' or 'Advance Australia Fair' (their home is girt by sea, you know). It was all just a little smaltzy, but I thought it worked a treat. The singers were excellent, and the anthems became a major signature of the tournament – the cameras always lovingly panned down the line as each team hugged and blubbed itself into a patriotic stupor, bawling tunelessly through. The prize for visible emotion during an anthem was hotly contested throughout, though an Englishman was to snatch it with a late, tearful bawl.

In these days of caps of convenience and poaching of players, it was often striking how many members of each team stood there mute, essentially because 'their' anthem was sung in someone else's language or because they felt false bawling and blubbing when they wore a jersey other than the one they were supposed to have been born into. But the pre-match festivities were often epic. If only the refs had ever sounded so good.

And to look around the Subiaco Oval as the teams followed the singers and the referees was a remarkable thing. It was a filthy wet Sunday night; torrential rain had fallen for hours (and how we laughed when we recalled the stories we had written about the likely weather: 'England face frying hell', and so on). It was a non-rugby city, as we knew. The Subiaco Oval is normally home to the West Coast Eagles and Fremantle Dockers, the Rules teams.

But over 40,000 came to watch, and gave the match a tremendous atmosphere. We had suspected from an early stage that Australia's rugby lovers, and also Australians in general, were in a fervent, wonderful party mood. They never let us down.

After three minutes and nine seconds, Jonny Wilkinson put England on the board with a penalty. After eight minutes and thirty-seven seconds, Malkhaz Urjukashvili put Georgia level with the equalising penalty. For five minutes, till Mike Tindall burst through to score with the same kind of weaving run he had unleashed against Ireland in the Grand Slam match, Georgia stayed level.

Thereafter, the size and power of England kept them hammering in the tries. Matt Dawson, who was not at his sharpest, scored the second and then the mighty Steve Thompson gave startling notice to the other teams of his prowess, blasting the remnants of the cover to score at the posts. Dad's Army provided two platoon members for the scoreboard soon after, with Back and Dallaglio scoring. Will Greenwood scored twice, Ben Cohen contributed another two – including one from a hanging diagonal kick perfectly measured by Paul Grayson. Cohen is a giant of a man, he is quick, he can jump, and he is dextrous. The hanging punt to the corner must have been in the nightmares of every wing he marked. Loose ends were tidied by late tries from Mark Regan, Jason Robinson and Dan Luger.

Of the twelve England tries, Wilkinson converted five from five, kicked two penalties from two attempts and as the television commentator said, 'This guy doesn't know how to miss.' He was to find ways of missing in the weeks ahead. But a rather handy knack of kicking those that truly mattered. He walked off after 46 minutes.

Paul Grayson added four conversions and Paliko Jimsheladze added a penalty for Georgia. In another era, England might have been inclined to allow Georgia the consolation score for which neutrals, and even the large English contingent at Subiaco, were desperate. Instead, quite rightly, they were clearly making a point of giving up nothing.

It was by no means a sensational performance but there was the satisfying impression that rust was being rubbed away and that something with a passable gleam lay underneath. There was also passable injury news. There were a few anxious moments with the scrum-halves but a hamstring injury suffered by Richard Hill, overwhelmingly a key man, would be right again, so the medicos confidently predicted, inside two days. They proved to be, however, the longest two days.

Yet Georgia, remarkably, kept their shape. Gregoire Yachvili reflected afterwards that he had never been called upon to tackle so much in his life. In the front five, Goderzi Shvelidze and Alexandre Margvelashvili, the props, held the scrum together valiantly.

Afterwards, Woodward was full of praise. 'It was just the kind of hit-up we wanted,' said Woodward, never knowingly behind with the latest item of state-of-the-art trendy sporting guff phraseology. 'I thought Georgia were marvellous.'

Johnson agreed: 'They played a very physical brand of rugby and made us work hard in the scrums and mauls. They put in some big tackles and their big guys caused us a few problems, especially in the second half.'

The Perth crowd gave the Georgians a wonderful reception at the end as they performed a mini lap of honour. To their great credit, Martin Johnson and the England team waited patiently at the entrance to the tunnel for the lap to be completed and clapped the Georgians from the field. Why should these things mean much? Who knows, but rugby is full of those touches, and they enrich the sport whenever they occur.

The day before, at Subiaco, South Africa had opened their tournament with a 72–6 win over Uruguay. Joost van der Westhuizen, the old stager at scrum-half, scuttled for a hat-trick of tries and South Africa looked fit and fast, especially with Joe van Niekerk and Juan Smith in the back row. They looked tall, rangy and dangerous.

England had six days' rest before they were to meet Rudi Straeuli's men. The pressure was already suffocating, and no one could even begin to ponder the rest of the World Cup till that world-turning match was over. Corne Krige, the South African captain and chief nutcase of Twickenham 2002, gave a press conference in which he offered the opinion that Martin

Johnson was the dirtiest captain in world rugby. Not while you live and breathe, Mr Krige.

15 October 2003 – Fiji 19, USA 18
(Suncorp Stadium, Brisbane)

But anyone concentrating solely on the major teams was missing a glorious World Cup. France had opened with a heavy defeat of Fiji by 61–18, though not before Rupeni Caucaunibuca, a remarkable, stocky and devastating wing, had burned them for a try. He then did more damage, lashing out at Olivier Magne, and was arraigned before the citing commissioner. He was suspended for two games, enough for him to contemplate the dangers of allowing a flaky temperament to hide a brilliant talent.

But France, lithe in figure-hugging Lycra, confident and measured, powered past, with Yannick Jauzion, the new centre, scoring a hat-trick in a vivid match. They played in smooth lines; they looked fitter and more disciplined than ever. We knew now that, barring some earth-shuddering upset, they would reach the semi-finals, and we knew also that they have a superb record in World Cup semi-finals. It seemed that every grudge from Agincourt to the British Beef BSE scare would be recycled shortly if England went through too.

Ireland had beaten Romania 45–17, and lovers of heroic resistance were thrilled to see Romania impose long periods of pressure. They were unlucky to score only two tries, a penalty try and another by Valentin Maftei. Ovidiu Tonita, the flanker, had a prodigious game for Romania. Ireland, with the driving force that is Keith Wood, desperate to bow out on a high and before bits of his battered body simply began to fall off, seemed as they always seem – keen, class in some positions, mediocre in others.

Their gem, their cutting edge, is always Brian O'Driscoll. In those early matches, he sported a trendy new hairstyle. Either that made his face a little fatter or he had put on a few pounds. Certainly, he was not himself. Form or pies? Who knew? I remember him discussing his glorious form on the 2001 British Lions tour where he had shredded Australia. His theme was that he had worked relentlessly, ferociously, on his fitness. 'But, of course, you can't work like that all the time.' It was something an England player would never have said.

The other two home countries had already raised hopes – in the hearts of all those who loved shock results. Wales, coached by Steve Hansen, a New Zealander who seemed to be trying to refashion the team and the country's domestic rugby in a Kiwi image, were turgid in victory over a very poor Canada, even though they came through 41–10; they were only average in beating Tonga by 27–20, scoring two tries against three in a match of pale colours.

At that stage, they were clearly inferior to Italy, who seemed better organised. Even if they beat Italy and sealed second place in Pool D, they would have to play the All Blacks in the final Pool game and, probably, the dreaded English in the quarter-finals. You could even have found a few Welsh followers who would have accepted an aggregate margin of defeat of 100 points from those two games, had you offered it to them at the time.

Scotland opened against Japan and shook them off only at the end, chiefly through a large surge inspired by Simon Taylor, their pedigree forward. They won 32–11, but at one stage, after a brilliant try for the effervescent and much-improved Japanese, from Hirotoki Onozawa, it was only 15–11. Ian Robertson, BBC Radio's commentator, sat in the media room receiving a savage verbal battering from his colleagues. He was white till Taylor struck late.

Japan's lack of physical stature militated cruelly against them – they would be driven off the ball in the tackles, although Masao Amino and Masahiko Toyoyama held on grimly to try to anchor their scrum. But they were dashing when they had the ball, and if they can find some size and power to graft on to their electric talent they might be in business. Perhaps Japan's womenfolk could strike up friendships with sumo wrestlers, in the national interest.

Italy conceded their match against New Zealand by keeping their top team off the field, and duly lost to the All Blacks by 70–7. But they revived to beat Tonga in Canberra, by 36–12. Denis Dallan was outstanding on the wing, but much of the new Italian power came from Sergio Parisse, the youngest man every to play Test rugby at number 8. Italy, like Argentina, usually looked a decent side desperately short of the oxygen of confidence. You feel that if they ever won three games on the trot, they would be off and running.

Fiji also recovered from their opening reverse against France, but they had to sweat buckets for it. Mac McCallion, the Fiji coach, claimed to have aged ten years on a fervent night in Brisbane – and at the beautiful, rebuilt Suncorp, everyone's favourite tournament arena, there was never any other sort of night. Kort Schubert, the Eagles' flanker, touched down a brilliant try at the very end and, with the clock having ticked down and out, Mike Hercus, the fly-half, had to kick the conversion for victory in the last act.

The poor man. Originally, he seemed to strike it well. But the ball never turned inwards, eased its way outside the far post and the Fijians had won 19–18. 'I can't put it into words how I feel,' he said afterwards. 'Could you?' Nope, mate. No one had the heart or the need to remind him that America had never won a match in the Rugby World Cup finals. They had one chance left.

It had been a fervent match and it also underlined the sheer box-office power and enthralment with the concept of the game clock. In European rugby and, indeed, almost everywhere in the world, the referee is sole judge of time and injury time. You never really know how long there is to go in a match until the final whistle blows. There is tension, but nothing gripping.

In the World Cup, there was a timekeeper off the field, operating digital clocks around the stadium. Whenever there was an injury or when the match had to stop for a referee's warning, the referee would signal and call 'time off' and then 'time on'. The clocks would stop on the time off and start clicking over on the time on. So you always knew precisely how long was left. It added greatly to the tension as the inspired Americans crafted their late try. It took years off the life of poor Hercus, as he knew that the clock had run down. And in a later match, you could have sworn that some cheating Aussie had slowed the tock so that it came too long after the tick.

One team was not scraping their victories. New Zealand demolished Italy by 70–7, with two tries each from their artists, Rokocoko, Howlett and Spencer; then they thrashed Canada by 68–6, with four tries from Mils Muliaina, the exciting full-back; and then Tonga by 91–7, with heavy scoring from their backs. They looked fast-moving and relentless.

All nice and sizzling. It is hard on any team, of course, to score nearly 230 points in three games and then you tell them they've proved nothing. But teams were clearly concentrating resources on winnable games, and, as yet, the New Zealand pack had not been tested. Not like their medical staff. Against Italy, Tana Umaga, the conscience of the team, had suffered a serious ligament injury falling over his own player. Conservative estimates held that it would take him three months at the very least to recover. Sad, and a pillar removed.

Oddly, next day, when we scanned the tournament's internal news service, there was no news of a replacement. Oddly, John Mitchell allowed himself to be persuaded that Umaga would be fit for the final stages. He stayed, hanging round, frankly, like an albatross. Umaga never played again in the tournament, and only Umaga, Mitchell and the doctors really know if they wasted time, stress and hope on a lost cause, and a distraction.

But the points avalanche at least showed that they could play rugby. One of the abiding images of the early weeks was of the New Zealand backs taking it in turns to score, and when one did, the others would come running up, beaming happily, to congratulate them. Perish the thought that they realised to be first on the scene after a try is to guarantee global television exposure.

But with a variety of photogenic dives and tosses of curls and dreadlocks, the likes of Muliaina, Howlett and Rokocoko soared to the top of the tournament try-scoring charts, and wouldn't you know it, they were still there at the end. Which was more than you could say, incidentally, for their team.

Australia were also treading water in the sense that their two middle Pool games, against Romania, when they scored 90 in Brisbane, and Namibia, when they scored 142 at the Adelaide Oval, were walkovers. Contrary to pre-tournament gloom, Namibia were the only team to prove seriously uncompetitive. But did this feast of Aussie tries (Latham scored five against Namibia) mean anything in the wider context of the event?

What did mean an awful lot, however, was the continuing colour and verve of the rugby and the backdrops, and the passionate drumbeat coming from the out-grounds.

25. HIGH ROADS

Woodward was always extremely protective about the inner workings of his team room. One day, for the sake of accuracy, I asked the team's media manager the name of the chef travelling with the team. He reacted as if I'd asked for a photostatted copy of the game plan for the Springbok game or if I was going to ask the chef to poison the team. 'Can I ask you what you are going to write about him?' I don't think he ever came back to me.

Woodward occasionally opened up. He was proud of his medical team. 'We pride ourselves on having a world-class set-up in every area, and the medical team is right up there.' Simon Kemp, one of the relative newcomers to the team, headed it. He had under him two physios, Barney Kenny, an amiable shaven-haired figure, and Phil Pask, formerly a very fine openside flanker with Northampton who had given up his practice to go full-time with England. You'd see Phil and Barney everywhere, prowling hotel pools as players trod water in rehab, putting them through silly walks to freedom from injury. There was also Richard Wegrzyk, who was masseur, father confessor and, even by the formidable work ethic of the whole party, on the driven side of industrious.

'The four of them work incredibly hard and work incredibly long hours. Their area of the medical room, I never go to, nor do the other coaches. It's their area and the players' area; we just keep our distance completely. I will meet with the doctor once a day and I totally trust what he says.' We were to let it pass when three weeks after the medical staff told us that Richard Hill would be available again in two days, he was still struggling to be ready to play any meaningful part in the World Cup. Injuries. You just can't rely on them.

Nevertheless, Woodward clearly revelled in the professionalism around him and rightly so, because it was he who had put the team together. He spoke in praise of Kemp, the doctor. 'We just call him . . . [everyone craned forward so they would not miss the gem of a nickname] . . . the Doctor.' Wow! Who'd have thought it? He also gave us an insight into Johnson's leadership. He was fulsome. 'And his famous words are . . . [everyone craned forward again in order not to miss Johnson's Churchillian epic lines] . . . let's get on with it.' Ah, well. Johnson was always a rather industrial gem. But still a gem. 'He never says very much,' Woodward said, 'but this week he's probably spoken more than I've heard him. That is the importance of the match.'

Any levity disappeared as the match approached. The South Africans were staying down in Fremantle, in an old colonial hotel with balustrades, and they were talking and training mean. Woodward revealed that he had come across the Springboks at the capping ceremony which had been held a week before the game. 'I don't think either side was too happy to be pitched together in the same room. But I shook hands with Corne Krige and Rudolf Straeuli, and had a few polite words. It was probably good because you do get a lot of things blown out of all proportion, especially in the media, going into these big games.

'But the bottom line with all these opposition players and coaches is still that rugby has got that ethos that you want to beat each other hugely during the 80 minutes. But I have never met a coach or player in the environment like last night who doesn't want to shake hands and have a chat. It did break the ice a little bit and it just proves that rugby does have this fundamental ethos, which is excellent, despite the history between the two countries, and long may that continue.' A day later, Woodward complained because the two teams had to stand in a narrow tunnel prior to taking the field.

Phew. In the past, players from the two countries that had met on Lions tours formed friendships that lasted decades into the future. Now, we had to celebrate a handshake and a few stilted words as confirmation of all that made rugby great. Ah, well.

There was one thing that was unlikely to continue – the World Cup campaign of tomorrow's loser was going to be permanently dented. It was reasonably effortless to make a case that proceedings at the Subiaco would constitute the most important match to date in England rugby history. At the time, it made even neutral pressmen feel sick with nerves.

There was also something vaguely disturbing in the air. Enormous numbers of rugby followers had come into town from the two countries, and Perth had large numbers of residents of English descent and probably even more of South African descent, escaping the crime of the Rainbow Nation.

I have always deemed it preposterous and patronising for rugby people to decry the arrival of non-rugby people in the ranks – how else is the game to grow? But it is also true that English sports followers abroad have been known to behave shockingly, that you would never have problems in any case distinguishing between a Springbok supporter in drink and a ray of sunshine. The fervent wishes of the home media that the English be thrashed also added an edge.

Walking to our seats, sensing a bite in the stands, and recalling memories of Twickenham 2002, we were uneasily aware that if a big rugby match was ever going to kick off both on and off the field, it was probably this one.

18 October 2003 – England 25, South Africa 6
(Subiaco Oval, Perth)

It did not. It was surprisingly calm on the field – ferocious, but hardly even testy, let alone violent. It was sweetness and light off the field, as Prince Harry danced up in his hospitality box whenever England scored. Jayne Woodward, wife of the coach, had clearly been put on to him as a minder and she was pictured in the papers next day locking him in a firm embrace. Good on them both, it was not the month for English reserve.

Yet all this was before the time when my colleagues and myself, and some team members, began to regard him as not so much a royal seal of England support than as a freeloading pain in the backside. Good old republican-leaning Australia, through a myriad of TV cameras and column inches and long lenses, remained as transfixed as ever by the spectacle of a royal making a spectacle.

At what was, essentially, not a spectacle. The result was everything, of course. England was launched on the high road to the knockout stages. This was the result which sent them careering along. The performance? Forgettable. England's defence was magnificent, but there was no rhythm to their play. The match itself was disappointing, halting and downbeat.

Next day, the *Sydney Morning Herald* ran a giant picture of a rather dishevelled Jonny Wilkinson. The heading ran: 'Is that all you've got?' The latest barb in the guerrilla media war. It was to rebound, spectacularly. The British redtops were only biding their time, and their time would come. But there was nothing bar the result at Subiaco that was definitive.

We had already learned from long experience that assessments of Jonny

Wilkinson are different to assessments of other players. Here, he was not impressive as a controller. He played 'as if careworn', I remember recording in my match report. He did not line up his juddering hits. So what did he do? Just kicked four penalties and one conversion from his five attempts, kept England churning forward in the bad times before finishing the Springboks off with two calm and beautifully struck drop-goals in the second half.

England's pace dipped, so did their continuity. They were so slow and inaccurate at the breakdown that they were turned over frequently, with Lewis Moody the main culprit. Quixotically, Woodward singled Moody out later as having had a wonderful game. Maybe turning the ball over was all part of the game plan, then.

Significantly, however, they did have a go-to area, a place where they could find sustenance in the shaky times when it seemed that even South Africa could beat them. The place was the mess room of Dad's Army. The home media had made fun of the average age of the team without mercy. But in Subiaco, Johnson and Dallaglio stepped up and took control. Yet the star was the oldest of them all – Neil Back, one awful pot shot at a drop-goal apart, was a revelation.

Perhaps most remarkable of all was the service from scrum-half. Matt Dawson's had been poor in the Georgia match and Kyran Bracken stepped up for the Springbok match as Dawson was injured. For a time, rumours swept the camp that Bracken's notoriously angry back was growling again. This, coupled with the fact that, for some reason he always kept to himself, Woodward did not really trust Andy Gomarsall in a major match, led to Martin Wood, the Bath scrum-half, flying down all the way from Heathrow to Singapore and Perth, being whisked to say hello to all the chaps then leaving for the airport, Singapore and Heathrow. Good for Air Miles.

Yet whether his back was sore or not, Bracken's service was laboured and variable, often scooped. His tackling was as good as ever, but Wilkinson was faced with a difficult assortment of lobs and stray rockets. Funny. If my Under-16 scrum-halves had passed like that we'd have taken them out of the next session and spent the whole time on their passing. Woodward was miffed when anyone mentioned it.

South Africa were dreadful everywhere apart from the scrum. The lack of real fire about them suggested to me that they had no confidence in each other and none in Rudi Straeuli, their coach. Something in the psyche of a team coached by a man who has lost its players prevents them from going to war on his behalf.

I had already drawn a savage assault on radio and television from South African followers with my assertion that a country of that size and rugby history must surely have been able to find someone to play at fly-half better than the truly, madly, deeply awful Louis Koen. Or not. Koen missed four shots at goal in the first half and he was clearly poised to make a match-winning intervention – on behalf of England – at any time. He did not keep us in suspense. After 63 minutes, Will Greenwood charged him down and the England centre carefully marshalled the ball over the line and scored.

Taken as an end in itself, it was a damp squib. Nor did it terrify any of the other camps. Unless it was terrifying that England could play so poorly, could throw away the ball, could have their scrum and their fly-half off key, and yet still beat easily one of the giants of the game.

They did not show much, but they hinted that, no, it was not all they'd got. 'We are so relieved,' Woodward said. 'But it was nowhere near the level of performance we can achieve.'

18 October 2003 – Subiaco Oval Media Centre

The late evening kick-offs meant that I would be still hacking away in the media centre well into the early hours, with people bustling around cursing malfunctioning modem connections, barking views on the game, vainly trying to discover from the locals if any restaurants stayed open till 4 a.m. England were beautifully embarked now. They would have to walk into some kind of catastrophe not to go through to the semi-finals, and, as near as dammit, Europe was guaranteed a finalist.

It was a matter of trying to shine up the last few words; check with London that they were captioning the pictures with the names of players who were actually in them; talk to the graphics department about our representation of the Greenwood try; have our Rugby Roundup man talk us through the other events of the day in the tournament; rewrite and retouch; making sure our preview material already filed referring to the next day's games still stood up. Then, dredge for nuggets from all our columnists – Lawrence Dallaglio, Jeremy Guscott, Malcolm O'Kelly and Chris Paterson all 'wrote' ghosted columns in some or all of our editions. Guscott is highly professional in his approach and Bob Dwyer, in my experience, easily the best match analyst in the media anywhere, worked for us throughout the tournament.

Sometimes, it falls into place. Sometimes, it is a long grind. At some time, when all the maelstrom of production of the first edition had subsided back in London, when the media centre bustle gave way to tired faces and a slow sense of relief, there would then be a check with the sports editor. Are we OK, have we covered the bases, have we missed a story that our rivals are running? No, as usual.

Just before I made that call, I took another. It was from a member of the Harlequins who told me that Will Greenwood, the try-scorer, was to leave for home the next day. Carol, his wife, had been admitted to hospital with complications early in her pregnancy. It was only just over a year ago that Will and Carol had lost Freddie, their son, who had been born 18 weeks premature.

It was a story. A profoundly upsetting one for the Greenwoods but in the sense that it was bound to come out soon (due to Greenwood not appearing in the team), still a story. I rang England's media people, who went deathly quiet. They refused to confirm the story.

'I know this is true, why are you denying it?'

Their answer was that Greenwood had already been booked to fly home from Perth the day after, at three in the afternoon, and the media announcement would be made at the same time, with him safely departed.

I had a sinking feeling as I apprised the hierarchy back in London. I knew they would be keen to run it. Essentially, I did not want to. I expect to be pushed hard by my sports desk. I push hard back at them. I try to be reasonably sanguine, always, if something that appears in the paper gives offence to the subject, and they are safely back at Wapping, I am in the field along with that subject. It's just tough luck. They also knew that there were many ways that the story could emerge that night and be run in any competing Sunday paper; they knew that Greenwood himself, under contract to the *News of the World*, may well be announcing it himself in his weekly column and that I, who knew it, would look silly for not filing it.

The exigencies of newspapers were one thing. But this was something else. Will Greenwood was not hiding a pulled hamstring; he was not hiding a positive drugs test. He was hiding, for the moment, the news that his missus was under treatment so that a second youngster was not born prematurely; and even though it was way past midnight and he would be in bed, all packed, the idea that the story might cause him inconvenience, cause him to be waylaid by hacks when his mind was elsewhere, caused me a considerable amount of unease. We ran a story, factual and unadorned.

Less than two weeks later, Greenwood was back in Australia. Carol was in excellent order and sent him back to play his part in a shot on glory. On 3 February 2004, Archie Frederick Lewis Greenwood arrived safely.

The *Sunday Times* reporting squad, as unimpressive a bunch at that time of day as you could find, arrived back at our hotel around three, shattered, and hoovered up a beer. I was starving. I ordered a steak sandwich from room service. I was almost too tired to eat. As it arrived, the office rang. 'The editor wants a 1,000-word feature on France. He thinks they will be England's next big game.'

France? I hadn't even seen them play. I didn't feel that 3 a.m. Perth time was quite the slot to call their media officer demanding an interview. It was something of a struggle. I put the steak sandwich down. My contact lenses were sticking to my eyes, so I was not inclined to unravel all the leads, the modems and the chargers, and to power up the laptop. I made some notes, rang the copytaker and started dictating off the top of my head. I dozed off completely at one stage and was woken after a few seconds by a tinny 'Hello, hello' on the line.

There had been nothing light about the day.

20 October 2003 – Sheraton Hotel, Phil Vickery

'Everyone's got their reasons for doing their sport,' Phil Vickery said. He had already explained his *raison d'être* for being on a rugby field. 'My reason for playing rugby was to find a channel for my anger, to hit into people, tackle, smash into things. That, to me, is what rugby is about. A lot of the time it is do or die, and that's what I most like. That pressure, those fears.

'I'm there, waiting for that first scrum, going through my little routine. Little checks, "Jonno, you in? Steve [Thompson], tight to Steve." We're ready; the referee is giving the order. We're ready. "Right," I'm thinking, "here we go, f*****g engage!" That first collision is a blackout moment, so much adrenaline you feel nothing.'

But here he had the honesty to admit that he had struggled against South Africa. It was not his fault, entirely, that he had come up against the only unit of the Springbok team which was any good, but Christo Bezuidenhout, the loose-head prop from the Mpumalanga Pumas, had given him a fair old working over, caused him to hang on in the scrums for dear life and drained him of some of the energy he uses to steam around the field. Vickery felt, at the end, 'just wasted, completely and utterly gone'.

'I had given everything I had, couldn't have wrung one more ounce out of myself and, even though we'd won, it hadn't gone that well for me,' says Vickery. 'At the end of the match, you hold your hands out but there's nothing there. You've given 110 per cent and you've got nothing to show. Everyone goes away from the game and they start going through the performances: "Ah, Vickery. Looked slow, a bit sluggish, a couple of dodgy scrums, a couple of good ones, average performance."

'God, it can be demoralising. Because then you've got to go back and face your teammates. There is no hiding place in this squad. You haven't had a good game, why haven't you had a good game? There's none of this "Ah, it'll be all right next week." No, it's how many times were you a fraction late getting to the rucks, why was there 12 minutes between tackle number five and tackle number six? Everything is on the video; every excuse you try can be checked. So you front up, and this is why not everyone plays for England.'

He revealed that after every game, he rings his family – mum, dad, brother and girlfriend. 'Last weekend one of them said, "Fantastic, that was fantastic" and I'm thinking, "What was fantastic? I've just been drilled for 80 minutes and you say it was fantastic?"'

This was not a potential weak point in the English make-up. England's scrum had had a bad day, but it seemed to me that no one else in the event, Argentina apart, came within a megaton of the South African scrum in terms of power. South Africa's rugby had declined, but they had retained enough of a historical perspective to realise that scrummaging was in their blood.

Perhaps Vickery's honesty, his Cornish directness and his angle on England's driven pursuit of some form of a sporting near-perfection (this in a thunderingly imperfect pastime such as rugby) was better news than the memory of his discomfort in one match.

20 October 2003 – Mile-high Mexican; Qantas flight 582

Walking through Perth airport, Greg Yachvili was downcast, more than 12 hours after the game. Georgia, again keeping their shape and again playing with courage, had lost by 46–9 to Samoa. It was, roughly speaking, a close match. The teams had been level in terms of courage, shape and intensity. Level, except that the Samoans had a monopoly in footballing dazzle. Georgia had the spadework, never the pretty shots.

A remarkable Sunday evening crowd of 22,000 at the Subiaco, happily seeing off the Rugby World Cup's Perth leg, loved it. At the end, the Georgians went to wave to a phalanx of supporters, some Georgian, some happily assuming their colours. Perth, the clean, spotless and not-quite-soulless city, had done the event proud as punch.

'If everything had gone well, we could have won, but if we expected to lose in our hearts, then we did not expect to lose so badly,' he said as he boarded the flight to Sydney, where the Georgians only had to face South Africa (naturally, the Springboks were already in their headquarters preparing for the match. Who cared about the Georgians having a fair crack?).

The crowd had been desperate to see a Georgian try, howled when they hacked on dropped passes towards the Samoan line. But the Samoans had ring craft and scoring power. Semo Sititi typified it, veering and weaving and sprinting for a gorgeous individual try, and there were six tries in all. Sailosi Tagicakibau, an import from Fiji, was deadly on the Samoan wing. Lima, the chiropractor, rearranged some more bones in the midfield.

Afterwards, the Georgians loaded up the end of their table for the press conference with massive props. Goderdzi Shvelidze and Soso Nikolaenko sat on the end, stone-faced and dark, glowering, unmoving, daring you to ask them something. I plucked up courage. 'Do the props feel,' I asked, 'that they were let down by the backs since they won their share of the ball?'

The interpreter provided by the media office absorbed the question. It was passed along the line from the English–French interpreter to the French-speaking coach, Claude Saurel, to the Georgian-speaker who understood French and who redirected the question to the top-heavy end of the table. The props muttered something, staring blankly in front. We waited patiently as the answer came tumbling back along the line to the output end.

'The props say that rugby is a team game, there are no backs or forwards, the team takes collective responsibility for the defeat.' A fair achievement that, media-speak retained through six separate translations. I wondered what question had really made it down the line.

I didn't have to wait long to find what answer had really come back. As the players filed out, Nikolaenko walked right past me, then stopped and turned. He held out his hand, tried to tear mine off in a handshake. 'Thank you,' he said, in English. There can surely be little doubt that he went off into a Georgian enclave with his fellow props and moaned heartily about the weaknesses and poncey qualities of backs in general.

The Georgian squad, it seemed, contained some of the least-convinced aviators in rugby touring history. A whole row of their players and back-up people had heads in hands during the take-off run, all looked in horror for comfort from the stewardess as the plane hit a bump in the climb-out. 'You're all a bunch of girls,' she called out to them.

However, when level flight was attained, they relaxed. They all stood chatting in the aisles, caused consternation by producing bottles of Heineken (not allowed to bring your own drinks on board). One high-spirited Kiwi girl in a micro-skirt distracted them by asking them to sign her legs in heavy black felt pen, and by the time she touched down it looked as if she had one of those impossibly complicated and mystical Samoan tattoos.

Soon, the Georgians began a Mexican wave, picked up by the rest of the passengers so that the lunging arms rippled back and forth from the business seats to the rear, and back again.

It was a two-tier tournament, but it was not all privation. Rugby touring is a wondrous bonding experience and Georgians seemed happy with it. England were in the air at the same time, bound for Melbourne, with (naturally) a full seven days to prepare for Samoa. I closed my eyes and tried to imagine Martin Johnson leading a Mexican wave on that flight. The image simply would not harden.

21 October 2003 – Roy and HG, *The Cream*

Here's a funny thing. We all pan the dear old BBC. It's just when you go abroad and watch television that you realise with a guilty thump how wonderful the BBC is. How funny.

One of the most famous double acts on Australian TV popped up in machine-gun bursts during the World Cup. They were called Roy and HG and their show was called *The Cream*. I supposed, if you delved down through the succeeding layers of pap risibility, which it comprised, you might have found a (long-lost) kernel of an idea that it should be a satirical, pungent and hilarious slant on current affairs, usually sport.

The two grinning Aussie nancies filled the screen, it seemed, almost every day. In the background, the studio audience wet itself with laughter and Roy and HG, apparently staring fixedly towards the autocue for their supposedly off-the-cuff comedic gems, took delight in what they clearly felt was a pointed assault on England, the nation and the rugby team.

They should have been on to a good thing – Australia, though it would never admit it for a second, is fascinated by England and all things English. If England never existed then neither would around nine-tenths of the columnists, social commentators and chat show hosts that the England industry spawns. Australians are more interested in the Royal Family than any Brit.

Roy and HG dribbled on. They are most certainly not the only Australians to become household names in their own country and yet find that the rest of the world is in utter and blissful ignorance that they even exist – there are media darlings, rugby league players, rock groups, businessmen and newspaper columnists in the same category. In the case of Roy and HG, a bloody good job.

Yet, as the World Cup wore on, as the visitors to Australia stared blankly, it became a point of honour not to miss them, purely because everyone was fascinated to see if they would say anything funny whatsoever before the final. They did not. They were arrantly unfunny. Insultingly bad. In fact, in the end they were absolutely hilariously bad.

They pulled out all the stops in the final week. They had as their guests Morgan Turinui, a reserve Wallaby squad player who they mocked because he wasn't in the team, but in a ham-fisted not a clever way; Rory Underwood, who'd popped into the country, a great player but a resounding non-interview from way back; then they hauled on Rob Andrew, who was commentating for BBC Radio Five Live.

Naturally, their fearless brand of anti-English satire waned even further when they actually had some Englishmen on the programme. All the anti-English fervour they hoped they were evoking died and was replaced by a cringing sucking-up. Poor Andrew sat there at first mystified by the abysmal questions and then, as his eyes suggested (and as he confirmed later), openly contemptuous about the whole unfunny charade.

The Cream? More like The Creeps. There, lads. Make a crap and scripted aside about that.

26. APPOINTMENT WITH THE CHIROPRACTOR

23 October 2003 – Emergency Department, Sydney Eye Hospital

The day after the England–South Africa game, I had been plagued with small black flies. I tried to grab them and wave them away with one hand as I brushed my teeth with the other. Maybe they'd been attracted by the half-eaten room service steak sandwich that was hanging around. They were persistent little things. They followed me to the lifts, through the foyer and down the road to Connie's, where the hacks always breakfasted. Connie had her six-inch eyelashes in but even they didn't brush them away.

Then I realised that the black dots were inside my eye and that something was happening to my vision. I put it down to the stress of the day before, which had ended at 5 a.m. with the last word of copy dictated to a copytaker operation significantly below world class. I passed myself fit to attend Paul Ackford's Sunday school outing that day, a decent lunch at Scarbrough beach, down the coast. But the black specks whizzed this way and that, great blobs also floated around, blurring my vision, like ghostly battleships across the viewfinders of a submarine. Next day, my black specks and I boarded the plane for Sydney.

Two days later, I was flat out in a dingy ward at Sydney hospital, both eyes bandaged, ordered to lie, unmoving, in the same position on my left side, disorientated, youngest in the ward by around 50 years, anxious about my sight but far more anxious that I might miss some work, even more anxious than that about whether the nurses or doctors (or worse, the anaesthetists) had ever read my articles on what a bunch of preening, navel-contemplating prats large numbers of Aussies were and how they cheated at the breakdown, about my family 12,000 miles away, about most of the lads being down in Melbourne, desperate for a piss but needing to be led by the arm to the loo to relieve myself while the nurses watched and waited for me to be ready to be led back. It was my first night, ever, in hospital.

I had a horseshoe-shaped tear in my retina. Retinal detachment is akin to wallpaper drying out, and beginning to peel from the top of a wall. And apparently, according to Dr Woo, the eye doctor in the emergency department, the retina was about to peel off something called the macula, and therefore, possibly, affect my sight for good.

He told me that I had to be admitted, that I needed an operation within 48 hours. Till then, I had to lie stock still, could not even walk slowly back to my hotel to pick up my things, or ring round my colleagues, in case I jarred myself or walked into a lamppost. I could not bring myself to tell him, since the situation in the eye was apparently so delicate, that the day before I had wheezed and crashed and bashed my way around the gym for two hours. Weights, ergometer, the lot. The only thing I hadn't done in the field of dramatically worsening the problem was to head-butt a flying medicine ball with my eye socket leading.

Dr Woo outlined the treatments. One possibility involved a bit of stabbing through the eye, some stitching and general poking about, and then the insertion of gas bubbles. 'They expand, press down on the repair and help the healing.'

Fantastic, except that when you have the bubbles you have to 'posture' – which means spending seven days lying in the same position for at least 55 minutes in every hour, and, because the bubbles explode in your head at altitude, you cannot fly for a month. That took me towards Christmas, marooned and lonely Down Under.

For a sports reporter at the World Cup, especially one whose life had revolved round the prospect of the assignment for three years, it was a glimpse of hell, total catastrophe. Yes, yes, yes. I know that there were people lying within yards of me who probably would have swapped, but fuck the always-someone-worse-than-you cobblers. At that moment, there was nothing worse. And think of the 'one-eye reporter' jokes I would have to face. Frankly, I was in abject misery and tears.

I heard the curtains twitch. Barry Newcombe, my dear friend and colleague, godfather to my son, Andrew, practically the only hack left in Sydney that week, came to see me. 'Fuck this,' I said, took the bandages off, sat up. We were soon laughing away. The curtain twitched again. It was some functionary asking for payment for their services. I dug out my American Express card from my pocket.

As she was running the card through the machine the curtain twitched again, to reveal a distinguished, grey-haired identikit portrait of a leading consultant. Was it mere chance, or the challenge of the horseshoe tear, or the scent, the glint of the American Express card? Barry was to swear later that the doctor grabbed the card, and said, 'That'll do nicely.'

Frankly, it was no time to stand on the principle of free health service treatment. Yes, Doctor, I would very much like to come to your private hospital. Dr Alexander Hunyor, who was to be my almost constant companion through most of the rest of the tour, and nothing but caring, spirited me away to a small hospital, blew the trumpet to summon his team, and next day I was operated upon.

Thank God, no gas bubbles. There was a small general anaesthetic, which knocks you out for just a few minutes while they plunged the needle containing the local anaesthetic into the eye. 'You'll be conscious during the operation,' said Dr Hunyor, 'but you won't feel anything, and afterwards you won't remember a thing.'

Remarkably percipient words, except for the fact that it hurt like hell and I remembered every last detail afterwards. Maybe the anaesthetist had read the *Sunday Times* after all.

Next day, looking like Mike Tyson had held me down while Lennox Lewis punched me in the eye, I rose, caught a taxi back to the hotel in Darling Harbour, shaky and quivering. It was a Saturday, a major workday. France were playing Scotland. I rang the office, which had been tipped off.

'Hi, lads, what's the wordage for the match report?'

'Fuck off and go to bed, Steve.'

I begged to work. I offered them a sidebar from the television coverage. 'I'm fine,' I said. I walked downstairs in the hotel to buy a rugby jersey for my son, whose birthday was in a few days' time. As I entered the foyer I cannoned into glass double doors, sending reverberations across the whole ground floor.

I went to bed, miserable as sin. Why? Was it that a sacred journalistic instinct to be on the story was being violated and, like the rather pompous John Simpson, did I have to put myself in harm's way no matter what the danger? Was work more sacred than sight? Or was it the anxiety of a soon-to-be 50-something, like most journalists around three times less assured than he sometimes appeared, that my employers and Fleet Street would deem me to be myopic, too old, prone to fold on the big stories? Well, it was all of these. Every one. But also, my eye bloody hurt.

24 October 2003 – South Africa 46, Georgia 19
(Aussie Stadium, Sydney)

Georgia had not scored a try against either England or Samoa. Their morale had suffered, too, in the heavy defeat against Samoa in Perth. It seemed doubtful if they could get themselves up for the next challenge. They were simply not used to backing-up in their international programme. They normally had a game and then waited six months at least for another. Here, they faced the merciless Springboks.

Well, around 35,000 refused to give up on them. They gave us one of the delicious treats of the World Cup. They reminded us, again, why we bother having World Cups. They competed toe-to-toe with the big Springbok pack and South Africa were so restricted that three of their seven tries came from big forwards driving over, with two from Danie Rossouw, who had been a find on the tour in a bristling tight flanker role.

Georgia unleashed series after series of forward drives and Aussie Stadium was willing them to score a try with desperation. But there are no easy scores, no gift-wrapped consolations. And so the stadium nearly levitated when Georgia won a close-range lineout, organised their drive beautifully, and with a rat-at-tat of mini surges, David Dadunashvili dived across to score. Only dullards were not dancing with joy.

With only 25 minutes to go, it was 29–16, and one of the biggest, most forbidding rugby countries in the world was having a battle with one of the smallest. The spiritual home of the scrum was struggling against a country that owned one scrummaging machine. I repeat. It was not some kind of vindication of the lack of funding. It was the most powerful indication of how the game will prosper if the second rank is nurtured. Wizened old hacks who'd seen it all reported back to headquarters with England in Melbourne next day.

'Jesus,' one of the real cynics said. 'I will never forget that match as long as I live.'

26 October 2003 – England 35, Samoa 22
(Telstra Dome, Melbourne)

Remember the callow Samoans training on the beachfront, interrupting their sessions to admire the local bathing beauties and so apparently inexperienced at the arts of lineout lifting that some of their jumpers sighed with relief when they were gently placed back on terra firma by their lifters?

Remember the beleaguered Samoans with no funding, with around 12 players from their top squad denied to them? Yes, that's the bunch. They took the lead at Telstra Dome with a penalty by Earl Va'a, and then England made the restart, trailing 0–3.

Samoa set up the ball. Then they started moving it wide, left and right. Phase after phase. From deep. Kas Lealamanu'a, the foursquare loose head, made a fierce burst and was to handle twice more in the move. Maurie Fa'asavalu, the young openside who played his rugby in Apia and who had been electric against Uruguay and Georgia, also appeared.

After around seven phases, Steven So'oialo and Va'a sent the ball wide one more time; Terry Fanolua, the pedigree centre from Gloucester, burst on to a short pass, Fa'asavalu backed him up on the left and then sent Semo Sititi, the captain, weaving his way for the try.

It would be lovely to think that not a single Englishman in the crowd of over 50,000 under the closed roof of the Telstra Dome failed to rise from his seat and cheer to the rafters. Certainly, one temporarily confined British writer rose from his bed.

After 18 minutes of this magnificent match, the statistics of possession came up on the big screens. England 10 per cent, Samoa 90 per cent. Well before the end, and for the rest of the tournament, England fans were thanking their lucky stars that Samoa didn't bring their first XV to the party.

A fluke? A one-off backs to the wall? Absolutely not. The Samoan nation is the richest repository of natural rugby talent. If it is unacceptable to lampoon national characteristics – shifty French, skinflint Scots, attractive cheery Welsh, etc. – then it has to be said that Samoans appear to have, as well as warrior spirit and pride in their nation that goes soul-deep, an innate ability to play, to make decisions, to run economical lines. Even their second XV does it well.

They also had, in this fifth World Cup, and still scaring the hell out of the ball carrier and anyone contemplating putting himself forward for the role, Brian Lima. The chiropractor, so called because he rearranges people's bones. Lima's most thunderous hit was still to come – he hit Derick Hougaard, the young South African centre, with such a frightening tackle in a later Pool match that television stations were loving replaying it frame by frame for about three weeks.

Lima levelled Jason Robinson and Wilkinson with more of his trademark shattering tackles. Good job, on the whole, that England didn't win more ball. Lima has given his guts for Samoa, and been a superb professional in domestic rugby in Australia, New Zealand, Wales and Japan. What a man, what an influence. World Cups were starting to give players like him a stage.

Ultimately, the Samoans simply ran out of steam. They were ahead at 10–0 when Va'a converted Sititi's stunning try, and they came again, in blue waves. England looked ragged, the non-English element in the crowd loved it, and the rising note of hope in the Australian TV commentary almost grew to a screech. Were England shaken? In the 16th minute, Wilkinson missed with a shot at a penalty goal. People looked at each other, incredulous – was the world ending? Then, from point-blank range, Wilkinson hit a post and the ball bounced away. Yes, apparently it was.

They struck back with the sort of try that gave the watching rivals their ammunition. They burrowed and blocked their way over for a Neil Back try with a forward drive, as humdrum an event as the Samoan try had been spectacular. By half-time there was no sign of English composure. Samoa still led 16–13 and they deserved it, too.

Woodward had seen enough and soon we heard the loud notes of the bugle summoning the cavalry. Steve Thompson, Lewis Moody and Phil Vickery arrived to replace Mark Regan, Julian White and Joe Worsley. The increased scrummage power told when England drove almost murderously for a pushover try, the Samoan scrum collapsed in a heap and the penalty try was awarded. Ah, well. That's the last we'll see of that lot.

Except that it wasn't. In the final quarter, thanks to two penalties by the immaculate Va'a, Samoa led 22–20 and launched a couple of surging attacks even though the flood of possession had been reduced to a drip.

And what was that useless Wilkinson going to do about it, then? Well, a fair bit. He stepped up to the scrum-half position with 15 minutes remaining and chipped over a goal that was neatness itself. Then came the dagger in the brave Samoan hearts. Wilkinson chipped high to the right-hand corner with his ever-improving right foot, Iain Balshaw came streaking, dazzlingly, out of everyone's peripheral vision, leapt and caught the ball and scored, unattended by defenders.

He had come from nowhere, so much so that we assumed that it was all a reffing blunder and that he had to be offside. So it was some tribute to the inch-perfection of Wilkinson's kick and the gas under the pedal of Balshaw that replays revealed him to be well onside. Later, Phil Vickery swerved and dummied his way over to score his first try for England. Interestingly, he scored on the end of a pass from Mike Catt, the last cavalryman, the last player to be chosen for the World Cup squad. Catt came on and looked sharp as a new pin.

The Samoans were beaten. But they had been wonderful, fast, brave, indomitable, clever. Appallingly, a member of the IRB was heard to dribble that this was the match that proved their measures to help the impoverished nations were working (what measures, and what, exactly, had worked?). This was the match that proved the potential of Samoa and offered a withering condemnation of the IRB's lack of effective help.

The Telstra Dome is an acquired taste. I do not think that its roof should ever be closed for rugby. But that night in Melbourne, it was rocking. The atmosphere and the match were sensational. Woodward was asked afterwards if this had been the match that set the tournament alight.

'If it was,' he said, 'I'm delighted for the tournament. But for me, it was scary.'

England were below par. Players like Matt Dawson, Lawrence Dallaglio and Wilkinson, key men in the spine of the team, had yet to assert themselves. Will Greenwood was missed for his quiet influence. Ben Kay and Martin Johnson gave England a powerful reference point but even the defence was ragged. The statistics showed that 20 tackles had been missed. The pace and the rhythm was missing. The World Champions-in-waiting were still, well, waiting.

After the match against Georgia, England was gracious enough to wait for the Georgians to complete their mini lap of honour so that they could clap them off. England were still waiting at the tunnel as the Samoans left the field. Whether it was good grace, or exhaustion, it was hard to tell.

The Neil Back grunt-and-groan try was significant in the context of the match and also in the way that it fed the wishes of those (Eddie Jones, the Australia coach, and every other living Australian, for example) who wanted to find aspects of England's game about which they could run bleating to referees.

Neil Back, who had the ball at the back of the heaving phalanx of his own forwards, scored the try. The ball carrier has to be securely attached in the driving maul. If he is detached at the back then all the forwards are obstructing and he is merely hiding behind them like a small American footballer running back behind his offensive line.

And it clearly seemed that Back was detached. He only put the odd shoulder or arm against the mass in front of him in a cursory attempt at some sort of propriety. John Eales, the spokesman for Visa (and, possibly on this occasion, the spokesman for Eddie Jones), proclaimed the try, the move, the English team itself, illegal. On this occasion he may have been right, though by the end of the tournament the only part of the England game which some Aussie commentator, player, coach or oaf had not declared illegal was the colour of their jockstraps. Amazing how often the referee of the next England match happened to be in the vicinity when they made their snipes, too.

What stuck in the craw with some was not the criticism of England or the unsubtle pressure on referees (nor even the fact that I did not trust many of them not to cave in to it). What was most distasteful to others was the unstated assertion that the poor old Aussie lads would never stoop to sharp practice on the rugby field, this a team which – in the eyes of just a few – cheated in the scrum, in their blocking runners and the operation of the flankers off their feet at ruck time. And what should have been obvious to all is that every team cheats, apart from yours.

John Boe was thrilled. And he took the chance to appeal, once again, to the rulers of the world game. 'There is a bloodline there that might be lost to rugby,' he said of Test rugby in Samoa. 'That would be a tragedy. These guys are born to play rugby. They develop physically earlier than Europeans and enjoy the smash element of the game. They have a natural instinct for the ball and are athletic on the move. Do we want to lose all that?

'Remember that rugby is not just a game in Samoa. It is a central part of their culture. It is one thing they have contributed to the world. They have taught me humility and respect, they never, ever complain. And their passion for the game, their commitment to one another and to their country, is truly uplifting.'

At the time of writing, around two months after those quiet and yet fiery words, no measures had been announced by the International Board, or any individual moneyed Union, to offer Samoa, or any other impoverished rugby nation, any help in any way.

27. ONE MAN, GOING SPARE

29 October 2003 – Chifly Tower, Sydney

Once, there was one man in the dugout. The spongeman. He'd run on with a wet sponge and hope you didn't have anything serious. Sometimes, he might be a qualified physio. But each team had one man, coaches sat in the stand, and the spongeman could not even cross the whitewash without express permission from the referee, in triplicate, and then only during a break in play.

Like most things, it's all gone wild. These days, the touchlines are almost as ludicrously crowded as in American football, with coaches, medical people, water carriers, supernumeraries and others who'd love us to think they are of any importance whatsoever. God bless the European Rugby Club, organisers of the Heineken and Parker Pen competitions, who've chucked off the field and into the stand all the non-essentials. Doesn't leave many.

They're a stroppy bunch, too. The medicos bawl their heads off at refs if they have gripes or if they see foul play. After South Africa had allegedly faked a blood bin injury in a match against England at Pretoria in 2000, Clive Woodward called for neutral doctors to be used at rugby matches, tacitly admitting that doctors are corruptible too.

As for referees, there are more out there these days than you can shake a stick at. There's the bloke in the middle with the whistle, there are his touch-judges (who prattled their way through games in the World Cup on the communications system. They should have kept quiet. They might then have stopped missing everything); then there are the third and fourth officials; they are each attached to one of the teams, they help to run the replacements bench.

When Mike Tindall was lying injured in the second half of the Samoan match, Dan Luger warmed up, ready to come on to the field. Dave Reddin, the England fitness supervisor, was the man running the replacements bench, with a microphone link to Woodward and the hierarchy who were up in the stand at the Telstra Dome. Woodward can be excitable. He was anxious for Reddin to get Luger on. Reddin, as all sides admitted later, was under pressure.

The official in charge of England's bench was Brett Bowden. In charge of the Samoan bench, therefore, with his New Zealand accent mixing with the many others of the New Zealand-based Samoans, was Steve Walsh. There was no reason whatsoever for Walsh to come into contact with England players or officials at any time.

Bowden told Reddin that permission was not yet granted for Luger's arrival. But, as Reddin was later to testify, because of confusion as to whether Tindall was off the field or not, confusion as to bylaws and because of pressure from Woodward up in his box, Reddin (and he always admitted it was a mistake) sent Luger on. There, Luger enjoyed 34 seconds at large. He made one tackle, departed after those 34 seconds and, even though Tindall was not actually taking any part in the match, England had 16 players on the field.

It was, categorically, a mistake, and a bad one. It did not remotely affect the game, and the Samoans did not complain. 'It was an error, I can assure you,' Woodward said. 'We will cooperate fully with any investigation.' One telling interlocutor asked the following question, a perfectly fair and even far-sighted one.

'Do you think that, because you are English, it might be blown up more than it should be?'

'I hope not,' said Woodward. The question reflected anti-English feelings in corridors of power.

I was torn. In a strong sense it was a storm in a thimble but there are times when justice must be seen to be done and where piffling misdemeanours must be jumped on to stop a slide into something altogether more serious. There is no doubt that modern-day coaching groups can be too intense, too full of themselves. I have enough knowledge of Reddin to say with confidence that he is neither a cheat nor anything other than a nice fellow, but he was flustered, Woodward made things worse, England were wrong.

The anti-English camp sprang into action. Toutai Kefu, the injured Australian number 8, was quite obviously wound up by persons unknown. 'They [World Cup officials] need to show courage over England's extra-man scandal and strip the Poms of their points,' he said. 'It makes no difference that the English sent out Dan Luger at the tail-end of the game when the result was already decided. The bottom line is that rules are rules.

'Even worse, England defied a tournament official. That is the key issue here. To suggest nothing should be done is a joke. They should be deducted the points they got from the game and the points handed to Samoa. England has got to take a real good look at itself. It showed lack of respect for the tournament official, and the whole thing just smacks of arrogance.'

Kefu smacked of someone missing the limelight, someone whose best days were four years behind him and a man from a country whose conversion to strict observance of rugby law could only be described as dramatically sudden. But there was always the chance that some anti-Pom grandee might hijack the process. In the end, after a formal hearing in Sydney's Chifley Tower, England were fined £10,000 and Reddin was barred from his place on the touchline for two games. It was a fair result.

Except for overtones a good deal more sinister than Toutai Kefu's desperation to remind us that he was still about. England were called to the judicial hearing to answer two charges: first, that they'd thrown on a 16th player without permission of the official; second, that Reddin had manhandled Steve Walsh.

Everyone's first thought was to wonder why on earth Walsh had come near enough to Reddin for this alleged assault to take place. We soon found out. Walsh had approached Reddin after the game, towards the tunnel area, even though he had nothing remotely to do with the 16th-man affair. One newspaper even alleged that he had called Reddin, subtracting rude words, a 'loser' and had berated him. Reddin, so witnesses claimed, merely put a placatory hand on Walsh's shoulder and was about to mumble some conciliatory words when Walsh stormed off, talking about possible charges of assault. It seemed he had lost it.

The complaint against Reddin was thrown out. 'There was a total conflict concerning the matters at issue relating to their respective involvements in the tunnel incident,' said Brian McLoughlin, the judicial officer, in his judgement. He also said: 'Mr Bowden, the No. 5 match official, with whom Mr Reddin had been verbally engaged, expressed a view of what he observed which I consider to be more consistent with Mr Reddin's evidence than that of Mr Walsh.' There is a clear implication there, which does not say an awful lot, shall we say, for Walsh's memory.

Woodward even had to give up a day's training to fly from the team's headquarters near Surfers Paradise to the hearing in Sydney. Poor chap. 'It was an extremely fair hearing and they did a very professional job,' he said.

Yet again, there was something dark lurking. Woodward had been taken to task on departure from England for the frippery of bringing Richard

Smith, a top-level QC, to the tournament with him. But again, he was proved correct. Friends of Woodward claim to this day that Smith's expertise was crucial in seeing off anyone lurking around the hearing with a separate agenda. 'He was like a top player,' Woodward was to say later. 'As soon as he crossed the whitewash he really started performing.' My interpretation of Woodward's words is clear – that if he had not brought a heavyweight with him, the tribunal may have come under pressure to expel Reddin from the event and docked England points.

England prepared for their match against Uruguay in Brisbane, the last of the Pool games. Suddenly, RWC Ltd themselves creaked and groaned into life and put out a statement. It was unsigned. Walsh was to be suspended for three days for 'inappropriate behaviour' at the England–Samoa match. That was that. As ever, there was no opportunity for a serious public examination of the verdict, or the procedure.

Inappropriate behaviour? Dave Reddin, verbally pushed by Woodward, had transgressed. They immediately admitted it, they were subjected to a draining series of formalities and an informal trial, they were rigorously examined, the proceedings were made public, the full judgement is still posted on the internet and the punishments handed down.

Whoever tried Walsh for his behaviour did so behind closed doors. No judgement was ever made public. We all had to guess. Or did we? I felt that Walsh's action should have barred him for life from refereeing international rugby. He tore up what had to be beyond reproach – his total impartiality between teams, something that has to be heard, seen and never violated. England's behaviour had got on his nerves. He left the familiarity of the Kiwi accents among his Samoan charges and engaged in hostilities with a team he may referee in the future.

So he missed one match. Soon, he was back in the tournament, refereeing Australia and Scotland, a disgraceful appointment. He refereed, in the view of the vast majority who attended, very badly.

The day after the Walsh verdict was announced, Woodward made a big deal of trying to express his sympathy. He revealed he had tried to ring the suspended official. Only Woodward and his maker will ever know if he did this for genuine reasons, or because he realised that the anti-England undercurrent sweeping the tournament at that time could easily deliver Walsh to him as the referee in the World Cup knockout stages.

Reddin partially bent the law that states that teams must play with a maximum of 15 men. Walsh transgressed something far more sacred.

28. THE ZIP ZIP MEN

28 October 2003 – Surfers Paradise

Ah! Surfers Paradise. For surfers, maybe it is. For that part of humanity which has managed to struggle on without strawberry sex wax and sewage waves, hell. It is a ghastly strip of neon-lit fast-food joints an hour north of Brisbane, a place without a noticeable centre or heart or soul.

The only attempt at culinary spontaneity we found was a Japanese restaurant in which the chef put on a display, cutting and slicing and sizzling bits and pieces on a hotplate integral to the table, with knives flashing and the accompanying mumbo-jumbo of a frustrated magician. You had to have ten on the table before he would start, so a self-effacing young couple on their anniversary were press-ganged to join eight voracious, spiky British hacks for whom the need to write the Queen's English without profanities in newspapers led to an urge to depart from the policy when not working.

There was some hilarity when the performing chef apparently slashed a little off target and projected a small segment of Japanese omelette onto Paul Ackford's shoulder. It was only the next evening, when another contingent of the English media munching squad went to the same restaurant, and reported back that the diner in the same seat had been hit in the same position by the same-sized omelette segment, that we realised it was all as mechanical an act as serving a box of KFC in one of Surfers Paradise's KFC outlets, all 11 of them.

England flew up from Melbourne to Coolangatta, the airport for Surfers, for what was seen as a week, if not of relaxation, then at least slightly more relaxed training, but never, in this passionately dedicated squad, for a moment taking their eye off the ball. After the hurry-up administered by Samoa, they were to meet Uruguay the next weekend. Dorian West, Martin Corry and Danny Grewcock were to make their first appearances, Grewcock after recovery – at least partly – from a broken toe

173

and Corry after a dash home for the birth of his new baby. Mr Wilkinson was to rest in his tent.

There was still no sign of Richard Hill, and we were now approaching the end of the third week since he had suffered an injury that would take two days to mend. And when it came time to name a captain for the match, in place of the resting Johnson, there was no sign of Lawrence Dallaglio, either, although he was chosen to play. At a press conference at Surfers, Woodward made a point of mentioning Dallaglio as a senior player not reaching his best, even though Dallaglio was only one of a raft of underachievers. He was not in the least happy when he found afterwards that his coach had singled him out.

Amazingly, and for the only time in the whole trip, the team and the media party were in the same hotel, one of those odd sprawling complexes with rooms scattered around small lanes in the middle of a golf course, a cross between a country club and toy town. Nothing was too much trouble for the staff unless you made impossible demands – such as wanting to be still eating at the restaurant buffet at one minute past nine, being debauched enough to want a beer at ten, or wanting to play a round on the hotel's own golf course without spending the equivalent of the gross national product of a small country.

At various times subsequently, Woodward was to refer to this confluence of players and press with affection. He said that it was good for the two sides to mix; at a point in the tour when Wilkinson was reckoned to be feeling the pressure, Woodward referred inquisitors to the Surfers leg when all the press had been able to see him smiling happily.

He was also happy to have a sounding board from outside the squad hothouse, as this was the week that England was arraigned on a charge of playing with 16. All this slightly jarred with the reality that, as soon as he heard that the media were in the same hotel (they had booked long before the team), he deputed minions to intercede with the media travel company (and they did so with real rudeness) to try to get the booking abandoned.

Focus and concentration was one thing. But a fear of the real world outside, and attempts to deny the human rights of people to book hotels wherever they bleeding well wanted, was another. Anyway, I'd been upgraded to an executive room. No way I was leaving.

Or seeing. My specialists had recommended prescription sunglasses to spare my eyes in the hot sun and, as the stitches in my eyeball meant that I could not wear my own contact lenses, I found an optician who could make them up quickly.

'What percentage of black do you want?' he asked. He explained that the strength of the black tint he was to apply could be varied. Well, my eyes were sore and sensitive, it was a beach resort. I opted for 90 per cent. What he failed to mention was that this was ridiculously high and through my prescription glasses, in the dazzle of a Surfers noon sun, all I could see were dim shapes. £220 they cost me, too.

It got worse. It was now a week since the operation to repair my detaching retina. The operation was such a success that Dr Hunyor had asked for my permission for colleagues to come and admire his handiwork. They hummed and hawed with clucks of congratulation when they put their eyes to the microscope and combed the repair area inside my head. A torrent of drops, judicious attempts not to walk into walls and the application of a Perspex shield at bedtime which made me look like the Phantom of the Opera had just begun to alleviate the fiery redness of my eye and its accompanying swellings. The other eye was bored stiff with taking all the laptop work.

However, strolling down a beach above Surfers, I became aware that the plague of flies had apparently flown over from Perth to be with me. Within two days, I was back on an operating table so that a small opening remaining from the original operation could be sealed down. Apparently, back-up operations are not unknown. I did my maths, calculated recovery times, begged the next consultant not to put gas bubbles in my eye.

Fair play, he ascertained when I had to fly next, decided to risk inserting enough bubbles to sort the problem but not so many that they would not all have disappeared by the next flight. He had a think, found a course of action, which – though treading a fine line – would enable me to work on the forthcoming weekend, a major week of Pool matches.

This time, there was to be no general anaesthetic. As I lay on the table, slightly sedated, a nurse came up and grabbed my shoulder and arm in a grip so tight that it was as if I were her long lost son. The grip was becoming slightly familiar and rather alluring when I opened my eye and found the reason for it. Someone in a mask was approaching me holding a long dagger, which he inserted in my eye through the lower lid. They sewed her arm back in a separate operation later that day.

When they took off the bandages hours later, I sat bolt upright. 'There's something in my vision,' I blurted.

'That's the gas bubbles,' they said. I never realised you could actually see the bubbles. For days, it was as if the lower half of my eye was filled with a moving bunch of large black grapes.

Stricken, I missed the off-field highlight of the trip – Zurich, one of rugby's most loyal sponsors, put on a splendid golf day down at Hope Island, provided everyone with a buggy equipped with a satellite navigation system to measure distance to the hole, a Texan scramble shotgun start, paired up hacks and players. It was, so everyone said, a welcome throwback to the old days of interaction with the team. Apparently, many of the England players turned out to be decent human beings.

I missed it. For three days, I had to lie in the same position on my left-hand side, rising only for essentials. The posturing process, lying still so that the bubbles do their work and expand to press down on the fresh repair, is stunningly boring.

Never mind, the lads said. You've had loads of practice at posturing. David Rogers, the photographer, went a whole five minutes the next day without cracking the ever-hilarious one-eye reporter 'joke'. I spent three days lying on my side with my laptop on its side too, tapping feebly with one hand, dictating stories to a sleepy copytaker in England and, thanks to the impressive travelling DVD collection held by David Norrie of the *News of the World*, watching *The Shawshank Redemption* endlessly, back to back three times.

What a film. What a pain.

29 October 2003 – Canada 24, Tonga 7 (WIN Stadium, Wollongong)

The best part of the pre-match rituals were the war-dances performed by the four teams of Pacific Islanders – Fiji, Samoa, Tonga and New Zealand (the latter tended to field a couple of white men just to give the impression that not all their squad comprised players their system had managed to filch from other countries. Only joking, boys).

They were all fiery affairs. When Tonga met New Zealand, both teams performed at the same time. The decision went to Tonga's Sipi Tau over the New Zealand Haka, because the Haka is meant to be performed while stationary while the Sipi Tau allows for an advance on the opposition. Just for a brief moment, it seemed the two teams were going to clash and have it all out before the first whistle blew.

Fiery stuff, and no doubt blood curdling in translation? I found translations. The Fijian effort, the Cibi, looks positively ferocious. Here's what it means. 'A cock and a hen, they attack, attack. It is taboo for me to slumber except to the sound of breakers. Your defence is just waiting to crumble when I prick it.' Don't know how anyone would summon the guts to face them after that.

The Siva Tau, the Samoan chant, says: 'Here I come completely prepared. The Manu Samoa, here I come.' Bit of a gap between gesture and threat, then. The Haka's words included: 'This is the man above me, who enabled me to live.' To think old Buck Shelford, the ultimate Haka leader, was chanting that claptrap all that time. The Tongan's Sipi Tau is a little bit more pointed. 'To the half-back and the backs, I have shed my human characteristics.' Although it does open with some stuff about a starving sea eagle.

I love all the rituals. The Haka and the others must always prevail. But no wonder they never do the words in English translation when they issue their challenges. The opposition and the crowds might fall about laughing.

The draw tended to ensure that major Pool matches came first. But the benefit of this was that it allowed some of the less-able teams to focus on their last match in the Pool; because often, they amounted to mini-finals against teams who had also struggled. We saw some marvellous mini-epics as a result – sometimes, in my case, through one eye.

Canada had been disappointing. They are another team which cannot quite reach the point of critical mass where confidence and funding and sponsorship and athletic prowess would begin to augment them, and they have never come close to reaching those heights of 1991 when they played New Zealand in an emotional quarter-final in Lille, scored two tries and slugged it out as if the match was between two equals in rugby history.

Yet they went out strongly, with Sean Fauth and Aaron Abrams scoring tries as they beat Tonga. One man, however, did not go out strongly. At this stage of the competition there were a large number of World Cup giants appearing in the event for the last time. A giant among these giants was Al Charron, who had played in that Lille epic, won nearly 80 caps for his country since, given up half his life and, probably, most of his money to play for one of the tournament's proudest teams.

If ever a player deserved to go out on a chariot, it was he. Instead, after a shocking illegal shoulder slam from Pierre Hola, the Tonga fly-half, he went out on a wheeled stretcher, neck in a brace, pouring blood. Some halfwit filling the position that day of citing commissioner did not see anything worth citing.

Next day, Canada had a boat trip around Sydney. They sat downing beers, reminiscing on an event which they had, despite their own disappointment, gilded again. Charron, a little shaky, mouth stitched, sat with them. 'He's OK as long as the beer goes down his throat, not out through his cut lip,' said a colleague. Great man.

One by one, other heroes of the smaller canvas of the tournament bowed out. Georgia and Uruguay had their sub-final in Aussie Stadium. All the comparative results so far had indicated that Georgia were the stronger of the two teams but when they met, it was Georgia's fourth match of the competition and Uruguay were only playing their third – what is more, Uruguay had not yet had their sapping match against England.

It was another gaudy triumph of an occasion, yet Georgia were out on their feet. They lost 24–12, could not begin to do themselves justice. Even Gregoire Yachvili, watched by both his parents, playing for the heroic memory of his remarkable grandfather, could do little to stem the tide. Alfonso Cardoso, Diego Lamelas and Nicolas Brignoni scored Uruguay's tries. It was decisive but it was also close. Tournament rules confined coaches to a glass-fronted box in each stadium, and they had to communicate via radio to their benches at pitch side. The television cameras would always pan frequently to catch the grief or the delirium up in the boxes.

When the final whistle blew and Georgia slumped to the ground, the cameras caught the Uruguay coaching staff. Diego Ormaechea, the coach, had been the oldest player in the 1999 World Cup, where Uruguay first tiptoed on to the global stage. Up in the box, he had gone bonkers. He and his coaching staff were enveloped in a great bobbing, jumping mass. Delirious. Back down on the field, Uruguayan players sprinted to a group of their supporters, jumped over the fence and embedded themselves in amongst the light blue phalanx. For a few seconds, we were all Uruguayan. Australia's *Daily Telegraph* placed these scenes as high as third in their top ten moments of the tournament.

Tasmania had its moment of glory, and so did Romania. At last, there was a victory to savour for two heroes, Romeo Gontineac, their worldly captain and centre, and Ovidiu Tonita, so relentless in adversity on the openside flank that more than one judge placed him in his eclectic team of the tournament. They beat Namibia by 37–7 on an occasion which drew a solid gang of the British media, sentimental softies that they were. Or maybe after the 300th Clive Woodward media conference they would have gone to watch Old Rottinghamians. The match was wonderfully well patronised by the people of Launceston, with 14,557 coming to watch. Local links were made between both countries and the hosts; club teams fixed to tour there, reciprocity of rugby feeling was powerful.

The mayor of Launceston, Janie Dickenson, played a major part in promoting the game. She said it was the biggest thing ever to happen to her city. Doubtless she received a full account of proceedings over the telephone – she missed the match to see her Canadian boyfriend in Singapore. Who could really fault her priorities? The World Cup was great. But it wasn't that great.

29. SHADES OF A RED REVIVAL

25 October 2003 – Wales 27, Italy 15
(Canberra Stadium, Canberra)

No one could accuse Italy of lack of foresight. It was more than six months since they had first spotted the disgrace contained in the fixture list, and the way that they had been stitched up in order to placate the tin-pot gods of television, who wanted decent British boys playing in prime-time slots, rather than dodgy Italians. Briefly, they even threatened not to come.

When they went to Canberra to meet Wales in the match that was always likely to decide second place in Pool D behind New Zealand, it was their fourth game in 14 days. Wales were only playing their third game in 14 days and the intensity of the international scene these days is such that to be robbed of recovery time so cruelly must have cost Italy at least 15 points.

Wales won at something of a canter and entered the quarter-finals. They had to, because a canter was all that they had been able to summon up in Pool action to date. Italy, as they often do, dominated both territory and possession for long periods of the first half of the Welsh match, with Alessandro Troncon at scrum-half and the explosive Andrea De Rossi on the flank desperately trying to inspire them.

But they probably realised that there was nothing in the tank; they certainly felt the lead in their legs. It was, in many ways, the most important match in their rugby history and they had produced four or five fine new talents earlier in the Pool. But there was an air of resignation about them at Canberra Stadium, and they first began to hunch their shoulders just before half-time. They knew that they should be responding massively, they just did not have the energy to do so. Afterwards, Syd Millar of the IRB admitted that Italy had been subjected to a horrendous programme. But then he gave that same shrug he produced when discussing the plight of the smaller teams. One of supine resignation.

Wales picked them off with a try by Mark Jones at the start of the first half, another by Sonny Parker just before the break, and they settled the match when Dafydd Jones, the tall flanker, scored after 64 minutes.

Even the Italians' most vital players, such as Sergio Parisse and Aaron Persico, seemed cowed by the end, and their only scores were five penalties kicked by Rima Wakarua, a one-footed (if you know what I mean) New Zealander unearthed by John Kirwan, Italy's Kiwi coach.

With respect, you have to hand it to New Zealand coaches wherever they appear in the world of professional rugby. They never stint in their effort to cure the problems of their team and New Zealand's employment statistics at the same time.

None of this was the fault of Wales, just their sheer good fortune. However, pessimists around their camp were not wholly convinced that this victory would do them much good in the long term. By a rather nasty aberration of the fixtures, their plodding team now faced New Zealand and England in successive matches, not only their two most deadly rugby enemies, but the two favourites to win the tournament.

2 November 2003 – New Zealand 53, Wales 37 (Telstra Stadium, Sydney)

It would be wrong to suggest that this was the match which electrified the tournament because there was a crackle in the air already. But here in the Telstra Stadium, we had a stunning spectacle. It was a match of quite magnificent skill, daring and pace, one in which Wales not so much stood toe-to-toe with their illustrious opponents, but ran through and around them to give them the shock of their lives.

The match went down a storm in Australia not simply because the Kiwis had been embarrassed but also because it was such a joyful affair. Wales thrived on extraordinary performances from Jonathan Thomas, the impossibly callow new flanker; from Shane Williams, the tiny and hitherto inconsistent wing; and from Gareth Thomas, the veteran wing who didn't even start the game but who came on and showed the wisdom of experience and the moves of a wizard.

Cold reality dawned when the vapour trails left behind had dispersed. The truth at the end was that New Zealand had still won; they had scored eight tries to four by Wales. But there was a massive element of good fortune in the way they sealed their win at the end – albeit, perhaps, a fortune which deserved to beam down on them, for their own effervescence brought even more tries to the free-scoring wings.

When Wales worked Shane Williams over in the left-hand corner in the final quarter of play, they took a 37–33 lead, a tribute to their ability to retain the ball and then for the likes of Gareth Thomas, Shane Williams and Mark Taylor to perform magic with it.

Even when Carlos Spencer, the fly-half, put New Zealand one point in front with the last ten minutes beckoning, there was no slackening of the pace that Wales had set. However, Justin Marshall made a break for the Welsh corner as he went for the try, which would tilt the match irrevocably. The Welsh defence appeared to have the situation in hand. Marshall was run down and tackled, and as he started to fall, Doug Howlett outside him was covered by a Welsh defender and no pass seemed on.

Except one. A forward pass. Marshall popped the ball around the back of the Welsh defender; every close witness and television camera brooked no argument that the try should have been ruled out. Yet all that appeared to concern Andre Watson, the referee, and Alan Lewis, the touch-judge, was whether Howlett had put a foot in touch. Subsequent reports even suggested that Lewis might have indicated a forward pass but that Watson, for some reason, ignored his call. Be that as it may, the refereeing authorities would surely take note of such a key blunder, and at least we would not see Watson again in the knockout stages of the tournament. Would we?

The other fascinating aspect of a terrific evening in Sydney concerned the roots of this staggering Welsh improvement. Coach Hansen had been in charge of Wales during a melancholy period. Some people held that his structures were too limiting and imposed an alien style. Yet, undeniably, he also had allies in the team who greatly admired him as a coach.

But this was a Welsh team playing without inhibitions, almost without structure and playing with devil. Was the improvement a tribute to Hansen? Or had a group of Welsh players, acting either as individuals or in combination, decided to play a game using native talents and cunning and skills?

And yet again, the All Blacks had not quite stated a powerful case. Not for a second could anyone in this tournament doubt their ambition. It was just that, occasionally, they looked flustered as Wales attacked, and they were unable to close the game down with a few lengthy, pulverising forward drives. Reuben Thorne, their captain, simply never looked the part. He tended to go through games with an air of quiet bemusement on his face.

The tournament moved on at high pace. England's Sunday match against Uruguay followed Super Saturday, one of the greatest days in the history of the tournament, and of rugby. There were three games of wondrous drama, tension and pathos, as Pool action reached a climax.

Scotland and Fiji played off for second place in Pool B, in a loser-goes-home match in Aussie Stadium. Scotland had not enjoyed a successful or an equable time, and Ian McGeechan's career as their coach seemed to be disintegrating rather than reaching a climax. There were even reports of unrest in the camp and the team had been murdered by an epic French performance at Telstra earlier. France scored five tries, and their back row, Imanol Harinordoquy, Serge Betsen and Olivier Magne, had played like three powder-blue and rather superior sports cars. France looked unflappable; a core of calm experience and discipline overlaid with some flashes from Frederic Michalak, apparently a new and less flighty young man.

There were few reports of dazzling Scottish play. At Aussie Stadium, Rupeni Caucaunibuca, back from suspension, savaged the right flank of the Scotland defence for two tries; Fiji could easily have scored twice more in the first half of a match which they dominated in terms of rugby class.

Yet in the second half, they lost composure when victory beckoned. They were also, clearly, undercooked in terms of endurance fitness. Tom Smith of Scotland drove over for the winning try near the end, but it was preposterous to see the match as some Scottish papers did, as a stunning comeback. Fiji faded and Scotland found that, fortuitously, they were left standing and had a path ahead to play Australia in the quarter-finals.

Super Saturday surged on. Samoa had given their classic performance against England in Melbourne, and they subsided to South Africa to the tune of 60–10. Derick Hougaard was tried at fly-half and made a reasonable fist of it, coming back well from Lima's explosion of a tackle on him. South Africa scored eight tries against one, finding some form.

If the game was not quite so stunning as the earlier epic, there were two items of considerable note afterwards. Australia's concept of the Nanny State fits perfectly in all this. If you have a laminated pass, you are able to wander round inside the fences, never mind how superfluous your task. But if any halfwit without a pass appears, interrupting the accredited halfwits, then he is immediately seized and brutally dragged off. The attack on David McHugh, the fine Irish referee, by a walking gutbucket of a Springbok fan in 2002 put everyone further on their mettle.

Given the dire warnings issued for people not to trespass, surely no one would even try it. However, as Louis Koen, on as replacement, was about to take a shot at goal for the final conversion, a lumbering fool called Tapumanaia Lautusi, a 29-year-old labourer, ran from the crowd and tried to tackle him. Koen got the kick away and turned to find that, amazingly, Lautusi had missed his tackle and knocked himself out as his head hit the ground. He even failed to mount the best defence – if only he'd pointed out that he'd seen Louis Koen kick before and he was going to offer him some help, he'd probably have been exonerated.

There was, almost immediately, an even more extraordinary sight. After the whistle, and the jersey swap, religious leaders on both sides suggested a pause for prayer. The two teams and their replacements formed a single colourful circle, at some points with the teams alternating, knelt and prayed. It was a wonderful image, and I imagine that you did not need to be a believer to find it so. It reminded me of the practice of Andrew Blowers, the superb and deeply religious New Zealander playing at Northampton, who is in the habit of apologising to opponents who have just been wiped from the face of the pitch by one of his special tackles.

1 November 2003 – Australia 17, Ireland 16
(Telstra Dome, Melbourne)

A nation shakes. The third element in Super Saturday produced yet another prodigious game and spectacle, and as David Humphreys, on as replacement for Ireland, took aim with a drop-kick right at the end, there seemed every chance that the hosts would be usurped at the top of the Pool and would have to go to play the streamlined French in the semi-final, rather than meet the struggling Scots.

However, Humphreys missed with the kick and Ireland lost composure in the dying moments as they tried to drive the ball up so that he could be brought into range for another attempt.

Frankly, the lack of real power in the Australian forwards and the bungling behind the scrum must have sent a cold sweat through Eddie Jones and his coaching staff. Australia still led by eight points in the second half, but by this time Brian O'Driscoll was beginning to stir himself, and after Joe Roff knocked on horrendously in deep defence, O'Driscoll made an absolutely magnificent job of reaching out for the line in a double tackle right on the touchline, with the ball controlled in one hand. It all seemed too good to be true but the video referee gave O'Driscoll the try, and quite rightly.

Ireland were never to lead, but the relentless passions of Keith Wood,

Malcolm O'Kelly and their pack, and the game of his life in a chequered career from Peter Stringer at scrum-half, caused desperate panic in the home ranks. There was absolutely no shortage in Australia at the time of old internationals desperate to be taken on as media punters to remind the world that they were still about and to earn a few dollars' drinking money. The avalanche of old Wallabies piling into Australia after this almost made you feel sorry for Uncle Eddie and his chaps. The Australian bookies also deserted their team, offering New Zealand at such dramatically unattractive odds for the forthcoming semi-final that it was hardly worth a dollar's investment.

Naturally, the country was solidly behind them but it was also true that their camp was, in the eyes of the rest of the rugby world, now to be ranked with that of England as the most-disliked. As far as I could see, England were disliked because they were England, Australia were disliked because they were rude. It was instructive, too, to see agreement voiced in the home media. 'Why doesn't anyone want to dance with the Wallabies any more?' asked Greg Growden, the doyen of Australian rugby writers, so he tells me. Growden was referring chiefly to the rather sour and grim outpourings which were coming from Jones and the camp. He quoted one media observer saying: 'At some Wallaby press conferences, the flowers instantly droop. The energy immediately goes out of the room.'

The truth was, as Growden pointed out, that while the 1991 Australians were the darlings of the British media en route to their World Cup win, everyone had become sick to the back teeth of the attempts by Jones, in the week before every game, to unsettle the opposition, needle their key players, suck up to the referee and even introduce an element of confrontation into proceedings, which could easily have led to warfare on the field.

The first reverse that Jones had suffered in his off-the-field battling, as previously noted, had come at the hands of Woodward when England thrashed Australia in the match at the Colonial Stadium, Melbourne, in June. When Woodward had walked into the post-match press conference, everyone expected him to speak honeyed words and to call a truce in the battle of words that Jones had begun before the Test. Instead, Woodward came in and absolutely lambasted the losing coach for the (admittedly, rather infantile) attempts at verbal warfare.

And it had all gone horribly wrong again for Jones just a week after the win over Ireland, as he was up to his usual media tricks before Australia were to play Scotland in the quarter-final. Jones harked way back to the 1989 British Lions tour of Australia. Undeniably, since they realised that the Australian pack were comprised largely of a bunch of nancies, the Lions, under Ian McGeechan's coaching, had decided to take the Wallabies on up front and the harsher the contest, the better they liked it.

There were grim incidents in all three Test matches and a ferocious barrage of criticism and hurt expressed in the Australian papers. To this day, there are people in Australian rugby who are still incensed at the memory of their being beaten up on the field of play.

The late Bob Templeton, an Australian and one of the greatest coaches of the era, saw it differently. He realised that the Lions had gone for the soft underbelly of his own countrymen, and he advised Australians to take defeat well and to stop whining.

Here, 14 years on, McGeechan – one of the true gentlemen of rugby, with a blanket refusal to involve himself in anything sordid – was bringing his Scotland team to meet Australia in the quarter-final. Jones immediately tried to draw parallels with the 1989 series, even though there were none to be drawn.

He warned the referee and the world in general that Scotland might be inclined to play 'last-resort rugby' in order to beat Australia up and upset them. It was an attack that evoked incredulity and distaste in almost every other camp and exposed what Jones clearly saw as part of his overall strategy to win games as an ungracious sham. Did it ever really gain him a point on the field of play? I doubt it. Back in 1991, the charming Aussies were so charming that they charmed England out of their game plan and won the game. Charming!

McGeechan's reaction was far more statesmanlike. 'Unless I'm mistaken, we are all playing last-resort rugby. If you don't win, you go home. I think that Eddie likes to try to influence referees wherever he can.'

Growden summed up by describing Australia as 'dim and dour. They have too much of a cynical crust. They are no longer the nice guys of world rugby. Instead, they protest too much.' He pointed out a view that, as far as Wallaby reaction is concerned, it was always the opposition, and never them, who used roughhouse tactics.

As the World Cup reached a conclusion, Jones clearly decided to change tack. He saw the error of his ways. The final weeks were conducted in an atmosphere of sweetness and light. Indeed, there was so little verbal punching to which the media could happily react that I was forced to take Growden to task for spoiling all the fun. Even Woodward used to say, as the anti-Pom tirades took aim at him: 'It makes us all laugh. It's just part of the fun and the crap that comes with it in this country.' But it was also, occasionally, tiresome.

Jones played it straight after his rudeness to Scotland. Essentially, he is a decent man, by no means the worst coach (if not the best). Somewhere in all this, somewhere in the fact that his tactics had even helped to stop loud Aussie propaganda, was another splendid result for Mr Woodward. He had heard enough Aussie claptrap and he found, when he barked back in un-English fashion, that it had all gone quiet over there.

30. CENTURIONS

2 November 2003 – England 111, Uruguay 13
(Suncorp Stadium, Brisbane)

Everyone out on the balcony to wave. England's second-ever century was duly run up, with 17 tries, of which five came from the razor-sharp Josh Lewsey. Normally, I detest these annihilations; detest the guilt it evokes (or should do) in the game whenever those who prepare in palaces play those who live in workhouses. But this time, it was not so bad. For a start, Uruguay never lost their shape, and Pablo Lemoine, the mountainous tight-head prop, anchored them with a heroic disdain for reputation and privation.

But it was a revelation to see the sheer attacking ability in the England ranks; to have proof there was class and pace to go with their more mundane but worthy qualities. That was so enjoyable. Lewsey, Iain Balshaw and Stuart Abbott provided an attacking pod on the right, which cut Uruguay to ribbons. Abbott, whose ability to make space in the packed midfield has been one of the key factors in transforming Wasps from sweating grafters to the verge of greatness, lacks only a yard of sheer straight-line speed. It was almost taking the mick when England drafted in Will Greenwood and Jason Robinson in the second half. All evening, they went zip-zip.

Perhaps the sharpest act, though, was Mike Catt. The Bath centre rippled with fitness, spraying glorious passes that dragged the recipient onto them and gave moves momentum. He looked as if he was revelling in the whole thing, even allowed himself a beam. Only Dan Luger struggled. You could almost touch the intensity and the willpower he brought to the occasion, the desperation with which he hammered on the door of the party. But Luger's famed busting running skills had deserted him, as had his confidence. It was not a happy sight.

Perhaps oddly for a match in which they conceded 100 points, Uruguay applied long periods of pressure. They spent ages battering away in the England corner, trying desperately to score a try from close range, and it was nothing more than they deserved when Lemoine crashed over.

The only other jarring note came when Worsley, who had been sent to the sin-bin, reacted to a mixture of jeers from Australians and roars from England fans by waving at the crowd as he disappeared. When he went into the dressing-room at the end, Woodward was waiting. 'I told him he was a complete prat for doing that. People out here say this England team is arrogant. We are in no way an arrogant team and that is why we have no place for behaviour like that.'

Diego Ormaechea, the Uruguayan coach, summed up the match to perfection. 'Against England, it was Formula One against a bicycle. A lion against a mouse. We are a soccer nation with 300 rugby players.' The mouse, by the way, would soon roar. Not as loud, however, as Woodward roared at Worsley.

Before I set out for Australia, I bought the Lonely Planet guide to the country. As a genre, I have very little time for the series. The editors always seem to be engaged in a reverse-pompous campaign in which they deride anywhere or anything on the lonely planet where large gatherings of other tourists might go. This is odd, because if large numbers of people go there, then there must be something worth seeing.

But flying down south, and in odd moments in hotel rooms afterwards, I enjoyed dipping into the book, enjoyed reading up on the vast panoply of Australian delights in the big cities, the endless outback and bush, the glorious warmth of Far North Queensland and the Barrier Reef, the flora and fauna and fierce animals of the hinterland, frontier mentality of the centre and north. And all the treats in between, with the mystical magic of Uluru in the centre. I knew some friends who were trekking round vast tracts of the country, allowing Australia to get under their skin. There was so much to see and to do. Endless Aussie.

But the ache of impending loss and waste struck early on. Western Australia is a vast area but, frankly, it is a place you can easily miss on your way to Sydney and the east coast, or if you are escaping from Australia on your way up to Europe. So the tourism people out there work their socks off, dragging big events and holiday packages to the far west. They negotiate aggressively with the Australian Rugby Union so that Test matches frequently come out to the Subiaco Oval. But whether they come for sport or sightseeing, I doubt if many people see the stop-off as a waste.

The Western Australian tourist board gave us a thoroughly agreeable breakfast briefing early in the tour. They took the opportunity because so many overseas travelling press were gathered in the same place, but to be fair to them, it was not all a hard sell. They simply wanted us as individuals to tap in to some of the delights of the region.

They kicked off by offering a comedy double act which made Roy and HG sound hilarious, but then they gave us a presentation which took in all the natural wonders of the whole state. It's one of those many places which is around 500 times the size of Wales. Or something like that. It was breathtaking. And what did we hacks do in the breathtaking state? I remember two walks on a beach near Perth. But of the wine valleys and mountains and parks and distant deserted beaches and all the other items in the panoply, we saw not a sign. It was a horrendous waste. There was barely a day when there were no rugby duties, either a match to watch or a press conference in which to fall asleep. The state of mind on the media trip was such that even if someone went to the toilet, he felt tempted to leave his mobile number with three other people just so they could let him know if he was missing anything important in the three minutes of his absence.

As the tour wore on, the sense that a wonderful country was passing me by became too strong. Nick Cain and I gave up on attempts even to make a one-day trip somewhere out there. Work, or preparation for it, or some angle on background, always intervened. The Lonely Planet guide simply became a reminder of what I was missing. I dumped it in a hotel wastebin, just as the knockout stages were starting.

I have no doubt that Australia is a wonderful place, and I made a resolution that, one day, I would see it for myself.

31. REAL RUDI! PACIFISM AND BETRAYAL

8 November 2003 – New Zealand 29, South Africa 9
(Telstra Dome, Melbourne)

People who ask me how their offspring can become sportswriters are unerringly pointed in the direction of Hugh McIlvanney's compendium *McIlvanney on Boxing*, the highlights of his reporting on the roughest trade. Not so much for a guide of how and where to start, but an illustration of the heights the hacks' trade can occasionally reach.

'But I don't like boxing very much,' my inquisitors often point out.

'You don't have to,' I always reply. One of my favourites is McIlvanney's report on the fight between Buster Douglas and Evander Holyfield in Las Vegas in 1990. Douglas came out bloated and unfit ('Holyfield may have wondered if he should be throwing punches or firing harpoons') and also, frankly, scared. A one-sided fight ended with Douglas knocked down but with senses intact, checking his face for damage but refusing to rise to beat the count. 'Pacifism,' wrote McIlvanney, 'is an honourable creed but a man's public espousal of it looks less than noble when he has just accepted $20 million to go to war.'

The pacifism of South Africa's rugby team in this abject afternoon at Telstra Dome was not born of physical fear. They had certainly not accepted in rand equivalent anything like $20 million dollars. But their culpability was even greater than that of the blustering Buster. By donning the green jersey for this match they had accepted a sacred duty to live up to those great men who had worn it for over 100 years with such distinction. They betrayed those great men.

They were also up against their oldest enemy and were one blasting performance away from the semi-finals and from erasing the dreadful memory of the racism, violence, incoherence and poor play of their recent history. And New Zealand was not Holyfield. They had the moves, but not the weight of punch. A true Springbok team would have scented glory and come out of their corner in a rage.

All morning, flying down from Brisbane with a plane-full of happy Leicester Tigers followers (obviously, they hadn't heard the Tigers' results from home), wandering the banks of the Yarra, arguing whether Melbourne was severely overrated, we looked forward to the match. All of us caught the satisfying scent of cordite. The prospect of the first few scrums was compelling, for the scrum was the stage for any attempt by South Africa to reverse the form book.

Yet there was something draining in the air from the start. For the first time, the marketeers had blundered somewhere; the stadium was not more than three-quarters full. At the first scrum, Christo Bezuidenhout and Faan Rautenbach, the two Springbok props, allowed New Zealand to form up right under their noses, a manoeuvre that gave them no space to surge into the scrum and put in a juddering hit. New Zealand easily held on. In the second scrum, Bezuidenhout's hit was almost apologetic.

Events were to prove conclusively that the New Zealand pack were of a standard in their tight forward play roughly akin to an English club team in the middle of the Zurich Premiership. Pacifist South Africa never budged them an inch.

South Africa were appalling. Derick Hougaard had come in at fly-half to replace the hapless Louis Koen and played like a startled rabbit. Joe van Niekerk was invalided out of the tournament, which was a body blow, but what did Rudi Straeuli do? He chucked Danie Rossouw onto the openside flank. Rossouw, strong and willing but tall and ponderous, tried to compete for the loose ball with the pedigree Richie McCaw. South Africa's back row was so waddlingly slow that when Justin Marshall, the New Zealand scrum-half, set off on sniping runs through which his aspirations were only to keep the back row interested, he found no back row even on the horizon. He had the freedom of the park, could graze his sheep there, and operate unmolested.

But it was not the dearth of pace or technique that chilled the blood. It was the supine acceptance of defeat, the fact that South Africa went through the motions. Victor Matfield, one of their class forwards, was a disgrace. Joost van der Westhuizen was playing the last game of a career so chequered that you could play draughts on it. When he was replaced at the end, he waved cheerfully to the crowd and did not look in the slightest put out. Frankly, he looked relieved.

Leon MacDonald scored a try in the first half; Keven Mealamu, the tiny hooker, scampered through some truly pathetic defence for another, and then Carlos Spencer, with one of those bits of play so beloved of people who judge class on flash, not substance, flipped the ball through his legs and Joe Rokocoko scored. The kicks made it 29–9 in a match which, apart from the travesty of a South Africa performance, was fading from the memory as the teams were still trooping off.

8 November 2003 – Telstra Dome Media Centre

There was no longer any doubt. Straeuli was a disaster; he had endured a personal nightmare away from the field as coach. The Lugubrious Moose was on his way out as coach and, categorically, had not proved to be the man I thought he was back in the genteel Edinburgh hotel foyer in the Middle Ages of one year previous.

He spoke drivel at the media conference. He did not appear to have noticed that his team had played badly nor could he possibly admit what was palpably obvious – that he had lost his men, that they did not want to play for him, even against the All Blacks in an eminently winnable World Cup quarter-final match.

'I am disappointed because we came here to win the tournament and did not. We won a lot of hearts on and off the field. Maybe [the team] has come together a year too soon, but I am proud of the boys, they are true ambassadors for South Africa.' Well, top marks for lack of honesty. The boys were a disgrace and every heart they won must have been an All Black heart.

Soon after Straeuli returned to South Africa, a probe was due into allegations of racism in the camp; another was due into the dreadful performances of the team and a new president, Brian van Rooyen, arrived as SARFU collapsed under the weight of failure.

Finally, an investigation was announced into a training camp that the squad had gone through before they left for Australia. What became known as the Kamp Staaldraad affair blew up when players broke ranks and spoke about the evil conditions and inhuman degradation they had faced in the name of preparing for a rugby tournament. A secret video was also released. Among the delights, the Springboks were doused repeatedly with ice-cold water while the English national anthem and New Zealand's Haka were played; they had to stand naked in a freezing lake; had to sit in a dark pit holding rugby balls in front of their private parts; and exercised in the nude.

In the video, one player was shown holding a bloody, headless chicken and another had an egg cracked over his head for a minor failure to perform some task. Officials of the South Africa Defence Force rushed out a statement declaring that such activities played no part in their own training. It smacked of some horrendous practices from a bygone age in the most backward and vicious English public school.

Racism, violence, sporting pacifism and surrender, disturbing rituals. Straeuli's year had the lot. That is before you even begin to scratch the surface of the team's failure in the field of coaching and team and unit development. This was the man I had identified as the future for a modern South Africa. I still meet those who knew him in his Bedford days, who admire him as a character, but if he was a New South African Man in any way, he had, in 2003, a bloody funny way of showing it. Within three weeks of the pacifism of Melbourne, he was dumped.

8 November 2003 – Australia 33, Scotland 16
(Suncorp Stadium, Brisbane)

The second quarter-final was never really riveting enough to make us sit up and take note in the media centre in Melbourne. Events at the Suncorp were all too predictable. It was obvious that, despite Eddie Jones' rudeness and silly prediction of a filthy match, it would be hard and fair, and so it was. It was highly likely that Steve Walsh, the reprieved referee who had no business being on the field after his irregular behaviour towards England, would referee abysmally, and he did.

And obvious that Australia would win. Their play had paralleled that of England so far. There was a decent side in there somewhere but they themselves could not release it. But it was their 11th consecutive World Cup win: a record. They struggled a little in the first half when Scotland, predictably, took the game to them, and Jason White and Simon Taylor played powerfully. But tries by Stirling Mortlock in the 47th minute and George Gregan on the hour, and then from David Lyons five minutes later, saw off the brave resistance. Mortlock's fine form after recovering from injury was a definite bonus, although his breakaway try came after Walsh had allowed Australia ridiculous leeway at the previous breakdown. Elton Flatley, fast making himself the equivalent of a Swiss Army Knife in his all-round usefulness (and notwithstanding the low reputation of the Swiss Army, knives or not), scored eighteen points with three conversions and four penalties.

Rob Russell scored a late try for Scotland, but their most remarkable moment, I felt, was a drop-goal. Chris Paterson let fly from only a yard or two inside the Australian half and the ball flew though the posts and landed around 15 yards behind the goal line. It was a stunning strike. People decry the value of the drop-goal but the skill involved in that kick was worth every point of the three.

It didn't mean much in terms of the match, but perhaps it was a little more significant in terms of Scotland's future. They have been so poor for so long and this tournament marked the final bow of Gregor Townsend, who played the quarter-final outside Paterson, who was installed at fly-half. Paterson has always been a superb footballer, not usually trusted, however, to play anywhere bar out on the wing. If he can add half of Townsend's tactical sharpness to his game, then maybe Scotland have a contender.

Bryan Redpath, their captain and one of their few pedigree players, spoke brave words later about Scotland's satisfaction at making the last eight. Frankly, they were awful in Australia 2003. All they did of any real significance was to beat a Fijian team which, had it been favoured with one-quarter of the budget and one-quarter of the preparation time for the tournament enjoyed by the Scots, would have taken them to the cleaners.

32. WALES ABANDONED

9 November 2003 – France 43, Ireland 21
(Telstra Dome, Melbourne)

There was never a time when I did not think England would win the World Cup if they played near their best. But this was the day when France probably overtook them in the betting and in the general perception. Was it their sleek jerseys, their unfussy demeanour, their discipline, their calm defence, their selection of options? Indeed, they played just like France in all their proud history, er, haven't.

And was the last piece of the jigsaw now in place? Frederic Michalak, when he had last played against England in Marseilles, performed as if the match revolved round him, and instead of providing a hub to keep the team humming, he would have a bite himself and then not so much set the ball on its way as discard it.

Here, he kicked 22 points. But it was his skills as a playmaker that were so striking. He was deft, unselfish. Fabien Galthié, the scrum-half, and the leader that France have always craved, was outstanding and the back row was magnificent. Here come Les Bleus. Gradually, most of the teams that had been knocked out took up the cause of anyone likely to beat England. Amazing how many ersatz French started piping up.

The final score indicates a fast and furious match with a decisive edge to the winners. It did not play like that. It was brutally one-sided. At one stage, in the third quarter, it was 37–0 to France. The French scrum and lineout was massively on top, and Olivier Magne, Christophe Dominici and Imanol Harinordoquy scored tries. Jean-Jacques Crenca, the French loose-head, then scored at the start of the second half and Michalak's kicking took them to 37.

Ireland came back, and good on them. But I am suspicious when coaches laud their team's courage at staging these late rallies. It is exceedingly hard to maintain your level of performance when you are crushing the opposition and I feel that Ireland only resurfaced because they were allowed to by a team that was, mentally, already playing their semi-final. It is the same principle as cricket's beer matches. The real thing's over. Big deal that you won the unimportant bit at the end.

Brian O'Driscoll scored two tries in the mini-revival, without ever suggesting that his fitness really was from the top drawer, and Kevin Maggs one. Maggs receives around one-fiftieth of the publicity of O'Driscoll, but his power in taking the ball up and his indomitable courage not only makes him an ideal foil but also ensures that he is highly rated inside the game.

It was the end for Ireland. Every team bowing out of Rugby World Cup 2003 made a lap of honour to wave goodbye. This was Ireland's goodbye, but it was also farewell forever for Keith Wood, the captain. There were not enough laps to honour him. 'I'd like to go on for a few more years,' he said, 'but the body's not there. It's gone.' By all accounts, the litany of Wood's injuries was so daunting that you hoped and prayed that he was not facing a painful and arthritic after-life.

On the final whistle, Wood and Galthié embraced. It was a gesture of mutual respect, unforced and graphic. Afterwards, the French hierarchy praised Wood to the skies. Wood has been an absolutely staggering player. Indomitable never summed him up. He was a true great, and people who assume that he was not quite the full biscuit in the tight because he was so prominent in the loose, really should have trusted their own eyes. He was the complete player and he was probably the greatest running hooker who ever played. He had the pace and skills of a centre. He may not have had the grace of a centre, but when did that count for much when giving it a thrash against all the odds?

He played in some Herculean games. Probably among the most magnificent were the first two Tests of the 1997 British Lions series. The first was won deservedly by the Lions and the second, which sealed the series, was won in the face of the run of play and one of the most ferocious South Africa onslaughts in history. If the Boks had played with that attitude in the quarter-final of the 2003 World Cup then they would have beaten New Zealand by around 65–0.

On the morning after that match, we encountered Wood walking stiffly about, clearly the worse for wear – and not just from a few celebratory drinks but also because of the colossal battering he had inflicted on his own body through the sheer devil will with which he had resisted.

'Get any sleep?' we asked him, after passing on congratulations.

'None at all,' he said. 'I was worried that if I got off to sleep I'd never have woken up again.' Talk about rugby being poorer for his passing. The

Six Nations will take years to recover, and I'd hate to be an Ireland hooker for the next decade, because the comparisons will be painful.

9 November 2003 – England 28, Wales 17
(Suncorp Stadium, Brisbane)

The Suncorp Stadium was boiling with emotion. They've revamped and resoared it since it was the plain old Lang Park and as unprepossessing as a 1960s tower block. Now, it is wonderful, airy, atmospheric. The two great rivals from Britain had transplanted their rivalry – sporting, sociological, historical – into this crowded corner of the Sunshine State.

It is the norm for coaches of teams favoured to win games to come out with all sorts of outlandish claims as to why the opposition must be respected and could even win. No doubt Eddie Jones had said it before Australia played Namibia. But in the week before this quarter-final, Clive Woodward's praise of Wales had carried a conviction. The extra pace of the men in red had given the whole culture of the tournament an acceleration and the scene was set gloriously for another attempt by Wales to run a top team to near-distraction.

Furthermore, it was now high time for England to produce something to file under the general heading of 'definitive'. Frankly, there were more emotions and contradictions circulating in me than I would normally endure without a bottle of Australia's best red or at least the best the *Sunday Times* would stump up for. When I first began to report on Welsh rugby matches it was an urgent professional duty to discard the vivid cloak of bias towards Wales that, like any other rugby fan, I had worn when I was a fan myself. Yet I suppose that, while observing the professional niceties, you can never extract from your own heart and soul matters so essential as the pride in your country. And especially the pride in your small country. In my teenage years this would often spill over into such a healthy dislike of England in general and the England rugby team in particular that it would spoil a whole year for myself and my school friends if the result in the annual confrontation went wrong. It was an affliction that I had cured in the first few weeks of life as a reporter, because I had to.

Today was my 50th birthday. That was something else to think about. I had also come to the game almost literally one-eyed since the latest application of the dagger had not allowed more than 75 per cent of the sight to return as yet in the offending eye. The media authorities were kind enough to allocate me a seat next to a television in the media box.

When Wales led 10–3 at half-time, my feelings were in turmoil. An enormous part of me was desperate for them to go on and win the match. My father was no longer around to have his whole week brightened by a possible Welsh victory but I could well imagine the scenes back at home on that early Sunday morning, with my old friends, now joined by their sons, agonising at the tension that was to come and recalling the mighty self-confidence which the rugby would spread around in its greatest days.

Blood, and nation, are always thicker than water. Yet I wanted a team from the northern hemisphere to win the World Cup. I wanted that to happen because the dominance of New Zealand and Australia and, less often, of South Africa had given the marketeers and technocrats involved in rugby in those countries the moral right to dictate the way that the game was going. In my view, they had made a total cock-up of it and had served only their own interests. They had almost produced a type of sport that had only sporadic reference points to real rugby as we knew and loved it. I had become a figure of some minor notoriety due to my attacks on Super 12 rubbish rugby in the mid-1990s; occasionally I would log on to message sections on websites and find that whole tranches of them would be savage verbal assaults on me. I loved it all.

The move back to rugby with forwards empowered was already in full swing, but it was important for the immediate future of the game, in my opinion, that New Zealand and Australia were exposed as empty shells representing a rugby philosophy that was shattering into small pieces. England had far more capability than Wales to complete that shattering process, so I feared, if Wales went forward from 10–3 and won, that they would subside readily to France in the semi-final, merely because they had already over-achieved and would be mentally sated.

The teams came back out for the second half. Perhaps the competing emotions inside me balanced each other out because I enjoyed the action hugely. My sorrow that Wales were dumped from the tournament was assuaged by the knowledge of the lift they had given everyone; and the fact that England were still winning while playing within themselves suggested to me that they were still on course. And in the final analysis I had followed their caravan up hill and down dale for what seemed like donkeys' years. I admired them as players, I admired their ferocious application and the way they conducted themselves, and I admired the way in which they played.

Style? Style was the first Welsh try. Mike Tindall grabbed a loose ball just inside his own half on the English left and projected a high, diagonal kick. As soon as he did so, we saw that Ben Kay was stationed on the England right wing and was the only immediate chaser. 'Kay's in the shit!' said Nick Cain on my right, almost as soon as Tindall had put boot to ball.

Indeed he was. Shane Williams caught the ball, murdered Kay on the counter attack, and a brilliant move involving Gareth Cooper, Gareth Thomas and the dazzling Williams again put Stephen Jones over for the try.

Wales showed another dimension just before half-time when an explosive driving maul from a lineout made space for Colin Charvis to lunge over. As they trooped off, Wales were no doubt torn between celebration and frustration from the belief that they could easily have scored two more tries.

That was their high point. Dan Luger, poor man, had endured a horrendous first half. Another problem was that Jonny Wilkinson could put no shape on proceedings. In comparison with the deadly Welsh, England's attack dithered. Wilkinson managed to hit the post and miss from bang in front in the first half, and struggled outside his kicking too. So Woodward applied the same panacea to both problems. He shunted Tindall to the wing in place of Luger, no doubt counting it as a short prison sentence – a punishment for his horrendous diagonal kick. And Mike Catt came on, grabbed the ball, and started spraying expert diagonal kicks down behind the Welsh defence. It seemed almost as if Catt had seen enough, that he was not even going to allow Wilkinson to stay in tactical charge. His arrival turned the game and by the end he was even making dazzling breaks.

The scores began to come quickly. Jason Robinson caught a deep Welsh kick early in the second half and ran it back with an absolutely breathtaking diagonal burst which cut up every rank of the Welsh defence. With a final expert pass, Robinson put Will Greenwood over on the right wing for the try. It was a sensational score.

Wilkinson yet again refound a strand of his considerable game that was in full working order. As England drove hard, and as Wales infringed in desperation, Wilkinson kicked six penalties and a drop-goal and a conversion, and even though Martyn Williams scored late on for Wales, the better team had reasserted itself.

Woodward was spectacularly rude in the post-match press conference. It was not so much what he said but the het-up, almost disdainful manner in which he said it. He was terse in the extreme with French journalists who asked him fairly mundane questions about the forthcoming semi-final. 'I believe that we will beat France,' said Woodward. 'The French fully know that England are going down to play against them in the semi-final of the World Cup, and it's about what happens during the 80 minutes of the game. I don't really care if they are favourites or not favourites. Clearly, we were not at our best today and we made some very fundamental errors, but I am also very confident that we can sit down, have a clear-the-air meeting next week, and beat France. We are disappointed how we played, but it's far nicer to be flying to Sydney than flying back home to London. We are not playing well, but we are winning these games through sheer bloody-mindedness.' And also showing the same quality in their press conferences, apparently.

Woodward laughed about his outburst later. I suppose it might just qualify as an occasion when the screaming pressure came to the surface. But there were few others.

11 November 2003 – Manly Pacific Hotel; Jonny Wilkinson media conference

It was not that Wilkinson was letting England down every match. Every time he had appeared in the tournament and, indeed, every time he had ever played for his country, so it seemed, at least one of the myriad golden strands of his game had been carefully wound around the neck of the opposition, until they choked.

Yet he had not quite delivered the all-round authoritative performance that he himself craved and it was possibly even salutary for him, as the ultimate team man, when Mike Catt received all the praise after the Welsh game for the way he had come on, grabbed the tactical tiller and turned it any bloody way he wanted.

By this stage of the tournament, the fascination with Wilkinson was still growing. He had minders by now, as, otherwise, merely to walk across the glamorous strand in front of the team's beach headquarters would have caused a riot. His weekly appearances in front of an increasingly large media mob were conducted even more in the vein of a sub-psychological examination into his character and a delving for signs of him cracking under pressure – an examination conducted by those of us who regarded ourselves as among the leading barrack-room psychologists that the world of sport had ever seen. Together with those who wanted to talk to him about his girlfriend.

There was no question whatsoever that the pressure on him was massive. It came from inside his own squad, from the sheer weight of expectation on a man for whom miracles were deemed to be mundane. But there was also the chipping away in the home media, the rigorous examination of his game and character, in an attempt to tease out any weaknesses for Australia to exploit.

Woodward was to claim later that Jonny never blinked in the tournament, was always on top of things. But both during the tournament and in what was otherwise a dazzling aftermath, you were always uneasily aware that the sporting gods were saddling one man with more responsibilities than was safe. As he sat up at the top table gently fielding questions, photogenic but largely expressionless, you realised that to expect golden soundbite nuggets was ridiculous.

What was Jonny like? The question was repeated to me throughout the tournament, as it had been from way back when he first sealed his England position. No one outside the squad and his family could truly claim to know, but my answer is that, as far as it is possible to judge, he is every bit as fine a man as he appears on his rather tortured television interviews and strangled public utterances. Certainly, he is revered as a character in the Newcastle Falcons dressing-room, where Rob Andrew has allowed a generation to grow up together.

There is no question in my mind as to my favourite interview memory of my long – and, no doubt, patchy – reporting career. Last year, I took the train from London to Newcastle to talk to him, and I was uneasily aware of his reputation as someone who was uncomfortable with the media, but very comfortable indeed stating his case on the field or on the practice ground. When I arrived at the Newcastle Falcons clubhouse, with a buzz of conversation rising from lunchtime diners, people rolled their eyes at me.

'You mean you've come all that way just to talk to Jonny? Best of luck to you, mate.' One short interview he conducted with local radio just before my slot was so full of spine-chillingly lame media-speak that I almost called a taxi and went back to London.

I am certainly not claiming that it was simply my journalistic techniques that drew him out. It could have been the fact that he was harbouring some guilt that the interview had been put back nearly two hours, a period of time he had spent on the pitch underneath the windows of the clubhouse, working endlessly on his kicking, assisted only by the giant and loyal figure of Ian Peel, the Falcons prop who was fetching and carrying the balls.

But when he sat down, he was wonderfully invigorating. He was mesmerising (and no, I am not even claiming that the subsequent interview, which appeared, did justice to the interview. But, if you insist). The standards he sets himself almost make you wince. Never mind about just demanding an almost infallible kicking percentage from himself. 'I look upon every individual tackle as a success or failure. I can depress myself by recounting exactly what went wrong.'

He spoke about the possibility of 'annihilating' opponents in the sense of wiping out the whole of an opposition attack with one thunderous tackle. Scary. 'It scares me too, when I am too fired up. I have to get the right angle, and the right control of the tackle.' These were words which I remembered and which came back to me after the World Cup, when he was struggling with shoulder injuries.

When we met, he was intent on adding what would be the final facet to the most prodigious all-round game that any player had ever produced. He was already the finest goal-kicker the world had ever seen, he was already the hardest tackler, pound for pound, in the game. He was already a splendid tactician, if not always infallible. Now he had hit upon the idea of improving his own skills as a cutting individual runner. He was already working furiously with Steve Black, the amiable and talented Geordie motivational/fitness/lifestyle guru (anything else I missed, Blackie?), who was one of his chief mentors.

He honed those new running skills in tight corners in a gymnasium. Black would hang row after row of heavy punchbags from the ceiling. He would set them swinging in random directions, and Wilkinson would have to side-step and whizz across the gym, avoiding the potential for heavy collisions. Next international after our interview, he came out and cut Ireland to pieces with ball in hand.

When he came to the World Cup, he had already superseded Jonah Lomu as the most famous rugby player in the world. When he left, and in the aftermath of his homecoming, it could be said that he had equalled the impact on sport itself of Lomu in the '95 World Cup – something which I always felt was impossible, because Jonah's impact was profound in so many ways.

Yet, both at that memorable interview in Newcastle and again as he murmured in Manly about pressure, coping, the search for the impossible goal of infallibility, I felt an anxiety on his behalf. Rugby will, I hope, always be a sport which would prefer its heroes to pass into contented and healthy retirement rather than sucking the nectar from them and discarding them.

He was asked if he grasped the dangers of his own intensity and his one-track sporting mind.

'I know that sometimes I get a little too involved and that I know I have to find some diversions from the rugby grind I impose on myself.'

We all sat up eagerly for details of these diversions. Which had he employed to date?

'Well, I haven't actually found any as yet, but I'm still looking.'

So it was indeed a pleasure to find that he had a formidably attractive and, as far as can be judged, entirely level-headed girlfriend with him for the latter stages of the tournament. I was inundated with e-mails from female acquaintances back at home, of all ages, who wanted me to slip something nasty into her Diet Coke.

Here was a man so good that he could endure what had been a patchy World Cup to date by his own standards (and yet something on the point of wondrous when judged by the standards of mere mortals) and still be there firing, almost lusting after the glory that was, by now, waiting to be won. Rugby was clearly lucky to have our Jonny and, before many weeks had passed, the old sport came to realise just how lucky it was. That billions of pounds would not have bought him, what he represented and the example he set.

But that was in the future. France were dangerous, they were to be faced in the semi-final in a few days' time, and Wilkinson, in all probability, prepared to prove the old adage about the tough getting going.

12 November 2003 – Dalcross Hospital, Sydney

By this stage, youngsters had almost stopped pointing at me in lifts. My eye had become slightly less scarlet and the swelling was receding. I still had to wear my Phantom eye shield at night but I could now use my laptop for several minutes without my eye streaming.

Two days after the quarter-finals, however, with the whole caravan relocated to Sydney and excitement rising, I woke to find that a curtain appeared to be rising from the bottom of my eye, and as breakfast and the day went by, the curtain was riding to a point where I had to peer over it to read or to navigate my way around.

By this time, endless poring over Internet briefings on retinal detachments had clued me up. At one stage I even considered myself sad enough to do what I had never done before and log on to an Internet chat room for fellow retinal sufferers. I managed to resist. But now I realised with horror, before I had even taken a specialist opinion, that I would soon be back on the operating table, and that people would be sticking needles in my eyes again. I had no nostalgia for that experience whatsoever. And with the semi-finals only five days away, I was in a truly desperate panic.

By this time, poor Dr Hunyor felt the pressure of the whole Murdoch organisation, channelled through me, to get one of their rugby correspondents fit for action. The poor chap had to abandon his daily surgery, had to summon all the troops into late-evening surgery. Frankly, I don't think I've ever felt more gutted in my life than when I was sitting on a wall outside his surgery, waiting for some loudmouth, semi-blind Croatian halfwit to find me and to take me to hospital in his taxi. He picked me up and started blathering. 'I don't want to talk,' I said.

I had not had a single retinal detachment in nearly 50 years, and now they appeared to be happening on a weekly basis. It was not comforting in any way to learn also that the operations would simply be piling scar tissue on top of scar tissue. This time, Dr Hunyor did not even bother telling me that it was not going to hurt and that I would remember nothing afterwards. I yowled with pain for most of the treat of an operation, felt all the daggers going in. Back in bed, feeling high on the morphine they had slipped me, I was very unamused to be visited by the anaesthetist.

'Sorry, I might not quite have got that right,' he said of the difficult task of giving the patient enough anaesthetic to ward off pain but not enough to send him out like a light. Oh, great. I was not churlish enough to complain, as they had torn up the waiting list so that I could stagger to the first semi-final in only three days' time. But a hefty invoice caught up with me soon afterwards, as rapidly as if it was Josh Lewsey chasing a fat prop.

33. DAYS OF THUNDER

15 November 2003 – Australia 22, New Zealand 10
(Telstra Stadium, Sydney)

So New Zealand were going to win the World Cup. Every Kiwi ex-great in the mass media was certain of it. Those of us who had said and written on a weekly basis that they were not good enough because their forwards were weak were drowned by a Kiwi caterwauling.

But Australia thoroughly deserves its reputation as a wondrous sporting country, and they are not especially inclined to lose to New Zealand in the semi-final of their own World Cup party. The Telstra Stadium was full and the city of Sydney was seething, with the streets surrounding the giant screens all packed and partying.

Australia, I felt, surely had a magnificent performance in there somewhere. Suddenly they came out and gave it. The scoreboard at the end said that they had dumped New Zealand out of the tournament to the tune of 22–10. But there was more to it than that. First, Australia's superiority, their magnificent defence, their wonderful flankers and their swarming and ambitious play with the ball in hand, deserved a margin of at least 20 points. And the sensational atmosphere drowned out the fluttering of chickens coming home to roost. The Australian front five were no great shakes in global terms but here, driven on by the giants in the second row, Justin Harrison, Nathan Sharpe and David Giffin, completely obliterated the feeble New Zealand pack, lock, stock and barrel. Richie McCaw, their only forward of note, must have known at the end precisely how the Dutchman felt with his finger in the dyke.

Two of the Kiwi talismen staged sensational disappearing acts. You could forgive the free-scoring back three because they were not given the ball – although Doug Howlett in particular appeared to have no idea how to make something happen now he was no longer on the end of a three-man overlap. But the two most sensational disappearances were those of

Jerry Collins at number 8 and Carlos Spencer at fly-half. Collins made a speciality of horrendous illegal tackles. One laid out Colin Charvis of Wales in a match last year and in this semi-final, driving in with no attempt to wrap his arms around, he knocked Sharpe senseless too. The only problem with Collins as a player was that if you tackled him, and therefore took away his ability to make ground in straight lines, he had no plan B, he had no offloading skills, and he was shut down and locked up.

Spencer, frankly, was never seen again in this tournament after the quarter-finals. Instead of stepping in and trying to take responsibility as New Zealand came under the hammer, he went further and further out, filling the position of sixth, seventh and eighth receiver. 'Where's Spencer, where's Spencer?' one of the TV commentators kept asking. The answer was that Spencer was imprisoned by his own lack of a basic game and his own lack of true heart when he was not strutting on a stage created by the weakness of the opposition.

It all blew apart for New Zealand when a hairy pass from Spencer was picked off by Stirling Mortlock, the recovered Wallaby centre who was in the process of playing a mountainous game. Mortlock sprinted nearly 80 metres to score. New Zealand were only in touch at all at the interval because Larkham, infuriatingly, decided to run a ball on the stroke of half-time, when he should have been nursing the lead. Spencer set off on the turnover and made a try for Thorne, the otherwise invisible New Zealand captain.

Yet, Elton Flatley carefully kicked Australia home in the second half, a period of play in which the intensity became ever more brutal, and in which a growing number of New Zealanders were ruthlessly exposed. So, frankly, was John Mitchell. It had been blindingly obvious from the start of the tour that Thorne lacked the stature as a player and a leader to exist at this level, let alone to thrive. In his heart, Mitchell surely knew that Brad Thorn, the giant former rugby league forward, was a better proposition.

But he never took the ball by the horns, kept throwing Thorn on in place of one of the two New Zealand locks. This has the effect of denuding a shaky lineout even further and of keeping an inadequate player on the field in the back row.

Australia celebrated widely. Legions of old Wallabies declared ringingly that they had been misquoted the previous week and that they knew that Eddie Jones was a form of deity all along. Back in New Zealand, the media had taken on a slightly different tone. 'World Chumps,' was one heading. All those people who bought into the myth of New Zealand superiority, and all the coaches and marketeers and referees who had arrogantly decided that rugby no longer needed proper forward phases, were confronted with this frippery of a New Zealand team, and confronted with the feeble reality that their next game would be a meaningless third-place play-off between two teams who had failed.

The only item of bad news for Australia came when Ben Darwin, the Australian prop, was caught at an odd angle as the scrum erupted and felt a horrendous grating in his neck. 'Neck, neck, neck,' he called out, and Kees Meeuws, his opposite number, was quick and chivalrous enough to stop pushing. Darwin slumped to the ground and there was a protracted stoppage while the rigmarole was observed of fitting a neck brace and strapping the poor man to a stretcher.

'I was very worried at first because I had lost feeling,' Darwin said. 'So I was very relieved when I started getting pins and needles in my legs and arms.' So was everyone else. Darwin was up and about, if still unsteady, within a few days, though he had to announce his retirement in February 2004. It was sad that someone who'd grafted through the preamble was unable to take the stage for the final, but it was wonderful that he had not become one of rugby's grievously injured.

34. FREDERIC'S LAST GAMBLE

16 November 2003 – Darling Harbour, Sydney

The Northern Hemisphere Championship was set for the Sunday. This conferred the not inconsiderable advantage that Australia would have had one extra day to rest compared to the winner of the second semi, but as the week of preview and growing tension passed by, all considerations appertaining to the future were cast aside. It was vanishing point.

The rather odd aspect of the knockout stages of the tournament was that both teams in every match had bookings to depart for home on the day after the match. There would be no time to absorb the pain of defeat before they packed you off home.

However, by this stage, and looking round the streets and bars and quays of Sydney, it was obvious that most of England had been evacuated anyway. There were a staggering number of English people in the city – to those who had bravely hacked their way around Australia for the whole lot were added the happy-go-lucky thousands who had descended via the organised package tours which hit town from the quarter-finals on. To these were added the latecomers who, either because they could afford it or because they had decided on impulse to come anyway, were gathering for a whistle-stop visit, taking in the last week.

From a distance, it did seem that the week before the England–France semi-final would be rather lurid in terms of the media coverage and the hostility from the camps. Agincourt was about to be invoked. But, in fact, apart from the ritual and rather laboured Pom-bashing in the Australian media, it was all relatively calm. Almost certainly, this was because any team reaching the semi-final and beyond deserves respect.

Possibly, the new deference to England and all things English had something to do with the fact that around 50,000 feasting and beasting England fans were delivering millions of dollars to the Australian economy. Some figures we saw suggested that every England supporter was consuming, on average, six drinks per day. Lies, damned lies and statistics. Most of the England supporters I came across were clearly averaging more than that.

For the last fortnight of our trip, the media party were incarcerated in the Star City, an establishment which towers above Darling Harbour in the western quarter of the city. Star City is a remarkable place. Essentially, it is a gigantic casino stuck there to drag in millions of suckers from the Asian market. One of the managers told me that it is worthwhile for the hotel to pick up guests at the airport in limos and put them up for free in a suite – the hotel still makes a hefty profit from their gambling losses. The casino floor was ringed with bars that stayed open till dawn – but if anyone got stuck in for a decent session they would be eased on their way by gangs of obnoxious heavies. The idea was that the punters would take quick refreshment and then scuttle back to the roulette and blackjack tables.

Yet the rooms were cavernous and the hotel manager, almost unique amongst his colleagues in Sydney, was not demanding a king's ransom per night and a minimum booking of six months before he would allow anyone in.

En route between reception and our well-appointed apartments, you had to pass through the ground floor of a lurid, 24-hour casino area. Here, there was a large sign giving the number for Gamblers Anonymous stuck above an enormous bank of cash machines where lines of mug punters lined up around the clock to replenish the dwindling stocks of cash. There was also a theatre which never spared itself in its efforts to give us the cutting-edge acts of the world. Engelbert Humperdink was playing at the time of the World Cup, and the preview material clearly indicated that he had spent much of the intervening time between his hits and his current status on the scampi-in-the-basket cabaret circuit having facelifts with increasing desperation. The Last Waltz would indeed last forever.

However, and despite a soreness in the eye region, it was still a wonderful time. The complex was so big that it even had its own landing stage, so you could catch a boat which went under the Harbour Bridge and dropped off at Circular Quay. And such was the sense of thrill that the big matches were upon us, that good old England were still going strong and that the sense of panic around amongst the host nation was growing all the time, that exhaustion was far from the mind.

And on match day, this after a humid Saturday for the Australia–New Zealand semi, there was something in the air. Yes, there was tension. But there was something else. Rain.

16 November 2003 – England 24, France 7
(Telstra Stadium, Sydney)

Probably, it was David Hands in *The Times* who expressed it best: 'The smooth roadster that has been France at this World Cup left the highway yesterday.' And with a reverberating crash. England dominated this semi-final. They did not score a try, but such was their authority that hardly anyone in the Australian press berated them for this, whereas normally we would have seen a barrage of headlines about the boring English. I think it's called respect.

In a sense, the wet and windy weather, apparently imported direct from England, helped Clive Woodward's men. But not because they played better in the wet; they did not. In the current multi-phased game, hardly any team plays better in the wet, anyway. The great advantage of the rain for England was that the French took one look at it, and turned into mental jelly.

This was a victory won on the scoreboard but, far more than that, it was a victory won in the heart. The France inner man collapsed like a shot drunk, and a great deal of the French improvement in technique and in mental matters was revealed to be a chimera.

Take Michalak. He reverted. He collapsed under the pressure of the occasion. His first tactical kick went straight up in the air; he missed two easy penalties in quick succession at a strategic time in the first half when six points would have provided France with real comfort. He played as if teamwork and team spirit was alien to him. In the final quarter, he departed and was replaced by Gerald Merceron.

At around the same time, France also took off Jean-Jacques Crenca, the fixer, the hammer-wielding heart of the French scrum. This was another change of massive significance. He was meant to be the game's enforcer.

Crenca and the French tight forwards clearly intended to get on top of England and although they did mess up a couple of early French scrums, it was England who gained ascendancy in the phase. England knew that if they could just slam the French scrum into reverse to the tune of only a few centimetres, then they would drastically reduce the effectiveness of the French back row. They did, and they did.

Long before the end, and when France were still comfortably within two scores, France had gone. Players like Aurelien Rougerie were skewing kicks horrendously off the sides of their feet and the air of resignation in the blue ranks was almost total. It was almost as if England had run on and held up the white jersey, and so France had run up the white flag.

In the final analysis, it had never been a brilliant England performance.

But they had done a spectacular number on the French team. Perhaps there had been a clue in the national anthems, because Lawrence Dallaglio had forced himself to the very front in the Anthem Stakes – the race amongst those deemed to be most passionate while singing. Dallaglio's face as he bawled 'God Save The Queen' was such an arresting and blood-curdling mixture of pure passion and intent that it was every bit as good as the most fierce Haka in transmitting a message to the opposition. Dallaglio, and the other senior England players, stepped forward boldly.

It was not all plain sailing. England had retained Mike Catt in the centre in place of Mike Tindall: rather an odd change, in that Woodward was never particularly keen on reacting simply to one performance in one game, notwithstanding the fact that Catt's cameo against Wales had been formidable. But it was rather bizarre to see Catt trying to bash the ball up the middle against a strong French defence in the first half and then, when Tindall finally arrived in the second half, to see him kicking the ball diagonally downfield in the wet. You might have thought that each player would have been better in the other role. Woodward was quite shirty with me after the match when I asked for his comments on the fact that England so rarely crossed the gain line in midfield.

But Matt Dawson was clever around the fringes, England's defensive organisation was splendid and the growing authority was inexorable. France had taken a lead at 7–3. Wilkinson dropped an early and warming goal before France struck. England made an awful hash of a long lineout and Serge Betsen snaffled the ball and ran on to the England line. The television match official took half the evening to find a good angle and England supporters were incensed because none of the camera angles demonstrated on the big screen at the Telstra Stadium could confirm that Betsen had indeed touched down. But perhaps the official had access to other angles, as he awarded the try. Michalak pulled himself together to kick the goal.

There was an outbreak of nonsense soon after when Jason Robinson attacked with the ball in hand. Christophe Dominici found himself off balance as Jason jinked, but, ludicrously, he lashed out with his legs with a blatant trip. The camera immediately panned to Woodward, fuming up in his box. 'Send him off,' were the words framed by his lips. Dominici was sent to the sin bin but he had also injured himself in the act and never returned. If anything summed up France's evening, it was that.

England led by five points at half-time; Wilkinson kicked a penalty to add to his earlier dropped goal, finding the mark well considering the poor conditions.

The second half belonged to England. It was not so much that they dominated possession or field position. It was just that they had decided that the match was theirs by destiny, and that France had no players with the stature to dispute it with them. France never scored again; Wilkinson kicked another two drop goals and four more penalties in the second half and England celebrations kicked off all round the stadium.

And at the end of it all, we would have what many people believed would be the dream final – the home team against the dreaded English. It was a wonderful prospect, and there seemed no chance that either side would win with much to spare. England were one step from heaven.

Bernard Laporte was whimsical, as well as shattered afterwards. 'Our kicker is not a machine, he is a mere man. Jonny Wilkinson is alive and well and kicking like a machine.' He also bought into the fallacy that the weather was crucial. 'England were spectacularly good in the rain.'

Woodward's rejoinder was curt. 'It rains in France, too; I've been there.' France's collapse came from within. 'I honestly believe we would have beaten France in dry conditions, too. They can't blame the weather.'

There was another in the series of departures after the match. Galthié was retiring from the French team. Johnson came over and embraced him as the teams walked off towards the end. He did not quite carry it off with the same warmth as had Keith Wood in his encounter with Galthié. Johnson really should take a hugger on the field with him to do the necessary. His heart's just not in it.

And what of the French heart? Galthié gone, burgeoning hopes crushed. The next Six Nations would be very interesting for them. There was always the possibility that they would splinter from the sheer shock of the reimposition of Anglo dominance.

In all the fury, we suddenly realised that Jason Leonard's arrival as replacement had made him the most capped player of all time.

19 November 2003 – Manly Pacific Hotel; England team announcement

England returned in triumph to their hotel on the sea front in Manly, a home from home where pine trees sheltered the walkers on the Strand from the sea breezes. Perhaps bizarrely, given their obsession with their own solitude and security, the closer they came to the bigger games in the World Cup, the more public their accommodation. Manly became a place of pilgrimage for the army of England supporters and, indeed, for the army of media people following the trip.

The *Sunday Times* even sent our sports news reporter David Bond on a lightning visit to file stories on the remarkable numbers and fervour of the England supporters. Bond, struggling past the most savage stick from colleagues reflecting his status as a Johnny-come-lately, had enough material from the fans for three features around two hours after touching down.

And the expected barbs and thunderbolts were simply not produced. One of the great joys of the semi-finals was that they threw up the two deadly enemies in a major clash of cultures, promising major antipathy as the old country faced the colonists. Frankly, it was such a fertile prospect that you would seriously have thought that Roy and HG would have thought of something funny to say about it all. They didn't, however.

But at least Windy Woody and Steady Eddie would come up with something tasty. Otherwise, the Aussie media would have to drum it all up on their own. Greg Growden, the foursquare man from the *Sydney Morning Herald*, was at his best with tongue in cheek, and he contributed a great line which suggested that England were adept in persuading Australia to give away penalties. Rotten swines. Bet the Aussies would never give away a single one unless England made them.

But what did we get? Silence. Almost bonhomie. Woodward and Eddie Jones had been among the prime antagonists of the last few years when it came to bickering between the camps but this time, Woodward was almost indignant when he was asked to give a date and time for the start of the sledging. 'The only time that Eddie and I have had cross words is the week before we play each other and it does all start with the media,' he said. Presumably, he was therefore accusing the media of making up the contents of the previous 45 press conferences from both camps, when they had chipped away at each other with vast enthusiasm.

But he went on: 'I have had nothing to say about them this week, everything is fine. I thought that in the match against the All Blacks they were absolutely tremendous. When Eddie and I meet at coaching conferences we have a cup of tea and if I met him this afternoon, I would go and have a cup of coffee with him.' Tea and coffee. The instruments of the peace.

Jones was similarly circumspect. He and his men had returned to their base way up the coast in Coffs Harbour, and squadrons of disappointed hacks were returning to base on a daily basis after failing to get Eddie to slag off England. If he still thought that they were boring, potentially dirty, illegal and overrated, then, sadly for us all, in the Fourth Estate at least, he was keeping it to himself.

But Woodward knew full well that his own attack on Jones in Melbourne when the teams met in the previous June had been carefully planned. He admitted it. And if one of the purposes of that tirade was to show that the English were not to be pushed around or belittled in the media, then his strategy was highly effective because Jones did not even try to bounce back.

All this supposed consumption of tea and coffee did not, however, remove all the suspicion. Woodward was asked to confirm or deny a rumour that all rooms in the England hotel were being swept for bugs on a daily basis. 'That is very melodramatic, but yes, we have a machine that anyone can buy in the shops that checks for bugs. It is a serious business and it resulted from the series between the Lions and Australia, when the Aussies purported to know the Lions lineout calls. We have this little device that is no bigger than a matchbox and Tony Biscombe, who is our IT man, goes round the hotel rooms and the team rooms to make sure there are no devices.'

Woodward, amazingly for so meticulous a man, had apparently failed completely to consider the possibility that Eddie Jones had placed bugs in the hotel toilets.

The occasion of the team announcement, the revelation of the names of the men who would at least start in the final, was both mundane and remarkable. There were absolutely no surprises, and the only change from the semi-final starting team was that Mike Catt returned to the bench and Mike Tindall, discarded chiefly on tactical grounds, came back to claim the place in the final he so richly deserved.

But this was all remarkable because it meant that England were going into the last match of the tournament with the same team that went into the first match of the tournament. They were fielding the team that most people would have predicted three or even six months before. It was a remarkable achievement, based on a large slice of luck but also on Woodward's planning and consistency and loyalty, and on the remarkable efforts of his training and medical staff. 'It was awesome,' Woodward was to say later, 'to get to that final week not only with the starting team that I wanted but also with all 30 in the squad available for selection.'

Australia decided to bring Justin Harrison back at lock for Giffin and Al Baxter, the young prop, came in for the unfortunate Darwin. Harrison had been lauded in 2001 as the young gun lock of the future after his role in the deciding Test against the Lions, although his career had stalled a little. But as a talisman, he was important. Could Australia rediscover the momentum of their hammering of the All Blacks?

One selection did not please Woodward at all. Even though Andre Watson, the South African referee, had not been allocated one of the semi-finals, even though he had messed up, in some assessments, the final of 1999 in Cardiff, here he was again, pulling out the plum match.

'Do you feel any unease, given the strength of your team in tight-forward play,' I asked Woodward at the time, 'that the referee is from the southern hemisphere, where they have not always been keen on what could be termed the English style?'

Woodward, I felt at the time, was a little too ready with his answer. 'We would be pleased with any of the top referees, we are pleased with the appointment of Andre and we look forward to a great game of rugby,' Woodward said. As he publicly admitted afterwards, he had assumed that Paddy O'Brien would referee the final and was severely taken aback when he heard that it was to be Watson.

35. RUGBY – GOING HOME!

22 November 2003 – Star City Casino Hotel, Darling Harbour

The day dawned with a feeling of death warmed over. It had been a harsh night's work. Nick Cain had been lying flat out on the floor, shattered, trying to dictate the last few paragraphs of a feature. Now and again, he dozed off completely and the copytaker had to shout down the line to wake him. I would have helped, but I was too busy sneaking back to my room to find a camera.

We planned a 24-page broadsheet sports section for that Sunday, almost all of which would be given over to the World Cup. After the match, on the front page of the sports section was something I rather enjoyed. Underneath a giant photograph of some bloke from the Newcastle Falcons who looked reasonably cheerful, there was the following tag-line. 'Inside: Eight-page pull-out with all the Premiership football action.' Rugby, for a day, had crushed dear old football.

If you consider that there are around 3,000 words per page on average, then we were faced with a fair amount of hacking. There was also the problem that an awful lot had to be prepared beforehand, with the rather significant disadvantage of not knowing who had won. So we sketched out two main features. 'Glory Glory England' and 'Go now, Woodward, you Turnip!' It's at times like those that you realise that the press can be a little taken in by the last result.

Still, I had no idea how big or how insignificant it all was at home. Everything was too busy and flustered for consideration of extraneous matters. There were also, I have no problem in admitting, gnawing nerves. Where that put the state of mind of the players themselves, God only knows. The tensions of the week were vast, the adventure was coming to an end, but everything was still to be settled. I wanted England to win because I believed in the way that England and the English – and, in fact,

Europeans – played the game and administered the laws. There was a certain vindication to be had should England confirm that superiority.

We could even contemplate a rag-out. That is a newspaper term for reproducing either a headline or a few telling paragraphs from the past which have been soundly vindicated by later events. Modesty forbids just a little but we'd been strong on the 'England to win' line for months. Amazingly, papers tend not to do the same when what we wrote once is revealed to have been a load of utter claptrap. I remember boldly stating that the 1984 Wallabies in Britain 'will struggle to win a Test'. We decided against a rag-out when they became the first Wallabies to win the Grand Slam.

There was also the fact that I admired the England operation: the team and the back-up people, in all my experience, amounted to a thoroughly decent and even outstanding bunch of blokes. By this stage of the trip, all the fine writers were amongst us – that is, the general sportswriters who flit from gorgeous exotic assignment to gorgeous exotic assignment. It was interesting to see the reaction of people who had a pedigree in covering major sports and following major teams. They seemed to think that the England lot were a decent bunch, too.

I admire Johnson as much as, if not more than, any sportsman I have come across and I have vast admiration for the attitude of a man like Dallaglio, who has a teak-tough attitude and self-belief. I have often felt that if you could transfuse Dallaglio's mental hardness into Tim Henman, into a few of the cricketers, or rugby league players, or even swimmers, then England might have a sporting reputation to compare with that of Australia. So all in all, the heart was plumping for one side.

And glory be, as we looked out of the hotel room to gauge which clothes were necessary, it was wet and windy. We had all expected to be brown as berries by this stage of our tour of Australia but, frankly, we were of exactly the same colour as all those who had come out from an English winter in the past few days. Never mind. The weather made no difference whatsoever to the match and did not hamper England's style in any way. But if enough Australians felt that the rain was an advantage to England, then all well and good.

At the due time, laptops packed, and with enough plugs and leads to strangle an army, a gang of us met in the lift to take our transport out to the Telstra Stadium. As we descended, the talk was all of rugby. 'It is absolutely amazing,' said one hack. 'The place is awash with rugby. You just cannot go anywhere without people talking about it.' As the lift door opened, around 30 Asians scuttled in, on their way to a hard afternoon's graft in the hotel's casino, utterly oblivious to the fact that English sporting history was about to unfold, just as they watched the roulette wheels whizzing.

The scenes at the stadium were amazing. You simply could not find a neutral. You could hardly find anyone who was not wearing a white shirt or a gold shirt. Even the race for match programmes was frantic. There were programme stands circling the stadium but it immediately became obvious that the organisers had blundered in not printing enough. Hordes of followers dashed from one stand to the next, devouring the available programmes like locusts, before rushing on to the next.

It was raining gently as the time came for the teams to take the field. The media people had even thought of that, and we all sat on the media benches, row after row of us, wearing extremely fetching transparent ponchos, which had a lifespan, given their rather ephemeral nature, of around 90 minutes. It was to be proved shortly that 90 minutes was not long enough.

Almost before anyone was ready, and with tension already gripping, the two teams walked down the tunnel. Martin Johnson, towering above George Gregan, was at the front for England. We did not know at the time that it would be the last time that he led his men into battle.

The soaring stadium went quiet for the formalities. Belinda Evans and James Laing, the two members of the World Cup Choir deputed to sing 'God Save the Queen', were cued in and did their stuff. This time, it was Ben Kay who took the title for most passionate and barely-in-control anthem bawling. Phil Waugh probably took the title for Australia, looking suitably fierce. Mind you, he does have the advantage of looking, even in repose, a little like one of the murderers in the Texas Chainsaw Massacre gang.

The final ceremonial act involved 20 giant cylindrical figures standing in a circle outside the perimeter of the pitch. There was one for each competing team and they were decked out in their country's colours. Each had one eye, representing the fans of that country. Then, 18 of the 20 made a slow plod out of the stadium, leaving the England Cyclops and the Australian Cyclops facing each other behind each set of posts.

The two one-eyed cylinders represented 82,957 one-eyed followers in the stadium. It was packed out, and while heady predictions that English fans would comprise half the crowd were optimistic, there were around 30,000 at least, almost all decked out in white. It looked wonderful, magnificent. It made Woodward call for the day when 'Twickenham looks like a wall of white, too'. Banks of green Barbour jackets just do not have the same effect.

Whatever you wore, you wore it with vast pride. This was emphatically not an afternoon where neutrals would be much of a consideration.

22 November 2003 – Australia 17, England 20 – after extra time – (Telstra Stadium, Sydney)

The evening in the Telstra Stadium was for cool heads. Shame, therefore, that off the field, there were none. Probably the worst moment of panic was to come in the second half of extra time. Suddenly, with the match tighter than tight, there was every prospect that the teams would still be locked together at the end of extra time, just as they were at the end of normal time.

I remember flapping. 'Where the hell are the tournament rules? Someone get the rules.'

'What happens if it stays like this at the end of extra time?'

'There is another period of extra time, and the first scorer wins.'

'But what if it's still level?'

'There is a drop-kick competition.'

'You must be joking. What are the rules for that? How many on each side have to kick? And surely to God, Jason Leonard won't have to do it. Will he?'

That was for the white-knuckled future. Almost from the start and even though they fell behind, England were convincingly superior. Johnson was to have a Herculean game, titanic in the loose and dominating Harrison in the lineout. And senior men such as Dallaglio, Dawson, Robinson and Greenwood were to step up to the plate.

England's defence hit hard and often, with Wilkinson, Tindall and Greenwood making those juddering keynote tackles that make you wince and which turn the game. Perhaps the biggest advantage England held lay in the scrum. The absence of Ben Darwin led to Al Baxter starting for Australia on the tight-head and from the moment he collapsed ignominiously in the first scrum, it was clear that he was out of his depth. Baxter was honest enough to say in public after the game that he realised how much he was lacking in terms of technique and experience, and how hard he was going to work to catch up.

It was therefore a good job for him that he had an ally. Someone to bail him out. Watson penalised England's superior scrum frequently, he fussed and fretted away at them in an unholy and inappropriate alliance with Paul Honiss, the New Zealand touch judge. You could hear Honiss yakking away to Watson on the electronic link, drawing his attention to supposed problems being caused by Trevor Woodman on the England loose-head.

Australia's try in the opening stages was quite beautifully done. Steve Larkham, the fly-half, put up a kick of inch-perfection above Jason Robinson in the England right-hand corner. Lote Tuqiri, on great form and with a good six inches on Robinson, raced up and jumped, took the ball and scored. Elton Flatley hit the post with the conversion.

Yet there were already signs that England were simply better. Wilkinson kicked two penalties to put them in the lead and then another to make it 9–5 as the half wore on and Australia faltered. England were also able to create some golden chances. Tuqiri went back to save brilliantly under the hooves of Lewsey when there was no more Australian cover, and then, on the stroke of half-time, Dawson wasted a golden chance when he chipped the ball into touch and ignored Ben Cohen outside him, when the Northampton wing appeared to have a yard of space. Cohen gave his clubmate the filthiest look of the whole tournament.

Yet the most horrendous, graphic waste of seven points had been committed by Ben Kay. Australia's defence was on the point of crumbling under pressure at the time and when Back and Tindall attacked the blind side, Dawson was able to hold the ball up for microseconds to draw the attention of Waugh, the final Australian defender, in order to give Kay the try in the corner. The pass was perfect, but Kay spilt it in his excitement.

When the whole match was over, Kay and his mates staged a re-enactment of the miss of the tournament with grins all round. Probably they realised that if England had not won the World Cup final, then Kay would have gone down in history as one of the country's most notorious sportsmen.

But England did score a try before half-time. They were already confounding those who called them boring by spreading the ball cleverly in the wet. Dawson sent Dallaglio away on a searing burst to the left of a ruck, Dallaglio absorbed the tackle and flipped the ball inside to Wilkinson. Wilkinson had an option to his right but he ran on, delivered the perfect pass and Jason Robinson went slithering over to score in the left-hand corner. The pocket battleship from Sale Sharks celebrated massively, by his quiet standards. Wilkinson missed the conversion but it was a healthy 14–5 at half-time. It was also a delightful, deft and skilful try.

England began the second half in assured form as well, putting together a splendidly sustained series. But gradually, with little mistakes in execution and tactics here and there, with Watson blatantly ignoring Australia's travails in the scrum, England, agonisingly, were unable to put Australia away. Gradually, with indomitable pride, Australia began to chip away at the lead, aided by a penalty awarded against Woodman on the loose-head, and not against the collapsible Baxter, Woodman's opponent. 'At one stage, Trevor was having to hold him up to stop the penalties coming,' said a senior England forward within two hours of the end of the match.

Yet Flatley brought it back to 14–8 and then 14–11 with the match staggering into the final quarter. For the first hour or so, there had been a magnificent atmosphere, with successive roared choruses of 'Waltzing Matilda' and 'Swing Low, Sweet Chariot'. But as the climax approached, it all became much more quiet. The truth is, it had all become too much. People who were at the ground that day and people I spoke to who watched it on television, or in rugby clubs and bars, simply found it all too unbearable to cheer or sing or do anything except bite their lips and pray.

And what of the hard-bitten hacks? It was almost impossible to work. People of all nationalities looked at each other and blew out their cheeks. What was unfolding was not the greatest game ever played, although it was certainly not negligible in technical terms. But it was the most outrageously, hair-raisingly agonising sporting encounter you could ever imagine. I've seen most things, but never anything like that.

It was all made even better (or worse, depending on how you looked at it) because the game clock loomed large on the scoreboards. You'd look up at the clock, look back 20 minutes later and find that only 30 seconds had ticked away.

Inside the last two minutes, a scrum went down near the England 22 on the right-hand side of the field. The front rows messed about a bit, Andre Watson spoke a few words, and when the scrums came down, Woodman was still standing up because he felt that Australia had engaged too early and he was not properly set. At an absolute maximum, a free-kick over a simple resetting of the scrum was all it really needed. Watson, unforgivably, gave a full penalty.

I then discovered that one of the most famous English referees watching back at home had nimble fingers. Before Elton Flatley had even placed the ball for the last kick of normal time, my refereeing friend had texted me the following message: 'Penalty? No way in a million years.' Immediately, I received another text from my friend Nicky. It said: 'I need a gin.' Both messages were entirely apposite.

Flatley stepped up, facing one of the most horrendously difficult easy penalties ever attempted. He drilled it straight down the middle, which was an absolutely fantastic effort. England's superiority had counted for nothing, it was 14–14 at the end of normal time.

The coaching staffs hurried on. Johnson, the Hercules, already had his men around him, speaking quietly but urgently. Woodward came trotting up and buttonholed Wilkinson, wanting his fly-half to drill the ball down field to the Australian corners, as a low-risk strategy to allow Australia to make the mistake.

'Suddenly, I realised that he was not even listening. He was miles away. He told me that he was sorry, but had to go off to practise his kicking. And off he went. I had to tell Mike Catt to make sure that Jonny had my message.' Catt, by now on the field for the limping Tindall, set himself to try to make a difference in a final of a World Cup he thought he would never take part in.

They will talk about a subsequent drop-kick by Wilkinson as long as the game is played. But after a couple of minutes of extra time, Wilkinson was given a penalty from near halfway, still in the murk and rain. He is not always regarded as a long-range kicker but here, he stepped up and kicked the most beautiful goal, arguably, of his whole magnificent career. It was easily his greatest kick of the day. The value was that it put England back in front, but also effectively built up a long lead – in the sense that Australia's attack had been so bottled up by the stupendous England tackling that, since the Tuqiri try, Australia had not come within a bull's roar of the England line.

The match went on and on, with every seizure of the loose ball a cause for celebration, and every dominant England scrum a possible platform for Watson to make another ludicrous decision. The game clock was ticking down into the last three minutes of the second period of extra time, and when Jason Robinson made a superb tackle on the impressive Tuqiri, it seemed that England were well set again.

Then, another thunderbolt. Watson penalised an England player for handling in a ruck, although there was a roughly equal chance that he might have penalised Australians for being off their feet over the ball. Flatley came up again. It was obvious that there was time for more action after the kick, but all of a sudden, the panic gripped that we had not properly studied the rules of sudden death and drop-kick competitions. Flatley, ice-cold, put the kick over and it was 17–17.

On these big occasions, it is always decidedly handy if you are stationed between two solid reporters with cool heads, soft voices and calm reactions. My colleague Chris Jones of the *London Standard* is one of the finest spotters around. Sadly, Chris was several rows behind and I was sandwiched between Tony Roche of *The Sun* and Nick Cain of the *Sunday Times*. Both know their rugby, but it would be an exaggeration of stupendous proportions to claim that they were cool, calm and collected. How much, even in the less stringent swear-box regimes, do you reckon is owed by someone who roars '**** off, you cheating South African ****!' About 1,000 rand, I'd say.

I have to admit that the three of us were now so thoroughly angered by Watson that we constituted a menace to any law-abiding citizens going about their lawful business in the nearby paid seats.

England had to kick off, back at level. Johnson decided to go for the long kick and the rapid chase, and it worked a treat. England pressurised Mat Rogers, the Australian full-back. Of the three Australians who had come over the wall from rugby league, Tuqiri had played outstandingly, but Wendell Sailor and Rogers had struggled to make any impact. The relieving kick delivered by Rogers really should have been the most almighty hoof of his whole career but instead, hampered slightly by the chasers, he drilled it into touch still within 35 metres of the Australian line.

Not more than, I'd say, 50 million minds then turned inexorably to Jonny Wilkinson. Line out, drive, bash it up a few times, get Jonny within range, drop-goal, glory. And do you know what? Despite rugby's capricious nature, despite the unpredictability of an oval ball, despite the rather mistake-laced nature of the play of both teams on that day, and despite the suffocating tension, that is exactly what happened.

England bravely called a long throw-in, fraught with danger. I had watched Steve Thompson spend hour after hour practising his throwing on a tennis court in Brisbane earlier in the tour, but how much easier was it to throw the ball through a high hoop held up by a coach, than when your whole sporting life was at stake in the final of the World Cup? Thompson delivered the perfect ball, Lewis Moody was lifted expertly and he flipped it down to win quick possession. Moody, on as replacement for Richard Hill, had played a major part in establishing the position by sprinting up to try to block the clearance by Rogers. 'I was still so fresh and had so much energy and just wanted to do as much as I could,' Moody said later.

Mike Catt was the man chosen to bash the ball up and he was given just a few extra feet of space because the throw to the end of the line had kept the Australian back row in their places just for a while.

Wilkinson was in the pocket, but still a long way back. 'I stepped back and thought that there was not long left, so would I try a shot from there?'

Wilkinson said. However, Matt Dawson had the skill and the courage to cut down the percentages. When the ball was recycled by Catt, Dawson set off through a tiny gap and made around ten or twelve precious strides. He set the ball back, Johnson took responsibility for the next charge, went up the side of the ruck and laid it back, with exaggerated care.

Dawson threw the ball to Wilkinson, who stepped inside so that he was set to kick off his weaker right foot. If there had been any time, no doubt so many lives would have flashed before the eyes of spectators. It had all come down to one moment at the end of a ferocious 18-month build-up for England and at the end of a great adventure for everyone. Riding on it were the hopes of, so we were later to discover, most of the English nation.

But if you had to choose someone to take the kick, you'd choose someone who'd practised it thousands upon thousands of times; a man who had never become flustered either when under pressure on the field from opponents desperate to disturb him, or from the baleful glare of the gigantic spotlight trained on all true superstars. What better man to be in that position than the fresh-faced youngster that Rob Andrew and Steve Bates had discovered in Surrey years before?

Naturally, the kick went over. It was the only predictable thing that had happened for ages. In the commentary box, Ian Robertson was delivering an absolutely classic commentary for listeners to Radio Five Live, and alongside him, giving a long screeching yodel of delight, was none other than Rob Andrew, the inter-round summariser. Some weeks later, the Woodward family sent out the most wonderful and over-the-top Christmas card. It showed the scenes at the end and, if you pressed a button, there was a replay of Robinson's comments on the drop-kick, complete with the screeching yodel in the background.

Wilkinson and Greenwood celebrated massively. 'We were shouting at each other: "World Cup, World Cup",' Greenwood said afterwards. Woodward would have been more sanguine if they had been pointing out to each other that there was still some dying seconds left on the clock. Australia kicked off and the time died away, but with the ball still in play. Trevor Woodman, who as far as Woodward can remember had never made a kick-off reception before, took the ball. England slowly recycled it, the ball was whipped to Mike Catt, Catt took aim at around the 25th row of the stand, drilled the ball into touch and Andre Watson's whistle blew.

Afterwards, I read quite a few magazine articles in which people had to answer where they had been when Jonny's kick went over. I was proud to say that I was in the Telstra Stadium. My friends at home asked me how I felt when the final whistle blew and what I did. My Welsh friends especially were intrigued to hear about my reaction. First, on hearing Watson's whistle, it was a pleasure to share a quiet few seconds of awed and wonderful reflection with Nick Cain, a splendid work colleague and my ambulance driver throughout the tour. 'They did it, they did it, they ******* did it!' I can put my hand on heart and say that I could not have been much more thrilled than if Wales themselves had won it.

All around me, people who had lived and breathed and grafted in the wake of England's progress looked quietly thrilled. For a few seconds only, the media neutrals had become English, and proud as punch of it.

I wondered how my two sons at home had reacted. The eldest has always felt his Welsh heritage most strongly; the youngest has tended to support whichever of those two teams were likely to win the next match. When I rang, the whole family was still shrieking deliriously. I found also that another friend had been hopelessly caught up in it all. Gary Stefan – born in Canada but one of the all-time greats in British ice hockey, a rugby follower simply because his son, Sam, had taken up the game – was so enraptured by the tension and spectacle that he was still shaking hours later. There were millions of such tales as people leapt to their feet in the late morning in all the small and large rugby clubs which had opened to eat brunch, all the pubs which had opened at dawn, and all so that the people could open their own square window on England's greatest sporting day since 1966. Dear old England.

There were absolutely no prizes for identifying the prime moment afterwards. The podium was quickly dragged onto the pitch and a presentation ceremony was set up. Johnson had already done his TV interview, appearing massively on the big screens inside the stadium as well as on the television sets all around the world. There was definitely the shake of emotion in his eyes and in his words.

Already seared on the retina were the dazzling moments in the immediate aftermath of the whistle. Incredibly, as Andre Watson blew the whistle, Ben Kay was almost standing on his foot. Kay, heroically maintaining the true spirit of rugby, clearly mouthed the words 'Thanks, ref', before joining in the delirium. The first man to reach Johnson was Neil Back, and the two veterans of a thousand battles embraced mightily. Jason Robinson, who'd had a wonderful tournament, raced up and hugged the giant figure of Dallaglio. The blond Ampleforth giant of Italian extraction, the glamorous Londoner, therefore linked arms with the ex-rugby league northerner, a man who, as he admits, had often been just a step ahead of the police in his early life. Catt and Matt Dawson found each other, and Jason Leonard, on the field as replacement for Vickery, was able to savour the culmination of the longest career any international rugby player ever had.

Jonny looked delighted, though in control. Glamour follows glamour. When the British Lions were playing in the Second Test in 1997 against the Springboks in Durban, it was tense and close, and the Lions trailed by two points. Jeremy Guscott was playing. Glamour. Back in Bath, some of his closest friends were watching on television. With a few minutes remaining, Chalkie Wardell, one of the pals, said: 'I bet that so-and-so wins it with a drop-goal. You wait and see.'

The rest was history. The same with Wilkinson. It had to be him. It was fate. It was glamour. World Cup over and done, and won.

The presentation itself was almost a shambles. The Australians came up first and, because of the extra time and rude TV directors chipping away at Syd Millar, demanding that he get a move on, Millar almost threw the losers' medals at the Australian team. John Howard, the Australian Prime Minister and a massive rugby fan, looked, as a colleague said with a cackle, like he had 'eaten a dogshit sandwich'.

Another anomaly was that every Tom, Dick and Harry was up there to get a medal. So both sides had to pack the platform with their team and replacements and squad members and coaches and medical staff and media officers. We looked for a bloke in a tall white hat lining up with England. If all that lot were up there, then why wouldn't the travelling team chef get his gong too? It was a little shoddy and should have been the preserve only of the players.

Then came the mighty moment. The England team were presented with their medals, and then Johnson stepped forward. The Australians, remember, call the trophy itself 'Bill'. Johnson hoisted it up to the skies, stood there with his brows unknitting, enjoying something that was probably indescribable and impossible to explain, then and afterwards.

Furthermore, he was marking the fact that the trophy had now reverted to its proper and full name. It was now, again, the Webb Ellis Trophy and Martin Johnson was bringing it home.

Long after a lap of honour, the players and coaches eventually filed into the media centre. 'I am over the moon,' Jonny said. Bless him. Don't worry about it for a second, mate. We weren't looking for stunning insights and soul-baring emotion. We didn't deserve them and rugby didn't deserve you.

But then, he had another think. 'It is not just winning the World Cup. It's being part of the team and feeling that togetherness and desire and those emotions and those dreams that everyone is trying to live out. We've attacked everything full on and we've taken our fair share of hits, but we've always believed in ourselves and we've stuck together.'

This is an era of spectacular lionisation of the individual over the team. Jonny, while he never asked for it, has been plucked out from any team he has played in. People have tried to Beckham-ise him, to set him above the sport, to talk about his earning potential. But here was Jonny receding into the background, receding into the team. Tiger Woods needs no one. Just some bloke to hand him a club. Jonny needed Lewis Moody and his lifting pod to win a lineout, needed Mike Catt to come steaming up, and then Dawson to show courage, Johnson to take responsibility. And he knew it.

Lawrence Dallaglio had waited for this moment. He was the only player in the tournament who played every minute of every match for his team. The player whose career had been afflicted by a severe knee injury, who had returned only slowly to top effectiveness and who had been criticised even by his own coach during the tournament, but who had come blasting through. He played like the giant he is and England traded on his supreme self-confidence. The heading on Lawrence's column in the *Sunday Times* did not pull a punch. 'Dad's Army insults were just one-eyed Aussie crap'.

He had clearly felt unable to just brush off some of the media barbs, especially the barb which had termed the England pack 'grumpy old men'. As he said: 'The Australian papers were wholly disrespectful to a lot of individuals and to us as a team. What did all the criticism achieve? It just gave us more ammunition. They got what they deserved yesterday.'

Perhaps I knew something more of the workings of the media mind, though I would not dream of telling Lawrence how to think. But I felt that almost all the Pom-baiting had been reasonably innocent. It was rarely particularly clever, either. And, indeed, the way to really get up their noses was to bat it all back with interest. Either in the media or on the field of play. I'd thoroughly enjoyed doing the former, and now Dallaglio had achieved the latter, and ultimate.

In any case, the Australian camp were outstanding afterwards. Gregan knew that he had never really fired in the tournament. He knew that his forwards had been beasted, that George Smith and Phil Waugh in the back row had been kept out of the game, and that Stirling Mortlock could not repeat the stunning performance of the semi-final. 'It was a massive final that came down to the last play in extra time. It's all I can ask and I was so proud of the efforts of every one of the Wallabies.' Fair comment, because whatever you thought about the superior team, it did go to the wire and Australia's attempt to defend their title was wonderful. They reached a greater height in the semi-final against New Zealand than they did at any point of their winning 1999 campaign.

And proud, too, was the Australian *Daily Telegraph* next day. 'Stand Proud' was the massive headline. At no point on the front page did the scoreline appear, nor, in a raft of pictures, was there any photograph of an English player. Bless them.

The *Sydney Morning Herald*, however, produced a front page of pure class. It prayed silence for what it called a 'public announcement to England and its sports fans':

> Re your magnificent football team's triumph in the Rugby World Cup final, November 22. On behalf of all Australians we would like to admit the following:
>> you were not too old (although we hoped you would be when the game went to extra time)
>> you were not too slow
>> you scored as many tries as we did
>> you kicked no more penalties than we did
>> you ran the ball as much as we did
>> you entertained as much as we did
>> you did it with one of your own as coach (even though he did spend some formative years playing at Manly)
>> you are better singers than we are (and, just quietly, 'Swing Low, Swing Chariot' is growing on us, as is Jonny without an h)
>> you played with class and toughness and grace
>> you were bloody superior . . . and
>> you are, for the first time in 37 years, winners of a football world cup.

Blimey. All that and they even liked 'Swing Low' – that put them ahead of me. They rounded up their page with the following:

> We are even prepared to stop calling on the IRB to change the points-scoring system. If you can guarantee a final as good as that, we will ask them to increase the value of penalties and the drop-goal.

They ended by congratulating the Australian team and fans for the way they had accepted defeat 'at the hands of you Pommy bastards'. Good job the Aussie team never found the same form as the chaps at the *Sydney Morning Herald*.

We knew our own tabloids would not let us down. Five weeks before, after England had been sketchy against South Africa, the Aussie paper printed their giant heading, 'Is that all you've got?' The *News of the World*'s front page on the day after the final was a giant photograph of Johnson carrying the Cup. 'This is all we've got!' said the heading.

Eddie Jones was to give by far the most interesting reaction. He conceded that European rugby had forged ahead. He conceded that the Zurich Premiership was proving a better preparation for international rugby than the Super 12. This was roughly akin to an Australian daring to admit that the quality of life in Australia was inferior to that of Britain.

But Jones warmed to his theme. 'We have put too much emphasis on entertainment in the Super 12. It has not become a soft competition, but too many easy tries are scored and there are not enough battles for the ball in the lineouts.

'We have eleven matches, but four of those are against South African sides who have fallen off the pace, while the Premiership is a tough slog from start to finish and we need to replicate that.'

Jones was gushing in his praise of Wilkinson and of the culture that had produced a man he described as 'a freak'. Jones added: 'He is a great example for young players, showing that if you want to be the best you have to make sacrifices. He is not just a kicker, but an outstanding fly-half who is a tough little character. England would still be a very good side without him, but what I imagine Clive Woodward is looking for is a number 2 in the position who can play in the same manner.'

Jones then looked ahead. 'I will be getting together with my New Zealand and South African counterparts to discuss making the Super 12 more of a contest in areas like the scrum and the lineout.'

Frankly, these were themes that I had been expounding for three years, often in the face of furious Kiwis and Australians who had no grasp of the fact that rugby was being sold down a marketing river amongst a candy-floss barrage of Super 12 tries, and that the whole mess was no way to produce proper international players and, especially, proper international forwards.

And here was Eddie Jones, formerly the high priest of endless continuity rugby, admitting, frankly, that everything I had ever said and written was true.

Good old Eddie had even caved in on another of my little – and possibly annoying – bugbears. I always hated the idea of people shutting the roof over rugby pitches, rendering rugby an indoor sport when it should be open to every element going. It happens at the Millennium Stadium, Cardiff, and it happens, always with the firm support of Australian coaches and administrators, at the Telstra Dome in Melbourne. But when Jones was asked if he supported the idea of a uniform international season, which could see most rugby played on hard summer grounds, he pulled back.

'Rugby is about contrasts and I would rather tour Britain in November than in their summer.'

Good on you, Eddie, and long may the English winter rain fall on your head. Perhaps Australia was not always overflowing with grace during the glorious eight weeks of the World Cup trip. But it pulled itself together and ended on the highest of graceful notes.

I already suspected that Clive Woodward was now in line for a knighthood for his services to rugby, and naturally, for my own game-saving contribution, I entertained fond and modest hopes of kneeling alongside him in front of Her Majesty at the earliest convenient date.

Strangely, as the players and officials stepped down from the podium and as everyone returned to their laptops, a sense of severe anti-climax hit me. I imagined that it was the same with a good few of the players. There was a sense of letdown that was almost painful.

Maybe it was because the Great Adventure was almost over and things might never feel so wonderful again. Maybe it was because I knew that 50,000 people were having a party in Sydney and that I had to sit in the media centre for hours as the party raged.

At around four in the morning, the last shattered remnants of a once-gleaming *Sunday Times* reporting squad, still steaming from the dampness of the day, packed into what was apparently the only taxi then operating in the whole of Sydney. There was a little more hacking back at the hotel, and at around eight in the morning, Sydney time, we had all applied a modicum of polish to our humble words, and sent them whizzing.

At that very moment of sheer relief, the phone rang. It was the sports editor. 'The editor wants a piece on the England lineout,' he said. I replaced the receiver and made for the door.

'Who was that?' asked Nick Cain.

'It was the editor asking for a piece on the England lineout,' I said.

'Are you going to do one?'

'No,' I replied.

Happily, even with the Sydney dawn having broken hours before, there was still a bar open in the lurid casino. We joined a happy band of rugby followers from most areas of the game. Rob Andrew, fresh from the screaming yodel, was happily holding forth on his own exultation, on the benefits to his beloved Newcastle Falcons of the World Cup in general, and on the young chap he had found in deepest Surrey some years before. He had already formulated a plan that Wilkinson would be driven round Kingston Park on the following Saturday. Still, we had no idea of the reaction back at home. Just that rugby was in for a boom.

It was no time for sleep. There was an enormous Australian breakfast, renamed for the morning as an English breakfast. We watched the live coverage of Great Britain's defeat at the hands of Australia in the third rugby league Test. Next morning, the *Australian*'s front page trumpeted their coverage of 'the one we *did* win'.

There was a wash-up media day promised over at the England team hotel and so, for the last time, we all boarded the *Narrabeen* for the trip across the harbour. The hotel was completely besieged by hundreds of England supporters, and the management had arranged for us to slip into a side entrance.

The English squad had always been famous for a lack of exultation, but it was clear from those wandering around the corridors, still in their nice grey suits with the dodgy brown shoes, that they had come direct from a formidable night of celebration. Indeed, even as we watched, a police van disgorged the remnants of a raiding party which had been led by Dallaglio and which had rampaged about the place until two policewomen had rescued them from a giant crush of supporters and driven them across the city to the north shore and sanctuary.

It was, for some weeks, appropriate for rugby to show a minor pomposity about its goodness. But you had to ask yourself in how many sports in how many countries would the world champion participants go out and drink and party in the streets and bars with their followers?

Various England players wandered in. All were raucously, lovingly cheered if they as much as peeped out of the window. Everyone wanted to know if Martin Johnson had finally found the fires dying inside him and would now call it quits. Johnson's answer was immediate. 'I would go and play this afternoon, if they wanted me to.'

There was an air of quite wondrous, if quiet, satisfaction amongst all the backroom staff. Phil Larder had produced an England defence which had conceded two tries in the semi-final and final combined. One was a rather freakish effort by Serge Betsen in the match against the French; the other was caused by superb Australian skills cashing in on a physical mismatch between Lote Tuqiri and Jason Robinson.

How did he feel about it all? 'The best thing is that we have done it here, in Australia. I admire Australian sport so much. I have been down here with so many league teams and we were beaten every time. Now, after this, I can die happy.'

It was a moving admission. Larder is known as one of the most professional, meticulous and parsimonious men in the game. I was thrilled for him that he felt such satisfaction.

And I was also thrilled for Woodward. It has always been incredibly tempting to poke fun at his back-room staff, from the coach to the visual awareness lady to the chef (there, I've done it again), but, looking around the room at them, you could find no one who had failed to do an absolutely world-class job.

As he had already said, it was a staggering achievement by Dave Reddin, his fitness coach, and by the whole medical team, that all 30 players had been available for the final. It was as staggering that, again with Reddin's expertise, the rather ageing pack had lasted the whole 18-month course. Neil Back, 35 just after the tournament, had plundered on throughout the tournament, throughout the final proper, and he was still electricity in person in the dying moments.

Obviously, Jonny Wilkinson had received help from many people, but there was no doubt that the kicking expertise of Dave Alred had been a major factor. If you took the final alone, you also had to concede that Alred had helped to make Mike Tindall, formerly a no-footed kicker, into a real contender, able to deliver booming diagonal kicks.

And so on throughout the whole squad. Andy Robinson had obviously produced a game plan to fit every different occasion. Phil Keith-Roach, responsible for the forwards, had helped produce the best scrummaging pack in the knockout stages. Simon Hardy, the throws coach, had produced Steve Thompson at a peak, so that the massive Northampton hooker could deftly pitch the ball onto the upraised fingertips of Lewis Moody in the fateful lineout at the end of the game.

Woodward had been criticised for extravagance in bringing a top QC, but then we found that he had played a huge role in heading off trouble in the 16th Man Horror. The chef? 'He was brilliant,' Woodward said. 'And he cost us nothing. There was a deal made with Uncle Ben's Rice and we actually made money out of having him here.' Woodward rewrote the World Cup preparation manual, and all coaches will be dipping into it for 2007, and for ever.

Indeed, Woodward appeared to have built a management team that came dangerously close to achieving an inch-perfect preparation. A team that contained no fripperies because he had identified well beforehand the difference between true improvement and silly diversions. No doubt, the chef produced magnificent meals.

27 November 2003 – Planet Rugby website

Stop, stop and stop. End all this adulation for Jonny, Johnson and the rest. Apparently, if his own testimony is to be believed, only one man had a perfect World Cup and so all the plaudits must now go in his direction.

All hail, Andre Watson. His own reaction to the criticism he had endured appeared on the Planet Rugby website.

Reading Watson's own account of what the rest of the world in general felt was a disastrous performance in the World Cup, we found that he admits to not one single mistake either in the World Cup final itself, or in the rest of the tournament. Golden memories only of a perfect performance. Give him a medal.

Indeed, Watson described the furore over what I felt to be a deeply distasteful afternoon of officiating as 'media-driven' and 'a storm in a teacup'. You wish, old chap, you wish. For a start, why should these things not be media-driven? The television branch of the media has 20 cameras at its disposal and, in the professional game, is perfectly entitled to point all 20 at a referee in a vital game.

The written media benches also have a perfect right. Those of us who have reported more than 250 international matches and have never seen a worse refereeing performance than in Sydney on 22 November are also entitled to drive matters as far as they can go. But that is not the point. If Watson, or any of the closed circles of referees who are tacitly supporting him by their own silence, seriously believe that the fuss is a figment of media invention, then they are deluding themselves.

Clive Woodward refused at the time to make any comment to me on the subject, but close friends and coaching colleagues indicated strongly to me that Woodward is still raging mad about Watson's performance. Later, Woodward was more expansive. 'Can you believe that in the final of the World Cup, we had to take off a player [Phil Vickery] because of the way that Watson was refereeing the scrummage? The scrum was one of our main weapons, and how can we have been penalised so often when we were superior?' Woodward could not even fathom how Watson had been appointed in the first place, and he had clearly rebuffed an attempt by Watson to strike up a conversation at a function the day after the final. 'I was polite but I suggested that if we spoke then I might have said something I regretted,' Woodward says.

Watson makes a big point of his grand gesture of telling Woodward to look at the video and then to call him. 'I've not heard from him.' Let us leave aside the sheer unctuousness of Watson's attitude and his apparent, and rather papal, belief in his own infallibility. Has he considered that Woodward had no intention of getting back to him because he has simply given up on any attempt at rationalising the irrational? I don't imagine Woodward would give him the satisfaction. Woodward later confirmed that no such promise had ever been given.

Yes, the rage extends far beyond the media. It extends to the England team and coaches. It extends to referees. In the week prior to the website whitewash (attempted), I had addressed a referees' society annual dinner and the jeer when I as much as mentioned Watson's name was deafening. One of the society's two Zurich Premiership referees, normally a mild-mannered sort of chap, let loose such a tirade at Watson's performance that only the Loyal Toast caused him to pipe down.

Media-driven? The *Sunday Times* sent copies of the video of the match to two leading referees, one a leading light in the Zurich Premiership, still active, and another, now retired, one of the most famous officials of this era. We asked their opinion. One referee reckoned that Watson had made 17 errors at a conservative estimate, the other firmly believes, at the very least, that Watson had betrayed the International Rugby Board Charter for the playing of the game, especially the section relating to the scrum.

Watson's defence of his attack on the superior England scrum beggars belief. He and Paul Honiss, the dire New Zealand touch-judge, were clearly bent on attacking the England scrum all afternoon. Just one example from Watson's feeble excuses. Apparently, the chief reason why he penalised Trevor Woodman at the very end of normal time was on safety grounds. 'Woodman didn't engage, which meant that his opponent hit a vacuum – it's usually a knee – and that's dangerous.'

Drivel. Frankly, for Watson to raise a safety issue as an excuse is deeply distasteful and his whole explanation clearly smacks of a finicky and one-sided assault on one team. Where, on God's earth, were the penalties against Australia? Al Baxter, the Australian tight-head, collapsed at the first scrum and collapsed at subsequent scrums. The whole world knows that Australia are not interested in engaging properly in the scrum, or standing square – one striking video produced during the World Cup showed the Australian props packing sideways at the same angle as the flankers. Frankly, Australia's scrum was crucified.

How well I remember the launch of the IRB Charter. It was a brilliant document inspired by Lee Smith, the splendid Kiwi. It was partly introduced to bring back the crunch of scrummaging and, as Smith said at the time, 'To stop the weaker side getting away with it. If one team comes to a match with a superior scrum, then why should they not be able to cash in on their superiority?'

Watson kept Australia in the game. Watson declares that: 'When I gave the penalty, I wasn't bothered about the match situation.' That's very kind of him not to make decisions depending on how many seconds were left. But it does not explain why, in the final of the World Cup, Watson went out and refereed just one of the participating teams. Nor does it explain how the feeble Aussie scrum got off scot-free.

These days, thank goodness, the people who harp on that referees are beyond criticism are dwindling in numbers. Every vantage point and every camera and every video must be used in the professional game to ensure that the referees are as good as the players. If Watson believes that the furore over his performance is media-driven, then more power to the media.

So it was a storm in a teacup? Hmm. If Wilkinson's drop-kick had not gone over, and if the inferior Australian team had somehow managed to escape, then Watson's storm would have filled a teacup of colossal proportions. It was a shame, given mistakes he made early in the tournament, and given his fumblings with the scrum in the 1999 World Cup final, that he was ever allowed another final. But he should thank his lucky stars that Wilkinson's kick went over. Otherwise, he would forever be known as the ref who won the World Cup. As it is, he will remain in my disbelieving heart and laptop as the referee who tried to win the World Cup.

36. THE FLIGHT OF THE CHARIOT

24 November 2003 – Sydney Airport

It was a strange feeling to be cramming the suitcase for the last time. Most certainly it would be a relief to be home and to stop living the false life of rugby's touring road. But I would miss Australia, every Australian (bar two or three), and there was also the rather depressing effect of landing on a dark English winter's morning, and the fears I had long held of reverting, feeling tired and old and sore, to mundane domestic rugby coverage.

Before we left, True Colours produced a whole raft of statistics from the tournament. The whole thing had made a profit of around £100 million. Roughly a third would remain with the host union, which would use it to fund its assault on the other two footballing codes in the country. Around £70 million would go to the International Rugby Board's developmental fund for rugby worldwide.

I had looked forward for weeks to the final tournament press conference at which, everyone confidently expected, a whole barrage of measures would be announced by the International Rugby Board so that the shocking, abysmal and immoral inequalities which the tournament had laid bare would be alleviated. The suspense, as it turned out, was absolutely pointless. Syd Millar, speaking for the IRB, merely referred vaguely to funding problems and then he delivered the most disastrous and myopic cop-out.

'We also have to look after the foundation unions,' he said. This was a reference to the fact that, unforgivably, the unions in Scotland, Ireland and Wales, despite their vast earning capacity, had got themselves into various kinds of financial problems. Mr Millar gave us to understand that unions which could derive half a million pounds from primary sources alone, from home internationals, would be hoovering up the cash that, morally, should have been devoted entirely to rugby countries which could not afford

more than one scrummaging machine and not more than one coach.
Shocking.

True Colours also revealed that 30 million television viewers had tuned in
for the final and that 82,957 people had actually attended the game, a
record for any Rugby World Cup match. No fewer than 96,000 foreign
fans, most of them English, had come from overseas and spent so much on
their trips that the Australian stock exchange had significantly risen. It
estimated that the fans had spent roughly £15 million.

There were statistics from back at home as well. Apparently, 15,000
English pubs had opened their doors at 7 a.m. on the morning of the final,
and Max Clifford, the public relations guru, was estimating that Jonny
Wilkinson's new annual earnings would be in the region of £3 million.
There were no statistics given as to how many times Wilkinson's employer,
Rob Andrew, gulped when he read that.

There was to be another significant statistic concerning the flight home.
It is generally regarded that the record for drinking cans of beer on flights
involving major sporting teams is the mark of 52 set by David Boon, the
Australian cricketer, on a flight between Sydney and London. Mike Tindall
made a magnificent attempt to create even more history, but on-board
statisticians reckoned that he came in two tins short.

And there was another great fat nil to contemplate. The number of
positive drugs tests. There had been stiff testing both in the pre-
competition period when testers arrived unannounced at the various
headquarters and during the event itself. Not one came out positive.
People who found it was all too good to be true kept imagining that,
somehow, the players had found ways of escaping and masking.

So why are there so many positive tests in athletics, where the level of
sophistication in the consumption of illegal substances and their masking
agents is light years ahead of the rugby player? Woodward spoke of his
experiences with drug testers. 'I don't ever get asked if they can test and I
don't want to be asked; they are welcome any time. They could arrive at
breakfast and say that they want to test all 30 players and the answer is: "Of
course you can."

'We had players tested in May and June, even in their homes, and this
is excellent. I don't want to be involved, apart from categorically saying
whenever asked that I will always ensure that they are available for a test
and to provide a sample. That is the kind of sport that you want to be
involved in.'

There is a reason for rugby players to take drugs – they provide shortcuts, so assist in securing careers and contracts and help recovery from injury. But rugby, dear old rugby, has an even better reason not to take them. It is, ultimately, a sport where honest competition is prized above anything, way above the preservation of market value and well above shortcuts.

England departed at lunchtime on Monday, 24 November. They had been in Australia for two months. British Airways renamed the aircraft 'Sweet Chariot' and even the homeward flight was to become part of the legend. The players, aware of their responsibilities, wandered round every row of the aircraft, showing off the cup to thrilled fellow passengers. It was just one of around 10,000 gestures which showed the squad for what they were – decent, straightforward, formidably dedicated and honourable blokes. 'I cannot see any of them letting this all go to their heads,' Woodward said. To those who knew their top rugby players, it was a prediction he did not even have to make.

Our own flight touched down at Gatwick around five hours after England had arrived at Heathrow, at a forbidding 5 a.m. We were still unsuspecting.

'Shame the boys got in so early,' we said as we left the airport in a taxi, a cold winter morning closing around us – and reminding us, frankly, of Sydney. 'There might have been a few hundred there to welcome them if only they'd got home at noon.'

Obviously, no one was going to see them in at 5 a.m. Oh no? When we heard about the scenes at Heathrow, it probably marked the moment when the Rugby World Cup was no longer a story simply for sports journalists, and it marked the moment when rugby finally confirmed its place in the national sporting consciousness.

Police estimates, you see, were to put the crowd who besieged the terminal and approach roads at Heathrow at between 8,000 and 10,000. I was staggered.

Two weeks later, a parade was arranged in central London, with the England squad to show off their trophy from the top deck of an open-topped bus, in a process intended to end in a rally in Trafalgar Square.

By then, I had become aware of the massive interest and understandable triumphalism that the World Cup had generated. People who had never heard of the game suddenly wanted to hear all the experiences. But was the parade a gesture too far, would it be embarrassing if only a few thousand lined the route?

The Rugby Football Union, who organised the parade, estimated that a healthy 20,000 would go to catch sight of the Webb Ellis trophy and would wave back at the players.

Wrong again. Police estimates of the crowd which brought life in central London to a standstill held that not much fewer than one million people turned out. The players were clearly utterly taken aback by their reception, and when the bus, nosing its way along, finally reached Trafalgar Square there were people as far as the eye could see, packing the square and all the surrounding roads, hanging off buildings and jumping in fountains. Woodward, Johnson and a rapturously acclaimed Wilkinson spoke to the crowds over the public address system. They were all en route to a reception at 10 Downing Street, an event which caused all kinds of political friction as politicians jostled to be bathed in the red-rose glow. Later that same day, there was an audience with the Queen at Buckingham Palace, and official photographs saw a clearly delighted Queen seated in amongst a formal team photograph of the whole squad, still wearing the dodgy brown shoes. The solemnity of the occasion had clearly been torpedoed by the arrival of an errant corgi, which duly appeared on the official picture.

It went on and on and on. The whole squad and the senior coaches (apart from the chef) were presented with MBEs in the New Year's Honours List, apart from Johnson, who was given a CBE, and Leonard, Robinson and Wilkinson, who were given the OBE. Woodward, the architect, was quite rightly knighted.

Heady, or what?

37. CALLING A HALT?

9 December 2003 – Welford Road, Leicester

Yet it had all raged on, through Christmas into the New Year. The players who had testimonial years staged dinners bursting with guests. Someone bought Dorian West's World Cup jersey for £500,000, staggering the country; the money was given to charity. At least it was clean. It had not even been worn in anger. My friend Ian bid £13,000 just to have a snap taken with the trophy and with his guests at a testimonial lunch for Mike Catt.

The trophy itself was sent touring round the country and, inanimate or not, was rapturously received. One day, Leicester fans queued to be photographed with it and the last in the queue took their snaps at two in the morning. At four in the morning, the next lot arrived to start queuing for the next day.

Editorials appeared eulogising rugby. Columns ranted away that the example of dedication, of putting the national team first, and of behaving like athletes and not brats, was a lesson England footballers could learn. The RFU hammered out the message and as thousands more came to watch live rugby, thousands of youngsters arrived to play it. The Zurich Premiership clubs, praised by Clive Woodward and his new pal Eddie Jones, began to panic simply because their stadiums had, apparently, begun to shrink. Sell-outs became the norm.

And poor rugby became a thing of the past. Every game was now full of glorious, attacking rugby. Except for those games that were not.

10 December 2003 – No one hurt as car stops safely, North Yorkshire

'Jonny escapes death,' said *The Mirror*. He'd been at the Palace along with the squad to meet the Queen after the parade. He'd done Number 10.

Two days later, he had to go back to the Palace alone for his MBE investiture. On the intervening day, he decided, on balance, not to hang out in the city consorting with royals and milking his cascading celebrity but to go back to Newcastle, to train with the Falcons.

While en route, his driver lost control at a speed described, valiantly, in the tabloids as 'up to 70 mph'. In other words, it could have been 10 mph. The car nosed through a few bushes, struck a tree a glancing blow and came to a stop, Jonny climbed out, rang his dad, who came to fetch him, and they all went home to bed. *The Mirror* was quite correct. Jonny had escaped death – along with millions of other motorists on the roads of Britain at the same time.

That same day, Mike Tindall had to deny in forthright terms rumours circulating in the gossip columns that he was the lover of Zara Phillips, daughter of the Princess Royal. Bet the team didn't give him any stick at all about that.

Also on the same day, Lynda Lee-Potter, the *Mail's* grande dame columnist, wrote a piece under the heading 'At last, some REAL men to shout about'. The England rugby squad, she trilled, 'know nothing of unisex. Unlike Rod Stewart, they do not wear silk knickers, get their hair permed, pluck their eyebrows or use their wives' Chanel No. 5 as an aftershave.

'Hopefully, the team will popularise the immaculate suit, the highly polished shoe, the short back-and-sides and the well-shaved chin . . . their masculinity enhances the femininity of their wives and girlfriends . . . when they are going out to dinner in the pouring rain they drop off their wives at the front door and then get soaked as they park the car. They don't like watching television on their own and always want their wife to sit with them, even when it's a programme she hates. If the doorbell rings they say: "Who's that?" and expect her to know . . . They can't stand slush and have no desire to get in touch with their feminine side.'

Bloody hell. Whoever's ringing the doorbell, let's hope it's not Lynda.

The boom in rugby would, no doubt, carry on. The William Webb Ellis Cup, with its heavies, prepared to continue its odyssey round England. England had lording rights for a glorious four years. Everything was bathed in a red, rosy glow. But thanks, Lynda, for showing everyone that it was time to get back to rugby, the week-in, week-out stuff, not the rugby-as-epitome-of-all-that's-heavenly-on-our-blighted-planet, Jonny's-a-story-because-he's-not-injured branch of it.

It was a rather gloomy and wet winter in the home of the world champions. Rugby weather.

The game I feared had already passed without problem. It was that dreaded first domestic game post-Australia, between Leicester and Bath on 29 November. It became part of the process. Who wanted to take a week's holiday, shattered though I was and being ordered by eye surgeons to recuperate? The walk on gilded splinters continued.

And Leicester even promised a glimpse of Johnno. He and Back and the others were rapturously acclaimed as they appeared to warm up, with no thought of resting. When Johnson arrived as replacement, the crowd stood and roared. For God's sake, when the announcer gave out the names of Mike Catt and Mike Tindall, Bath's heroes, they roared as well. That's Bath men. Being revered at Welford Road.

I was still caught up. It was a dark day, average floodlights, and every bone in the body and mind, so to speak, was weary. I sat next to David Norrie and Paul Ackford, all three fresh, if that is the way to put it (and it isn't), from Australia. We peered sleepily into the gloom. We hardly saw a single incident all day. We had to tour the press box.

'Who scored then? Who gave the scoring pass? Who was sent off just then?'

That Sunday, my Maidenhead Under-16 team played Wasps. Their season had been fractured by, of all things, matches off because of hard grounds and because of county calls. They played delightfully, with real skill, and afterwards were laughing and jesting in the changing-rooms.

That evening, I attended The Greyhound pub quiz for the first time for nine Sundays. 'Steve. Are you back from Australia, then?' asked Clive, who'd answered one question in two years. 'No, he's obviously still out there, you silly ****,' said Tommy Keys.

Clive Woodward officially declared World Cup fever over and done on 1 January. On 12 January, he was at the Rugby Writers' Dinner receiving an award for his achievements. Johnson was there too, to pick up the main award as the club's Personality of the Year. Other players, notably Jason Leonard and Lawrence Dallaglio, appeared, if they do not mind me saying so, to have mislaid the sheet from Dave Reddin warning that alcohol interfered with training.

A few days later, after the Leicester–Ulster European Cup game, a press conference was called at Welford Road. Johnson, as had been widely predicted for several weeks, announced that he was retiring, at 33, from international rugby. For some time, I had concluded that he was the greatest lock who had ever played. The World Cup indicated that he was the game's finest leader. So much of my own reporting career had run in parallel with his glories, and gave me such rich material, that I felt the loss as keenly as any Tigers tragic or England nutcase. I recalled the first time I'd seen him play, years ago for England Schools. And all the times he had been to war since. I also worried for him – where does all that surging, and yet now surplus, adrenalin go?

But it was not the only story buzzing. Leicester were having a disastrous season, had been thrashed over in Ulster the previous week. Phew! Rugby World Cup Ltd, the organisers, were refusing to accept the blinding evidence of their own eyes that the triumph of Australia 2003 lay in the fact that one country was the host – RWC were still bumbling along with the plan to waste a World Cup by scattering the 2007 event to the four European winds. I was determined that I would rant away till they went deaf, or reconsidered.

More yet. There was the onrushing Six Nations, with the world and his wife desperate to topple England, and with new players about to wear the now-hallowed white. That day at Leicester, too, I had a rather sharp argument with the sports editor about the fact that he had cropped away a little of the rugby space that week.

It seemed strange, even after the stresses of the 18 months of England build-up, that I had seriously, anxiously, genuinely doubted the properties of the old game to regenerate itself, and the spirits of others, on a beach in Scotland, a million words ago. Anyway, one thing my various experiences, good and bad and painful, had reminded me of is that even rugby is an empty vessel without the comradeship, support, barbed relationships and rock-solid friendships of the people in it, and admiration for the people who play it – in England's case, play it better than the world. I woke from the World Cup dream feeling hungry.

Anyway, in 2005, the British Lions are due to tour New Zealand. Jesus. What a trip that promises to be.

38. WEARING DOWN

29 August 2004 – Cookham High Street

Nine months after the World Cup, I was commanded to attend Sir Clive. Not in his quarters, but in his local pub. And not via an equerry, but via a text message. 'Let's catch up,' it said. Our homes are only a few miles apart (his is bigger than mine). His book *Winning!*, a weighty, excellent, anecdotal and insightful work about his coaching philosophies, was about to be published and I had rendered the state some service by reading the final page proofs (on the beach in Tenby) to try to spot any howlers before printing. I assumed he wanted a beer to see if I liked the book. Anyway, I like him and which anxious hack was going to knock back an audience with the man who was contracted to coach England till 2007?

In those nine months between the end of November 2003 and the end of August 2004, the World Cup team had broken up. Woodward was later to suggest that he regretted allowing it to break up so quickly and that he wished he had kept the likes of Neil Back, especially, in the fold. Bravely spoken, because England played without a real openside flanker for the whole post-Sydney year.

By the time we spoke in the pub, Martin Johnson had been followed into retirement from international rugby by Back, Jason Leonard, Kyran Bracken, Dorian West and (I first heard this from Clive as we sat down in the pub; I was stunned, but not half as stunned as I was to become one minute later), Lawrence Dallaglio.

In addition, Jonny Wilkinson had not yet returned to rugby after a serious shoulder operation. He played just a few minutes of his comeback game after the World Cup in December 2003, before having the operation to try to repair damaged nerves and tissue in his right shoulder. He had missed all the Six Nations and the 2004 summer tour to Australia and New Zealand. He was to return only for the start of Newcastle Falcons' 2004–05 Zurich Premiership season.

Even his absence had been typically Jonny. Medical reports were pored over, cutaway diagrams were provided in newspapers. His shoulder was prayed for. A wondrous rumour machine sprung from nowhere. Every week, or more often, you would hear from someone that secretly, the medical staffs at Newcastle and England were saying that he would never play again. Everyone knew a bloke who was the dentist of the partner of the physiotherapist who was treating Wilkinson who insisted that the injury was far worse than anyone was admitting. Maybe. Maybe. But he was shirking very little as the new Falcons season began brightly. One day at Bath, he stood and signed autographs for over two and half hours. Rugby's one-man goodness machine.

And yet the wheel of injury fortune had turned viciously. In the nine months since the World Cup, Iain Balshaw, Mike Tindall, Mike Catt, Matt Dawson, Phil Vickery, Julian White and Lewis Moody had all been absent for prolonged periods. It was as if the fates, having relented for 2003, had come to deliver their invoice. In any case, even the fit and able-bodied were diminished. A large group of the rump of World Cup heroes had played either significantly or dramatically below their best form in the 2003–04 season, among them Will Greenwood, Steve Thompson, Jason Robinson, Ben Kay and Ben Cohen. Three of those – Greenwood, Kay and Robinson – have been excused the summer tour to try to revive their spirits, legs and form.

Bearing all this in mind, it was palpably the biggest non-shock in the history of rugby that England's results had been poor in 2004 so far, with only a scruffy mid-table finish in the Six Nations following a wipe-out by the vengeful down-under teams. But those observers and England fans who panicked were completely missing the big picture. Woodward's team was designed to win the World Cup. It was an old team when the tournament came round but it lasted till the last seconds of extra time when all the ambitions were realised; it was blindingly obvious that the team would break up, that some of the sporting codgers would depart.

It was also highly likely that a swathe of the team would suffer a drop-off in form. It was all very well to laud the revival of the New Zealand team which beat England 2–0 in the 2004 tour; all very well to laud the South African team which, at the longest last, revived and won the 2004 Tri Nations in great style. But it was the coaches of those two nations who had bemoaned the lack of experience in their teams during the 2003 World Cup (and who picked the team, anyway?) and who had predicted that their teams would peak in a year or two. Big deal. Woodward's team peaked for the big one.

However, throughout all the misplaced criticism, Woodward remained (as far as the prospects for his team went) bullish. In *Winning!* he expanded yet again on his vision that he could take the England team onwards. He had declared that England's autumn international series against Canada, South Africa and Australia would see a major leap forward and that England's followers need worry only if those matches went horribly wrong.

He bought two pints of bitter. We sat down at a table by the door and I waited for the traditional gush of rampaging enthusiasm to swamp me.

'I've resigned,' he said.

There is, of course, when I last looked, only one Sunday in every week. And, therefore, only one *Sunday Times*. I was absolutely stunned and frankly, the journalist's reaction in me was even stronger. There would be six days to pass before I could reveal, embellish, analyse the biggest story rugby had seen for donkey's years. It duly appeared, day by day of those six days, leaking inexorably out, great chunks bitten off in various media outlets. The man with the exclusive and nowhere to stick it.

Woodward also told me that three days previously, Lawrence Dallaglio, his mighty captain and one of the very few people the game had seen who had the presence to compensate for the loss of Johnson, had met with him in an emotional state and told him that he was standing down from England. 'I told him that I had some news for him, too,' Woodward said. By now, it was not so much the gradual break-up of the World Cup juggernaut as its disintegration

One of the tabloid papers carried a story 48 hours after Woodward had first confided in me. The topspin exerted on the *Daily Mail*'s story, carried as the sporting splash, purported to reveal that Woodward was switching across to football to revive a long-held ambition to manage at the top level in the sport and to indulge an almost fanatical interest in the round-ball code. *Winning!* revealed that his father, a naval officer, had sent him away to HMS Conway, a bizarre naval boarding school with echoes of *Tom Brown's Schooldays*, in his later teens and that football was banned there, rugby compulsory. Woodward, a promising footballer and inveterate football lover, was to run away three times in protest that he could not carry on with his football and had to play the alien game.

Now, the Mail, suggested, it was all coming home to roost. His ambition was to coach at top professional level and to coach the England football team, and the clear implication was that he had done everything in rugby and was now swanning off to right the wrongs in the bigger sport. 'Woodward to Succeed Sven?' was one of the headline questions posed.

For almost a week, this football angle raged. Football managers, coaches and players were canvassed. Some rather liked the idea of a fierce, well-organised, driven man stepping across to galvanise the national team, which was in a trough; others pointed out that Woodward had never even coached a professional football team, let alone the national team. 'It was kind of people to say that I'd never coached a pro football team,' he told me later. 'But I have to point out that I knew that already.'

It was all poppycock, in the sense that the change in direction of his career path towards football had no bearing at all on his leaving of rugby. Yes, he did intend to try out at football. He did intend to take every football coaching certificate going, including that needed to coach in the Premiership. He did see a chance that he could bring his organisational and motivational skills to bear and perhaps at some time in the future obtain a senior post in which he worked alongside a top-line football coach – 'An Andy Robinson kind of figure in football.'

He had already stuck up a relationship with Rupert Lowe, the chairman of Southampton, and the pair had agreed that Woodward would move to the club in the medium term to work with academy players as a first step.

But all these connections were forged after he had decided to leave rugby. And despite all the loudly trumpeted implications, despite the suggestions that he was following a long-planned career path, the truth was that he had been forced out. His conscience, his sense of what it would take to prepare an England side in the seasons up to the defence of the trophy in 2007, could no longer allow him to stay. It was not football which dragged him away, it was principle.

In terms of England's results, the wheels began to fall off when Ireland came to Twickenham for the first home match which England had played in the Six Nations tournament – and it was to become the first match they had lost in the competition at Twickenham for seven years. People cast about for someone to blame, purporting to find evidence of terminal decline as Ireland swept to a momentous 19–3 victory, culminating in their own riotous celebrations.

And, God bless them, the Irish played well, sealing their victory with a try in the corner by Girvan Dempsey. However, there was more, or perhaps less, to their victory than met the eye. England had a staggeringly calamitous day in the lineout. Steve Thompson could not find the farmyard let alone the barn or the barn door with his throwing and Ben Kay and his supporting cast of lifters and jumpers were also way off with their timing. England had around 13 of their own lineout throws either poached or spoiled by the inspired Malcolm O'Kelly and Paul O'Connell, and such is the structure and dynamic of modern rugby that everything collapses under the weight of those kind of lineout statistics.

England had opened decently in this Jonny-free period, winning by 50–9 in Italy thanks chiefly to a sharp hat-trick from Jason Robinson; and they also beat Scotland 35–13 in Edinburgh, with four good tries, although, admittedly, the Scottish team was a lamentably poor one. By this time, the Six Nations title was already looking beyond them. A rather downbeat and even turgid air had enveloped proceedings and although they managed to beat Wales 31–21 at Twickenham, they went to Paris for the final game as underdogs. Even though the final score of 24–21 looked reasonably respectable, the fact is that they were 24–6 down at one stage; they came back in only because France, ludicrously, appeared to declare their innings closed in the final quarter.

It would be silly to pretend that this was all some kind of sweet revenge for France after the horrors they endured in the World Cup semi-final, because nothing could have erased that particular memory. But the victory gave France a Grand Slam. One of the main differences between the teams lay in the relative zip of the back-play. France had Damien Traille and Yannick Jauzion in the centre. The pair would easily have been big and strong enough to play international rugby in the second row in most other eras of the sport's history but as they showed at the Stade de France, they had glorious skills to burn and they put the fumblings of England's backs into sharp relief. The fact that England were now down to their fourth-choice fly-half in Olly Barkley was not, in itself, sufficient excuse for the painfulness of the comparisons.

The disintegration in terms of results went on. Woodward allowed Robinson, Greenwood and Kay to miss the summer tour but he knew full well that many of the players he had to take were either carrying injury or suffering a devastating loss of form. He was also to blame himself (unfairly) for Dallaglio's shock autumn departure. 'I should have left him at home,' he said of Dallaglio and the summer tour. But how? It would have sent the wrong signals, and others would then have withdrawn.

Such is Woodward's natural ebullience that he left for two Tests against New Zealand and another against Australia in a positive frame of mind, talking about an ambition to win all three. But by the time England trotted out onto that dreadful, gloomy arena called Carisbrook in Dunedin for the first Test, many illusions had been blown away in a New Zealand autumn. They lost 36–3 to a new-look New Zealand team. Newish forwards such as Keith Robinson and Jono Gibbes had been drafted by Graham Henry and all the talk was of Kiwi revival, of the building of a new superpower pack and the resumption of New Zealand dominance over the whole world.

I shared very little of this new optimism, and pissed off several million New Zealanders, it seemed, when I humbly suggested that, once again, they had all gone off the deep end in their overrating of their blessed team.

The second Test in Auckland was a write-off. By now, England were being held together by hope and tape, but they did open brightly. Then, the whole match was invalidated by the ludicrous sending-off of Simon Shaw in the first quarter. Shaw approached the back of a ruck and appeared to lead, gently, with his knee. He may or may not have grazed a prone and offside New Zealand forward with the aforesaid knee but if I were the aforesaid forward, I would have been considerably pleased not to have received from Shaw the kind of good kicking that I would unquestionably have dished out had the roles been reversed.

From around seven miles away, Stuart Dickinson, the Australian touch judge, not only ruled that Shaw had indulged in gross foul play, but told the referee, Nigel Williams, that Shaw should be sent off. The replays revealed an offence by Shaw which may just have been a penalty, but was never, ever a yellow card – let alone a red card. Dickinson's appalling, pompous overreaction ruined the game and England lost 36–12, thanks notably to a striking hat-trick of tries from Joe Rokocoko.

Afterwards, Shaw escaped without punishment because the officials had made a procedural mess-up. They had gone upstairs to the television match official to confirm the identity of the 'miscreant'. They were not allowed to do that and they therefore grossly compounded the original error by Dickinson. However, many in the England camp were annoyed that Shaw had escaped merely on procedures. For my part, I was absolutely intrigued to find out what the disciplinary panel would have done had they sat in judgement on the issue itself – had they not completely exonerated Shaw, they would have made total prats of themselves and would have confirmed in bold type the anti-Englishness still running rampant through rugby.

The All Blacks duly subsided in the 2004 Tri Nations tournament, fading to second place with their forwards, as usual, ropey as anything. And so there was one match left in the longest season for England, and as we were to find out later, one match left in the whole Woodward era. The match between Australia and England at the marvellous Suncorp Stadium was billed as a revenge mission for the Wallabies. Not even their most driven marketeers bought into that, because England had incontrovertibly won the Big One and they were down to third and fourth and even fifth choices in some positions as they took the field.

They lost 51–5, and if their heads never dropped, the comparisons were nonetheless brutal in terms of freshness, athleticism and ideas. Joe Roff was in brilliant form for Australia and Clyde Rathbone, a South African crudely transplanted, came into the side just before kick-off, when useless Wendell Sailor withdrew, and scored a superb hat-trick.

That was that, the season was over and the Poms were in retreat. Woodward faced the travelling media in a conference room of the Hilton Hotel, Brisbane, the day after the Test disaster. He was clearly furious at the three defeats he had suffered. But he was also, it seemed, positive. 'There is no need for anyone to panic. When we get home and when we get all our players back and firing for the autumn internationals, we will have a better idea of where we are. I will only be really worried if things are still going wrong in the autumn.'

As an afterthought, Woodward was asked his opinion on some excited outpourings from Twickenham, which had reached us in the Deep South. An agreement had been signed, so media releases ran, between the RFU and the Premiership clubs. It was called the EPS (Elite Player Squad) agreement, and it set out plans for training days and a whole raft of other measures through which Woodward would be granted access to players and preparation time to continue the job. We expected Woodward to greet this warmly. Yet he was dismissive of questions concerning the agreement.

Ah well. Maybe he's depressed by the tour.

However, I was later to find that his reaction to the EPS agreement had nothing whatsoever to do with poor England results. Not only did he hate it with a passion, but it came to represent a total and fierce dissatisfaction with his whole situation, with the lack of prioritisation given to the national team. Indeed, it was at the very root of his departure.

He expanded on all the reasons for his stunning exit as we sat in his garden at the start of September 2004. We sat in the same garden, and indeed in the same seats, where he had expanded on his vision for the World Cup 18 months previously. The garden still looked wonderful but the backdrop had become, for want of a better word, evil. He told me that he had resigned three weeks earlier but had asked Francis Baron, chief executive of the RFU, to keep the matter secret for the time being.

Woodward revealed that the 'World Cup factor' had lasted around 10 seconds. Before the tournament, he had had to battle fiercely against the major clubs for what he saw as proper preparation time for his men. He had believed that his own voice would grow in strength and influence after he brought home the Webb Ellis Trophy, that all disagreements as to priorities would be a thing of the past as the game in England realised what it took to win a World Cup, and, therefore, what it took to retain it.

No such luck. 'I realised when I came back that the clubs felt they had done their stuff and that now it was their turn. I realised, when I put in a World Cup report with some serious recommendations that was completely ignored, that people were listening to me less than they had before the tournament. I found that very strange and disturbing.'

And with the break-up of the team and with players making decisions beyond his control, he was reminded once again of the weaknesses of a system where the players are contracted to the clubs, and not centrally to the national team. 'I understand that the players are the property of the clubs, but if we had them under our control, then think what we could do. We could manage them all properly as a squad. We could manage their fitness and we could manage things like their welfare, their retirements, even their testimonials. But we have no control over our elite athletes.'

Woodward expanded on his dislike of the EPS agreement – he explained that he had not been properly consulted about it, that most of the main measures were unenforceable, and that in any case, he felt that he should be above all the petty bickering and negotiating. 'I told them that I wanted 26 training days for the season ahead,' he said. 'I saw that as an absolute minimum. We are trying to put a new team together with a large number of new players. This cannot be done overnight. The agreement seems to give me 16 training days. But it is not about training days. It is infinitely wider than that. It is about me being allowed to prepare these elite athletes in the way they should be prepared.'

Woodward expanded, too, on the vast minefield lying between him and his aspirations for his team: there were no 'A' matches arranged; he did not agree with the siting of the academies that had been established; he felt he was given no support from the club directors of rugby. 'Nine of them are foreigners and the other three want my job,' he said, rather clumsily but memorably. He was dismissive of the club negotiators. It went on and on.

Woodward revealed that the opening bid in terms of training days from the club sides had been, believe it or not, a princely none. Zero. Zip. And perhaps most remarkably of all, as Woodward expanded on his own hurt, I realised that the man who had accepted the adulation of a million people in Trafalgar Square when the Cup came home was now almost completely alone in the corridors of power.

He clearly felt abandoned by Baron, an old ally. Fran Cotton, another old ally of Woodward's in his post as chairman of Club England, had moved on to the International Rugby Board. Chris Spice, the RFU performance director who was meant to be Woodward's right-hand man, had apparently quailed in the face of club intransigence and even though Woodward was too polite to say so, it was clear that professional respect and a working relationship between the two had utterly broken down.

Woodward felt that it was he against the world. It was not so much that he quailed in the face of the fight and the enemy. It was just that he did not see why on earth he should have to battle so that the England team could be properly prepared. I did point out that I felt him too hawkish or, even, too principled. He kept on bringing up the examples of Ireland and Scotland and New Zealand, where the players are centrally contracted. I told him that England was not Ireland or Scotland or New Zealand. It was England, good old England, and it had a thriving professional rugby game.

But I did have vast sympathy with Woodward about the total disappearance of the World Cup factor, the bunglings and jealousies of the major clubs, the brutalisation of his vision, and the operation of what Australians call the tall-poppy syndrome. I simply could not believe that Woodward's staggering contribution to the health and glory of English rugby meant so little that hardly anyone had even come to him to ask him to change his mind about resigning in the three weeks since he had decided, still less to try to mediate in the dispute, to give him an ally.

So he was gone. The media frenzy lasted for ages. For some reason no one really understood, Woodward, Baron and the wholly ineffective Graeme Cattermole, the RFU's chairman of the management board, sat together at a press conference to announce formally his departure. Negotiations had been bitter and the electricity crackled as Woodward expanded on the crushing of his vision.

Later that day, I asked him about the human cost. His home had been besieged by cameras all week. How might his family be affected? Typically, he had even prepared for that. 'When we were all celebrating on the beach at Manly the day after the World Cup final, Jayne and I told the kids that this was the upside, these were the great bits, we told them to make sure they enjoyed it all because there would be the other side, the down times.' Those times had arrived, bitter and ridiculously premature.

England's most recent rugby results had been awful, but I could see no reason why Woodward could not revive them, and he clearly had, underneath all his misgivings and principles, the strength and motivation and ideas to restore the bandwagon to its tracks.

8 September 2004 – Pennyhill Park Hotel

And so, on a sunny Indian-summer morning, we were all back at Pennyhill Park, the Palace of Sweat. Andy Robinson was to be revealed as Woodward's successor, at least on a temporary basis. I had rated Robinson as player or coach for as long as I could recall but my immediate impression was that he needed a coach, almost a father-figure. Robbo was not the man to spend hours, as had Woodward, in forced-polite negotiation.

As I drove in past that welcoming/warning sign on which the registration number of your car is suddenly illuminated, I found it hard to believe that it would not be Woodward who sat at the media table at the press conference, with his scattergun approach to new ideas, and wisdoms and oddities causing us all to duck in a kind of resigned, familiar and even comforting fashion.

Woodward's involvement in rugby would still be heavy. He had long ago been announced as head coach for the 2005 British Lions tour. At first, a few dire Celts on the Lions committee raised objections. They reasoned that since he had a tortuous relationship with the England directors of rugby, who were going to provide a large chunk of the party, he was no longer the best man for the job. It was tripe, and indicative of a few months when all those people who had been forced to bite the bullet as Woodward and his men swept through planet rugby popped up their heads and allowed the bile to flow freely.

His appointment was confirmed when people realised that it was all to the Lions' advantage. Now, he would be completely free to concentrate on the Lions; frankly, I was always doubtful if there were enough hours in the day to allow him to prepare both England and the Lions in tandem.

Soon, he was off and running. This most English of rugby coaches agreed to spend a week with the Italian squad as they prepared to play New Zealand in the autumn of 2004. He arranged to spend a week with Wales as they worked up to their own autumn programme and Mike Ruddock, the Wales coach still finding his own way, had the humility and good sense to buy into the idea with complete warmth. I sent Clive a note pointing out that, in case he had never been to Wales before, it was £4.80 to cross the Severn Bridge.

All very well. But as he prepared to meet his new charges, and as distance lent perspective to some newsy early weeks of the new season, the sense of incredulity left me only very slowly. It was still much less than a year since England had won the World Cup and, frankly, turned all known rugby history on its head, reversed a strong trend in British sport itself; Woodward himself tended to see the staggering run of 13 successive victories against the giant South Hemisphere nations as an achievement greater than the World Cup, and I tended to agree.

Naturally, the fallout from the World Cup had been profound and wondrous. Numbers of those who played and coached and refereed and sponsored rugby had risen dramatically; everyone, including the Zurich Premiership clubs, was basking in the warmth of the World Cup factor. Yes, the game had settled down. Rugby is not the type of sport to preen itself for too long, there is always the next crushing tackle to negotiate. But history had been rewritten and Woodward' s part could never be erased. It had been a magnificent journey for everyone, and I felt nostalgic about it as soon as it had ended. A few weeks after Woodward departed, Wilkinson, the man Woodward had plucked from nowhere, was made captain of England.

Could England pick up the pace, could they re-establish that momentum, that scoring power, that un-English expectation of victory, that self-belief? Andy Robinson clearly has his work cut out, but under Woodward, England rugby had improved no end and it was ironic that many of his harshest critics were those who were taking the most advantage of it all.

'You'll laugh at this, ' Woodward said when we met in the pub, 'but deep inside, I have an ambition to be England football manager.'

I looked back on the final three years of Woodward's reign: the relentless driving of his team and coaches, the increasing confidence, the zany new ideas which actually bore fruit, the victorious march, the part-frozen moments as Jonny's drop kick went steepling forwards, and between, the posts in Sydney. The way in which the talented Woodward tended to confound the sceptics, whether or not he made enemies of them.

'I'm not laughing,' I said.

APPENDIX

Tour Test: 9 November 2002, Twickenham

England 31 (2G 3PG 1DG 1T) **New Zealand 28** (4G)

England: J. Robinson; J. Simpson-Daniel, W. Greenwood, M. Tindall, B. Cohen; J. Wilkinson, M. Dawson; T. Woodman, S. Thompson, P. Vickery, M. Johnson (captain), D. Grewcock, L. Moody, L. Dallaglio, R. Hill

Substitutions: B. Johnston for Greenwood (40 mins); N. Back for Hill (temp 49 to 62 mins) and for Dallaglio (70 mins); B. Kay for Grewcock (61 mins); A. Healey for Simpson-Daniel (77 mins)

Scorers – Tries: Moody, Wilkinson, Cohen; Conversions: Wilkinson (2); Penalty Goals: Wilkinson (3); Dropped Goal: Wilkinson

New Zealand: B. Blair; D. Howlett, T. Umaga, K. Lowen, J. Lomu; C. Spencer, S. Devine; J. McDonnell, A. Hore, K. Meeuws, A. Williams, K. Robinson, T. Randell (captain), S. Broomhall, M. Holah

Substitutions: D. Lee for Devine (30 mins); A. Mehrtens for Spencer (40 mins); M. Robinson for Umaga (temp 37 to 40 mins) and for Lowen (47 mins); B. Mika for K. Robinson (62 mins)

Scorers – Tries: Lomu (2), Howlett, Lee; Conversions: Blair (2), Mehrtens (2)

Referee: J. Kaplan (South Africa)

Tour Test: 16 November 2002, Twickenham

England 32 (2G 6PG) **Australia 31** (2G 4PG 1T)

England: J. Robinson; J. Simpson-Daniel, W. Greenwood, M. Tindall, B. Cohen; J. Wilkinson, M. Dawson; J. Leonard, S. Thompson, P. Vickery, M. Johnson (captain), B. Kay, L. Moody, R. Hill, N. Back

Substitutions: L. Dallaglio for Hill (temp 41 to 51 mins); A. Healey for Tindall (80 mins)

Scorers – Tries: Cohen (2); Conversions: Wilkinson (2); Penalty Goals: Wilkinson (6)

Australia: S. Larkham; W. Sailor, M. Burke, D. Herbert, S. Mortlock; E. Flatley, G. Gregan (captain); W. Young, J. Paul, P. Noriega, D. Vickerman, J. Harrison, M. Cockbain, T. Kefu, G. Smith

Substitutions: D. Giffin for Vickerman (55 mins); A. Freier for Paul (69 mins); D. Croft for Harrison (temp 70 to 80 mins) and for Smith (80 mins); M. Giteau for Herbert (73 mins); B. Darwin for Noriega (77 mins)

Scorers – Tries: Flatley (2), Sailor; Conversions: Burke (2); Penalty Goals: Burke (4)

Referee: P. Honiss (New Zealand)

Tour Test: 23 November 2002, Twickenham

England 53 (6G 2PG 1T) **South Africa 3** (1PG)

England: J. Robinson; B. Cohen, W. Greenwood, M. Tindall, P. Christophers; J. Wilkinson, M. Dawson; J. Leonard, S. Thompson, P. Vickery, M. Johnson (captain), B. Kay, L. Moody, R. Hill, N. Back

Substitutions: L. Dallaglio for Moody (15 mins); A. Healey for Wilkinson (44 mins); A. Gomarsall for Dawson (57 mins); D. Grewcock for Kay (71 mins); T. Stimpson for Greenwood (72 mins)

Scorers – Tries: Greenwood (2), Cohen, Back, Hill, Dallagliope; Conversions: Gomarsall (2), Stimpson (2), Wilkinson, Dawson; Penalty Goals: Wilkinson (2)

South Africa: W. Greeff; B. Paulse, R. Fleck, B. James, F. Lombard; A. Pretorius, B. Conradie; W. Roux, J. Dalton, D. Carstens, J. Labuschagne, A. Venter, C. Krige (captain), J. van Niekerk, P. Wannenburg

Substitutions: N. Jordaan for Conradie (11 mins); R. Russell for Paulse (47 mins); A. Jacobs and L. van Biljon for Pretorius and Dalton (55 mins); C. van der Linde for Carstens (62 mins)

Scorer – Penalty Goal: Pretorius

Referee: P. O'Brien (New Zealand)

Six Nations: 15 February 2003, Twickenham

England 25 (1G 5PG 1DG) **France 17** (1G 2T)

England: J. Robinson; D. Luger, W. Greenwood, C. Hodgson, B. Cohen; J. Wilkinson, A. Gomarsall; J. Leonard, S. Thompson, J. White, M. Johnson (captain), B. Kay, L. Moody, R. Hill, N. Back

Substitutions: G. Rowntree for Leonard (33 mins); L. Dallaglio for Moody (44 mins); D. Grewcock for Kay (84 mins); M. Regan for Rowntree (temp 47 to 56 mins)

Scorers – Try: Robinson; Conversion: Wilkinson; Penalty Goals: Wilkinson (5); Dropped Goal: Wilkinson

France: C. Poitrenaud; A. Rougerie, X. Garbajosa, D. Traille, V. Clerc; G. Merceron, F. Galthié (captain); J-J. Crenca, R. Ibañez, C. Califano, F. Pelous, O. Brouzet, S. Betsen, I. Harinordoquy, O. Magne

Substitutions: S. Marconnet for Califano (62 mins); S. Chabal for Betsen (62

mins); T. Castaignède for Rougerie (64 mins); J-B. Rué for Ibañez (74 mins)
Scorers – Tries: Magne, Poitrenaud, Traille; Conversion: Merceron
Referee: P.G. Honiss (New Zealand)

Six Nations: 22 February 2003, Millennium Stadium

Wales 9 (3PG) **England 26** (2G 2PG 2DG)

Wales: K. Morgan; Gareth Thomas, M. Taylor, T. Shanklin, R. Williams; C. Sweeney, G. Cooper; I. Thomas, J. Humphreys (captain), B. Evans, R. Sidoli, S. Williams, D. Jones, Gavin Thomas, M. Williams

Substitutions: G.J. Williams for Humphreys (57 mins); C. Charvis for Gavin Thomas (57 mins); G. Jenkins for Evans (57 mins); M. Watkins for Shanklin (65 mins); I. Harris for R. Williams (66 mins); G. Llewellyn for S. Williams (73 mins)

Scorer – Penalty Goals: Sweeney (3)

England: J. Robinson; D. Luger, W. Greenwood, C. Hodgson, B. Cohen; J. Wilkinson, K. Bracken; G. Rowntree, S. Thompson, R. Morris, M. Johnson (captain), B. Kay, R. Hill, L. Dallaglio, N. Back

Substitutions: P. Christophers for Robinson (39 mins); J. Worsley for Back (56 mins); D. Grewcock for Kay (63 mins); J. Simpson-Daniel for Hill (temp 40 to 50 mins) and for Wilkinson (77 mins); A. Gomarsall for Luger (77 mins)

Scorers – Tries: Greenwood, Worsley; Conversions: Wilkinson (2); Penalty Goals: Wilkinson (2); Dropped Goals: Wilkinson (2)

Referee: S.R. Walsh (New Zealand)

Six Nations: 9 March 2003, Twickenham

England 40 (5G 1T) **Italy 5** (1T)

England: J. Lewsey; J. Simpson-Daniel, W. Greenwood, M. Tindall, D. Luger; J. Wilkinson (captain), M. Dawson; G. Rowntree, S. Thompson, R. Morris, D. Grewcock, B. Kay, J. Worsley, L. Dallaglio, R. Hill

Substitutions: C. Hodgson for Wilkinson (47 mins); O. Smith for Hodgson (53 mins); S. Shaw for Kay (57 mins); M. Worsley for Morris (59 mins); M. Regan for Thompson (65 mins); A. Sanderson for Dallaglio (temp 19 to 26 mins) and for Hill (65 mins); K. Bracken for Lewsey (71 mins)

Scorers – Tries: Lewsey (2), Thompson, Simpson-Daniel, Tindall, Luger; Conversions: Wilkinson (4), Dawson

Italy: M. Bergamasco; N. Mazzucato, P. Vaccari, G. Raineri, D. Dallan; R. Pez, A. Troncon (captain); G. De Carli, C. Festuccia, R. Martinez-Frugoni, C. Bezzi, M. Giacheri, A. De Rossi, M. Phillips, A. Persico

Substitutions: A. Masi for Dallan (16 mins); M. Bortolami for Giacheri (temp 6 to 11 mins; and 47 mins); L. Castrogiovanni for De Carli (49 mins); G. Peens for

Vaccari (65 mins); M. Mazzantini for Troncon (68 mins); S. Palmer for Phillips (71 mins); F. Ongaro for Festuccia (74 mins)

Scorer – Try: M. Bergamasco

Referee: A.C. Rolland (Ireland)

Six Nations: 22 March 2003, Twickenham

England 40 (4G 4PG) **Scotland 9** (3PG)

England: J. Lewsey; J. Robinson, W. Greenwood, M. Tindall, B. Cohen; J. Wilkinson, M. Dawson; G. Rowntree, S. Thompson, J. Leonard, M. Johnson (captain), B. Kay, R. Hill, L. Dallaglio, N. Back

Substitutions: D. Luger for Tindall (56 mins); D. Grewcock for Kay (62 mins); P. Grayson for Wilkinson (66 mins); T. Woodman for Rowntree (66 mins); J. Worsley for Dallaglio (74 mins)

Scorers – Tries: Robinson (2), Lewsey, Cohen; Conversions: Wilkinson (3), Grayson; Penalty Goals: Wilkinson (4)

Scotland: G. Metcalfe; C. Paterson, J. McLaren, A. Craig, K. Logan; G. Townsend, B. Redpath (captain); T. Smith, G. Bulloch, B. Douglas, S. Murray, N. Hines, J. White, S. Taylor, A. Mower

Substitutions: S. Grimes for Murray (51 mins); K. Utterson for McLaren (56 mins); R. Beattie for Mower (67 mins); G. Kerr for Douglas (72 mins)

Scorer – Penalty Goals: Paterson (3)

Referee: A. Lewis (Ireland)

Six Nations: 30 March 2003, Lansdowne Road

Ireland 6 (1PG 1DG) **England 42** (4G 1PG 2DG 1T)

Ireland: G. Murphy; J. Bishop, B. O'Driscoll (captain), K. Maggs, D. Hickie; D. Humphreys, P. Stringer; M. Horan, S. Byrne, J. Hayes, G. Longwell, M. O'Kelly, V. Costello, A. Foley, K. Gleeson

Substitutions: P. O'Connell for Longwell (57 mins); R. O'Gara for Humphreys (63 mins); A. Quinlan for Costello (68 mins); J. Fitzpatrick for Horan (75 mins); G. Dempsey for O'Driscoll (81 mins)

Scorers – Penalty Goal: Humphreys; Dropped Goal: Humphreys

England: J. Lewsey; J. Robinson, W. Greenwood, M. Tindall, B. Cohen; J. Wilkinson, M. Dawson; G. Rowntree, S. Thompson, J. Leonard, M. Johnson (captain), B. Kay, R. Hill, L. Dallaglio, N. Back

Substitutions: J. Worsley for Hill (temp 22 to 29 mins); K. Bracken for Dawson (temp 25 to 34 mins and 68 to 71 mins); T. Woodman for Rowntree (temp 37 to 40 mins and 45 mins); D. Grewcock for Kay (temp 45 to 51 mins); P. Grayson for Wilkinson (temp 54 to 60 mins); D. Luger for Tindall (68 mins)

Scorers – Tries: Greenwood (2), Dallaglio, Tindall, Luger; Conversions: Wilkinson

(3), Grayson; Penalty Goal: Wilkinson; Dropped Goals: Wilkinson (2)
Referee: J. Kaplan (South Africa)

Tour Test: 14 June 2003, WestpacTrust Stadium, Wellington

New Zealand 13 (1G 2PG) **England 15** (4PG 1DG)
New Zealand: D. Howlett; J. Rokocoko, M. Nonu, T. Umaga, C. Ralph; C.
Spencer, J. Marshall; D. Hewett, A. Oliver, G. Somerville, C. Jack, A. Williams,
R. Thorne (captain), R. So'oialo, R. McCaw
Substitutions: S. Devine for Marshall (48 mins); K. Mealamu for Oliver (56 mins);
M. Muliaina for Rokocoko (72 mins); J. Collins for So'oialo (73 mins)
Scorers – Try: Howlett; Conversion: Spencer; Penalty Goals: Spencer (2)
England: J. Lewsey; J. Robinson, W. Greenwood, M. Tindall, B Cohen; J.
Wilkinson, K. Bracken; G. Rowntree, S. Thompson, J. Leonard, M. Johnson
(captain), B. Kay, R. Hill, L. Dallaglio, N. Back
Substitutions: P. Vickery for Leonard (40 mins); J. Worsley for Hill (72 mins); D.
Luger for Lewsey (77 mins)
Scorer – Penalty Goals: Wilkinson (4); Dropped Goal: Wilkinson
Referee: S. Dickinson (Australia)

Tour Test: 21 June 2003, Telstra Dome, Melbourne

Australia 14 (3PG 1T) **England 25** (2G 2PG 1T)
Australia: C. Latham; W. Sailor, M. Turinui, S. Kefu, J. Roff; N. Grey, G. Gregan
(captain); W. Young, J. Paul, P. Noriega, D. Giffin, N. Sharpe, D. Lyons, T.
Kefu, P. Waugh
Substitutions: D. Vickerman for Sharpe (44 mins); B. Cannon for Paul (53 mins);
M. Rogers for Turinui (58 mins); B. Darwin for Noriega (65 mins); L. Tuqiri
for Grey (65 mins)
Scorers – Try: Sailor; Penalty Goals: Roff (3)
England: J. Robinson; J. Lewsey, W. Greenwood, M. Tindall, B. Cohen; J.
Wilkinson, K. Bracken; T. Woodman, S. Thompson, P. Vickery, M. Johnson
(captain), B. Kay, R. Hill, L. Dallaglio, N. Back
Substitutions: J. Worsley and M. Dawson for Hill and Bracken (53 mins); S.
Borthwick for Kay (temp 62 to 67 mins)
Scorers – Tries: Greenwood, Tindall, Cohen; Conversions: Wilkinson (2); Penalty
Goals: Wilkinson (2)
Referee: D. McHugh (Ireland)

World Cup Warm-up Test: 23 August 2003, Millennium Stadium

Wales 9 (3PG) **England 43** (3G 3PG 1DG 2T)

Wales: G. Williams; Gareth Thomas, M. Taylor, S. Parker, M. Jones; S. Jones (captain), G. Cooper; I. Thomas, R. McBryde, G. Jenkins, R. Sidoli, C. Wyatt, C. Charvis, D. Jones, M. Williams

Substitutions: G. Williams for McBryde (61 mins); J. Thomas for Wyatt (62 mins); A. Jones for Jenkins (72 mins); Gavin Thomas for D.R. Jones (72 mins)

Scorer – Penalty Goals: S Jones (3)

England: D. Scarbrough; D. Luger, J. Noon, S. Abbott, J. Simpson-Daniel; A. King, A. Gomarsall; J. Leonard (captain), M. Regan, J. White, D. Grewcock, S. Shaw, M. Corry, J. Worsley, L. Moody

Substitutions: D. West for Regan (37 mins); O. Smith for Luger (57 mins); A. Sanderson for Moody (62 mins); D. Walder for King (71 mins); W. Green for White (72 mins); S. Borthwick for Shaw (temp 11 to 16 mins)

Scorers – Tries: Moody, Luger, Worsley, Abbott, West; Conversions: King (2), Walder; Penalty Goals: King (3); Dropped Goal: King

Referee: P.C. Deluca (Argentina)

World Cup Warm-up Test: 30 August 2003, Stade Vélodrome, Marseilles

France 17 (3PG 1DG 1T) **England 16** (1G 3PG)

France: N. Brusque; A. Rougerie, Y. Jauzion, D. Traille, C. Dominici; F. Michalak, F. Galthié (captain); J-J. Crenca, Y. Bru, S. Marconnet, F. Pelous, J. Thion, S. Betsen, I. Harinordoquy, O. Magne

Substitutions: B. Liebenberg for Traille (54 mins); R. Ibañez for Bru (54 mins); D. Auradou for Thion (65 mins); P. Tabacco for Betsen (65 mins); O. Milloud for Crenca (temp 5 to 9 mins, 38 to 41 mins and 66 mins); S. Chabal for Magne (75 mins)

Scorers – Try: Brusque; Penalty Goals: Michalak (3); Dropped Goal: Michalak

England: I. Balshaw; J. Lewsey, O. Smith, M. Tindall, B. Cohen; P. Grayson, A. Healey; G. Rowntree, D. West (captain), J. White, S. Borthwick, D. Grewcock, M. Corry, A. Sanderson, L. Moody

Substitutions: S. Thompson for West (50 mins); J. Noon for Cohen (temp 10 to 16 mins) and for Balshaw (54 mins); J. Leonard for White (temp 6 to 8 mins) and for Rowntree (61 mins); S. Shaw for Borthwick (61 mins); A. Gomarsall for Tindall (76 mins)

Scorers – Try: Tindall; Conversion: Grayson; Penalty Goals: Grayson (3)

Referee: S. Lawrence (South Africa)

APPENDIX

World Cup Warm-up Test: 6 September 2003, Twickenham

England 45 (4G 4PG 1T) **France 14** (2PG 1DG 1T)

England: J. Robinson; I. Balshaw, W. Greenwood, S. Abbott, B. Cohen; J. Wilkinson, K. Bracken; T. Woodman, S. Thompson, J. White, M. Johnson (captain), B. Kay, R. Hill, M. Corry, N. Back

Substitutions: M. Dawson for Bracken (34 mins); P. Grayson for Wilkinson (43 mins); S. Shaw for Johnson (43 mins); L. Moody for Corry (57 mins); J. Lewsey for Cohen (temp 47 to 53 mins) and for Abbott (60 mins); J. Leonard for White (63 mins); D. West for Moody (temp 68 to 72 mins) and for Thompson (73 mins)

Scorers – Tries: Cohen (2), Robinson, Balshaw, Lewsey; Conversions: Wilkinson (3), Grayson; Penalty Goals: Wilkinson (4)

France: C. Poitrenaud; X. Garbajosa, Y. Jauzion, B. Liebenberg, C. Dominici; G. Merceron, D. Yachvili; O. Milloud, R. Ibañez (captain), J-B. Poux, D. Auradou, O. Brouzet, P. Tabacco, C. Labit, S. Chabal

Substitutions: A. Rougerie for Dominici (40 mins); O. Magne for Chabal (50 mins); F. Pelous for Brouzet (58 mins); Y. Bru for Ibañez (70 mins); I. Harinordoquy for Tabacco (73 mins); S. Marconnet for Milloud (temp 62 to 73 mins) and for Poux (73 mins)

Scorers – Try: Rougerie; Penalty Goals: Merceron (2); Dropped Goal: Jauzion

Referee: N. Williams (Wales)

World Cup Pool Match: 12 October 2003, Subiaco Oval, Perth

England 84 (9G 2PG 3T) **Georgia 6** (2PG)

England: J. Robinson; J. Lewsey, W. Greenwood, M. Tindall, B. Cohen; J. Wilkinson, M. Dawson; T. Woodman, S. Thompson, P. Vickery, M. Johnson (captain), B. Kay, R. Hill, L. Dallaglio, N. Back

Substitutions: D. Luger for Tindall (35 mins); A. Gomarsall for Dawson (35 mins); M. Regan for Thompson (40 mins); P. Grayson for Wilkinson (46 mins); L. Moody for Hill (51 mins); J. Leonard for Woodman (temp 28 to 29 mins) and for Vickery (51 mins)

Scorers – Tries: Greenwood (2), Cohen (2), Robinson, Tindall, Dawson, Thompson, Dallaglio, Back, Luger, Regan; Conversions: Wilkinson (5), Grayson (4); Penalty Goals: Wilkinson (2)

Georgia: B. Khamashuridze; M. Urjukashvili, T. Zibzibadze, I. Guiorgadze, V. Katsadze (captain); P. Jimsheladze, I. Abusseridze; G. Shvelidze, A. Guiorgadze, A. Margvelashvili, Z. Mtchedlishvili, V. Didebulidze, G. Labadze, G. Chkhaidze, G. Yachvili

Substitutions: S. Nikolaenko for Margvelashvili (40 mins); V. Nadiradze for Didebulidze (43 mins); D. Bolghashvili for Yachvili (66 mins); D. Dadunashvili for A. Guiorgadze (72 mins); B. Khekhelashvili for Khamashuridze (75 mins); M. Kvirikashvili for Jimsheladze (75 mins); I. Machkhaneli for Chkhaidze (80 mins)

Scorers – Penalty Goals: Urjukashvili, Jimsheladze
Referee: P.C. Deluca (Argentina)

World Cup Pool Match: 18 October 2003, Subiaco Oval, Perth

England 25 (1G 4PG 2DG) **South Africa 6** (2PG)
England: J. Robinson; J. Lewsey, W. Greenwood, M. Tindall, B. Cohen; J. Wilkinson, K. Bracken; T. Woodman, S. Thompson, P. Vickery, M. Johnson (captain), B. Kay, L. Moody, L. Dallaglio, N. Back
Substitutions: D. Luger for Tindall (70 mins); J. Leonard for Woodman (73 mins); J. Worsley for Back (temp 46 to 51 mins)
Scorers – Try: Greenwood; Conversion: Wilkinson; Penalty Goals: Wilkinson (4); Dropped Goals: Wilkinson (2)
South Africa: J. van der Westhuyzen; A. Willemse, G. Müller, D. Barry, G. Delport; L. Koen, J. van der Westhuizen; C. Bezuidenhout, D. Coetzee, R. Bands, J. Botha, V. Matfield, C. Krige (captain), J. Smith, J. van Niekerk
Substitutions: J. Smit for Coetzee (temp 44 to 51 mins and 57 mins); L. Sephaka for Bands (6 to 13 mins and 68 mins); D. Hougaard for Koen (68 mins)
Scorer – Penalty Goals: Koen (2)
Referee: P.L. Marshall (Australia)

World Cup Pool Match: 26 October 2003, Telstra Dome, Melbourne

England 35 (3G 2PG 1DG 1T) **Samoa 22** (1G 5PG)
England: J. Robinson; I. Balshaw, S. Abbott, M. Tindall, B. Cohen; J. Wilkinson, M. Dawson; J. Leonard, M. Regan, J. White, M. Johnson (captain), B. Kay, J. Worsley, L. Dallaglio, N. Back
Substitutions: S. Thompson for Regan (48 mins); P. Vickery for White (48 mins); L. Moody for Worsley (48 mins); M. Catt for Abbott (71 mins)
Scorers – Tries: Back, penalty try, Balshaw, Vickery; Conversions: Wilkinson (3); Penalty Goals: Wilkinson (2); Dropped Goal: Wilkinson
Samoa: T. Vili; L. Fa'atau, T. Fanolua, B.P. Lima, S. Tagicakibau; E. Va'a, S. So'oialo; K. Lealamanu'a, J. Meredith, J. Tomuli, O. Palepoi, L. Lafaiali'i, P. Poulos, S. Sititi (captain), M. Fa'asavalu
Substitutions: D. Rasmussen for Fanolua (45 mins); S. Lemalu for Tomuli (52 mins); K. Viliamu for Poulos (62 mins); D. Tuiavi'i for Lafaiali'i (65 mins); D. Feaunati for Tagicakibau (72 mins); D. Tyrell for So'oialo (75 mins); M. Schwlager for Meredith (75 mins)
Scorers – Try: Sititi; Conversion: Va'a; Penalty Goals: Va'a (5)
Referee: J.I. Kaplan (South Africa)

World Cup Pool Match: 2 November 2003, Suncorp Stadium, Brisbane

England 111 (13G 4T) **Uruguay 13** (1G 2PG)

England: J. Lewsey; I. Balshaw, S. Abbott, M. Catt, D. Luger; P. Grayson, A. Gomarsall; J. Leonard, D. West, P. Vickery (captain), M. Corry, D. Grewcock, J. Worsley, L. Dallaglio, L. Moody

Substitutions: M. Johnson for Corry (43 mins); J. Robinson for Balshaw (43 mins); J. White for Vickery (52 mins); K. Bracken for Gomarsall (61 mins); W. Greenwood for Grayson (61 mins)

Scorers – Tries: Lewsey (5), Balshaw (2), Robinson (2), Catt (2), Gomarsall (2), Moody, Luger, Abbott, Greenwood; Conversions: Grayson (11), Catt (2)

Uruguay: J-R. Menchaca; J. Pastore, D. Aguirre (captain), J. de Freitas, J. Viana; S. Aguirre, J. Campomar; E. Berruti, D. Lamelas, P. Lemoine, J-C. Bado, J-M. Alvarez, N. Brignoni, R. Capo, N. Grille

Substitutions: M. Gutierrez for Grille (43 mins); R. Sanchez for Berruti (43 mins); J. Alzueta for Alvarez (52 mins); D. Reyes for de Freitas (temp 5 to 10 mins) and for Viana (52 mins); J-A. Perez for Lamelas (56 mins); G. Storace for Lemoine (69 mins); E. Caffera for Menchaca (71 mins)

Scorers – Try: Lemoine; Conversion: Menchaca; Penalty Goals: Menchaca (2)

Referee: N. Williams (Wales)

World Cup Quarter-Final Match: 9 November 2003, Suncorp Stadium, Brisbane

England 28 (1G 6PG 1DG) **Wales 17** (1G 2T)

England: J. Robinson; D. Luger, W. Greenwood, M. Tindall, B. Cohen; J. Wilkinson, M. Dawson; J. Leonard, S. Thompson, P. Vickery, M. Johnson (captain), B. Kay, L. Moody, L. Dallaglio, N. Back

Substitutions: M. Catt for Luger (40 mins); T. Woodman for Leonard (44 mins); S. Abbott for Greenwood (52 mins); K. Bracken for Dawson (67 mins)

Scorers – Try: Greenwood; Conversion: Wilkinson; Penalty Goals: Wilkinson (6); Dropped Goal: Wilkinson

Wales: G. Thomas; M. Jones, M. Taylor, I. Harris, S. Williams; S. Jones, G. Cooper; I. Thomas, R. McBryde, A. Jones, B. Cockbain, R. Sidoli, D. Jones, J. Thomas, C. Charvis (captain)

Substitutions: G. Jenkins for A. Jones (28 mins); G. Llewellyn for Cockbain (48 mins); M. Williams for J. Thomas (57 mins); D. Peel for Cooper (64 mins); M. Davies for McBryde (64 mins); C. Sweeney for S. Jones (temp 58 to 72 mins)

Scorers – Tries: S. Jones, Charvis, M. Williams; Conversion: Harris

Referee: A.C. Rolland (Ireland)

World Cup Semi-Final Match: 16 November 2003, Telstra Stadium, Sydney

England 24 (5PG 3DG) **France 7** (1G)

England: J. Lewsey; J. Robinson, W. Greenwood, M. Catt, B. Cohen; J. Wilkinson, M. Dawson; T. Woodman, S. Thompson, P. Vickery, M. Johnson (captain), B. Kay, R. Hill, L. Dallaglio, N. Back

Substitutions: M. Tindall for Catt (68 mins); K. Bracken for Dawson (temp 39 to 40 mins and 69 mins); L. Moody for Hill (73 mins); J. Leonard for Vickery (temp 4 to 5 mins) and for Woodman (78 mins); D. West for Thompson (78 mins)

Scorer – Penalty Goals: Wilkinson (5); Dropped Goals: Wilkinson (3)

France: N. Brusque; A. Rougerie, T. Marsh, Y. Jauzion, C. Dominici; F. Michalak, F. Galthié (captain); J-J. Crenca, R. Ibañez, S. Marconnet, F. Pelous, J. Thion, S. Betsen, I. Harinordoquy, O. Magne

Substitutions: C. Poitrenaud for Dominici (33 mins); O. Milloud for Crenca (61 mins); G. Merceron for Michalak (63 mins); C. Labit for Betsen (63 mins)

Scorers – Try: Betsen; Conversion: Michalak

Referee: P.O. Brien (New Zealand)

World Cup Final Match: 22 November 2003, Telstra Stadium, Sydney

England 20 (4PG 1DG 1T) **Australia 17** (4PG 1T)

England: J. Robinson; J. Lewsey, W. Greenwood, M. Tindall, B. Cohen; J. Wilkinson, M. Dawson; T. Woodman, S. Thompson, P. Vickery, M. Johnson (captain), B. Kay, R. Hill, L. Dallaglio, N. Back

Substitutions: M. Catt for Tindall (78 mins); J. Leonard for Vickery (80 mins); I. Balshaw for Lewsey (85 mins); L. Moody for Hill (93 mins)

Scorers – Try: Robinson; Penalty Goals: Wilkinson (4); Dropped Goal: Wilkinson

Australia: M. Rogers; W. Sailor, S. Mortlock, E. Flatley, L. Tuqiri; S. Larkham, G. Gregan (captain); W. Young, B. Cannon, A. Baxter, J. Harrison, N. Sharpe, G. Smith, D. Lyons, P. Waugh

Substitutions: D. Giffin for Sharpe (48 mins); J. Paul for Cannon (56 mins); M. Cockbain for Lyons (56 mins); J. Roff for Sailor (70 mins); M. Dunning for Young (92 mins); M. Giteau for Larkham (temp 18 to 30 mins; 55 to 63 mins; 85 to 93 mins)

Scorers – Try: Tuqiri; Penalty Goals: Flatley (4)

Referee: A. Watson (South Africa)

BLACKIE

The Steve Black Story
**Steve Black
with Arthur McKenzie**
Foreword by Jonny Wilkinson

'Blackie is an inspirational character with a totally unique gift.
He is a true friend.' – Jonny Wilkinson

Steve Black is commonly regarded as one of the most inspirational fitness gurus in the world. He has worked with the finest sportsmen in both rugby and football, while his advice and motivational skills have been sought by many, including Kevin Keegan, Peter Reid and Paul Bracewell.

The pinnacle of his career so far came when he was selected for the British Lions tour of Australia in 2001. More recently, he has been named as one of the key factors behind the success of Rugby World Cup hero Jonny Wilkinson.

This engaging biography documents Black's journey from life as a bouncer on the streets of Newcastle to the global sporting achievements that followed. *Blackie* is an inspirational read for anyone who seeks success, be it in sport or life in general.

ISBN 1 84018 828 6
Now available
£15.99 (hardback)

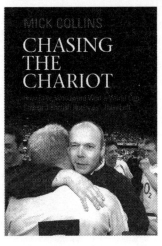

IN STRENGTH AND SHADOW

The Mervyn Davies Story
Mervyn Davies and David Roach
Foreword by Willie John McBride

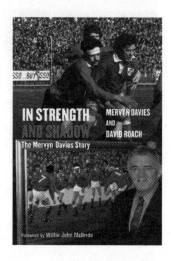

In what was a remarkable but short-lived career, Welsh rugby legend Mervyn Davies won two Grand Slams, three Triple Crowns, earned 38 consecutive Wales caps, was captain of his national team and played in two victorious Lions tours. From the tail end of the 1960s through the first half of the glorious '70s period, 'Merv the Swerve' cut an iconic figure in the world's great rugby arenas.

Then, in March 1976, Mervyn suffered a massive brain haemorrhage on the pitch. Against all odds, however, he recovered.

In this candid biography, Mervyn writes about his many highs and lows, and recounts how he lost rugby but regained his life. From locker-room tales to the loneliness of rehabilitation, *In Strength and Shadow* is funny, moving and honest.

ISBN 1 84018 865 0
Now available
£15.99 (hardback)

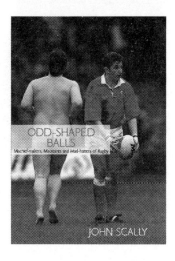